Praise for *Fire and Rain*

Named one of the "Best Rock Books of the Year" by *Rolling Stone*, the *Kansas City Star*, and the *Financial Times*

"A refreshed view of the moment when the counterculture allegedly went soft. Browne's finely detailed, engrossing narrative . . . reveals the decade to be one as complex and artistically rich as was the one that gave us the British Invasion and the Summer of Love."   —Ann Powers, NPR

"A scrutiny of a significant year of transition that holds its own against any other year in terms of its dramatic tensions and creative output. A worthy addition to anyone's collection of such music histories . . . I couldn't help but be riveted."
—Associated Press

"What was going on with those artists and, more broadly, the culture of America at that time. . . . A fun read."
—Demetri Martin, *Time*

"Browne is an incredibly intelligent writer. . . . His considerable narrative skills make *Fire and Rain* one of the most entertaining and informative books of the year. It's bound to be enjoyed not only by rock fans   sted in popular culture and social chang   NPR, "Books We Like"

"[A] juicy history   —*New York* magazine

"Nobody has done a better job chronicling that moment, with its cultural and chemical chaos, than Browne."   —*Rolling Stone*

"Compelling . . . attention to detail lends this compelling book a depth and richness rarely found in rock biography."
—*Financial Times*

"Browne employs a smart narrative style to make such well-worn stories as the Beatles' breakup fresh again. . . . A fascinating look at an era when an artist's reputation was built not on social media sites, but on the music itself."   —*Publishers Weekly*

"Fascinating doesn't even come close as we get the intertwining, almost incestuous connections between all four of these artists, not to mention the tremendous cultural tremors going through the body politic as a whole and how this informed their music."
—*Huffington Post*

"Intimately familiar with the music, fully comprehending the cross-pollination among the artists, thoroughly awake to the dynamics of the decade's last gasp, the author expertly captures a volatile and hugely interesting moment in rock history. A vivid freeze-frame of Hall of Fame musicians."   —*Kirkus Reviews*

"Absorbing . . . Browne avoids sentimentality and nostalgia, aiming instead at a fresh look at the bands and their milieu. Some of the period details are almost astonishingly apt."   —*Boston Globe*

"A fascinating look at a pivotal year."   —*People*

"Exhilarating and meticulously researched . . . Browne is a superb chronicler of popular music and a fine social historian."
—*BookForum*

"*Fire and Rain* works as a history lesson but is foremost a fast-paced music fan's appreciation of the brilliance of that era's artists."   —*Miami Herald*

"Browne's engrossing account of this fertile but volatile period sets the standard by which comprehensive musical histories should be judged."   —*BookPage*

"This juicy, fascinating read transports you back to a turbulent year. . . . Browne artfully describes the creation of these classic songs in a way that makes them seem brand-new."   —*Parade*

"A watershed year in the development of rock & roll music, as the 'We' decade morphed into the 'Me' decade, drugs went from sacrament to scourge, and the notion of bands as inviolable units was blown to smithereens. . . . Browne has already covered the '80s with Sonic Youth and the '90s with Jeff Buckley; he now puts his mark on yet another transition period in rock and roll."
—Roy Trakin, *Hits*

"Browne vividly recreates a time when popular music, as a communally shared pastime, really mattered . . . a clear and brisk journey through one of the most catastrophic years in rock history."
—*Pop Matters*

"As a reporter [Browne] is dogged and earnest; as a profile writer, crisp and professional. As *Fire and Rain* jaunts from London to Laurel Canyon, he drops in memorable details."
—*New York Times*

"Excellent . . . Browne renders this somnambulant period with such care that he makes it seem alive."
—Michelangelo Matos, *Chicago Reader*

"Rich anecdotes and incisive analysis . . . The form of the book, told chronologically over four seasons, lends it the compacted, real-time drama of an episode of *24*."   —*New York Daily News*

"Browne's absorbing tapestry of the times is hard to put down."
—*Portland* (Oregon) *Book Review*

"Browne engagingly illuminates many overlooked stories that may not be familiar to even dedicated rock enthusiasts. Highly recommended."   —*Library Journal*

"An irresistible page-turner, a gossipy, scholarly account of an explosive rock moment, as organized as the times were chaotic—as well-crafted as a Beatles tune. The book is a brilliant lens on a time you only thought you knew."   —*The Hollywood Reporter*

"If you liked Keith Richards' *Life*, then try *Fire and Rain*."
—*St. Petersburg Times*

"A classic."   —*CityView*

"Totally entertaining . . . There are drugs, love affairs, and infighting behind the music, a story Browne smartly sets against the backdrop of a culture emerging from the turbulent '60s. . . . I was hooked from the minute I opened it."
—Caryn James, Indiewire.com

"Masterfully researched and written . . . the sort of book that should have come along much sooner than it actually did. . . . [A] compelling, thought-provoking read."   —Blogcritics.com

FIRE AND RAIN

ALSO BY DAVID BROWNE

Goodbye 20th Century: A Biography of Sonic Youth

Dream Brother: The Lives & Music of Jeff & Tim Buckley

*Amped: How Big Air, Big Dollars and a
New Generation Took Sports to the Extreme*

FIRE AND RAIN
The Beatles, Simon & Garfunkel, James Taylor, CSNY, and the Lost Story of 1970

DAVID BROWNE

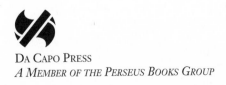

DA CAPO PRESS
A MEMBER OF THE PERSEUS BOOKS GROUP

Designed by David Janik
Set in 10 point Janson Text by the Perseus Books Group.

Cataloging-in-Publication data for this book is available from the Library of Congress.

First Da Capo Press edition 2011
First Da Capo Press paperback edition 2012
ISBN 978-0-306-81850-9 (hardcover)
ISBN 978-0-306-82072-4 (paperback)
ISBN 978-0-306-81986-5 (e-book)

Published by Da Capo Press
A Member of the Perseus Books Group
www.dacapopress.com

Da Capo Press books are available at special discounts for bulk purchases in the U.S. by corporations, institutions, and other organizations. For more information, please contact the Special Markets Department at the Perseus Books Group, 2300 Chestnut Street, Suite 200, Philadelphia, PA 19103, or call (800) 810-4145, ext. 5000, or e-mail special.markets@perseusbooks.com.

10 9 8 7 6 5 4 3 2

For my sisters, Linda Virginia and Colette:
Without you and your record collections, this book wouldn't exist.

INTRODUCTION

This book has its roots in that most devastating of traditions, classroom humiliation. One Christmas long ago, my parents asked me for a list of possible gifts, so I gave them the names of a few records. Only months before, for my twelfth birthday, I'd received my first LP, making the momentous transition from singles to albums—a twerp-to-cool-kid rite of passage that's since gone the way of the turntable. Since my older sister Linda had already introduced me to the music of Simon and Garfunkel, I asked for one of their albums for my own.

Our first day back after winter break, my classmates and I at our elementary school in Hazlet, New Jersey, filled each other in on our presents. When my turn arrived, I proudly announced I'd been gifted with an album. What one, they asked? Simon and Garfunkel's *Sounds of Silence*, I replied. Their aghast looks—the way they pulled back from me as if I'd admitted I couldn't *wait* to get home to start homework every day—was the first sign something had changed. Then one of them said, in a tone equally puzzled and contemptuous, "Why do you want that *old* music?" All my surrounding classmates then turned, en masse, away from me.

Yes, the album *was* six years old, an eternity for a teenager. But from my friends' reactions, you'd have thought I'd been given a collection of Stephen Foster parlor songs from the middle of the previous century. Hadn't the '60s just ended?

I had to admit those years already felt farther away than they were. Repeatedly, those of us who came of age in the '70s were reminded we'd missed out on the most astounding era in history, a flowering of culture, society, and mankind like none before (and with girls in mini skirts to boot). Compared to that, our era was an even darker Dark Ages: Welcome to a world of Watergate, KC and the Sunshine Band, '50s nostalgia, and gas rationing, we were told. Personally, I loved hearing early disco songs on the radio and happily watched Fonzie say *"Aaayyy,"* yet I still wondered: What happened, and how did it happen? When did the hopeful sensibility of one era give way to the dimmer one of another?

The question has tugged at me ever since. If friends my age are drawn to the '70s, it's generally the second half—the momentous years of punk, Studio 54 disco, the original cast of *Saturday Night Live*, the films of Lucas and Spielberg. But the messy conflicting signals of the first half of the decade have always haunted me: utopian music like prog rock alongside post-utopian movies like *Deliverance*, men-pushed-too-far action films like *Billy Jack* and *Walking Tall* next to an antiestablishment, pacifist-central TV series like *M*A*S*H*. And everywhere was the fragmentation of so many of the classic bands of the '60s, replaced by flaxen-haired troubadours sweetly serenading the ladies (the "Frisbee Guys," as my friend Tom and I call them). After *Sounds of Silence*, some of the first LPs I ever owned were all the other Simon and Garfunkel albums (*Bridge Over Troubled Water* spun regularly on the close-and-play stereo in my bedroom), the Beatles' *Let It Be*, and everything recorded by Crosby, Stills, Nash & Young, together, separately, or in duo form. I didn't have to buy James Taylor's *Sweet Baby James;* I always seemed to hear its low-maintenance melodies drifting out of my sister Colette's bedroom.

Many years later, during a brainstorming session for my next book, my wife suggested I write about the music I loved in my childhood, meaning not just Simon and Garfunkel but Crosby, Stills, Nash & Young, the Beatles, James Taylor, and so on. As she rightly pointed out, I was still giving cursory listens to those musicians' new releases, attending their reunion concerts, even interviewing them for one outlet or another. When we wondered aloud whether they had anything in common, one thing came to my mind: 1970. Here was the year in which two of those groups fell apart, one achieved critical cultural mass and *also* collapsed, and another broke through to a new level of mass acceptance. Further researching those twelve months, I was reminded what a turbulent year 1970 truly was. I'd remembered Kent State and Charles Manson's trial, but I'd nearly forgotten about the Southern Strategy or the brownstone that exploded in New York's Greenwich Village, right down the street from an NYU dorm where I would later live. It was a year—a strangely overlooked one, in some regards—of upheaval and collapse, tension and release, endings and beginnings.

Combined with the music and musicians who provided the soundtrack to those events, a story—the one I'd been wondering about since those grade-school years—started to take shape. Many have rightly argued that the dawn of the '70s began in 1972 or 1973, just as the '60s didn't genuinely launch until JFK's inauguration in 1961. Yet the more I thought about it, the more 1970 felt like the lost year: the moment at which the remaining slivers of the idealism of the '60s began surrendering to the buzz-kill comedown of the decade ahead; each subsequent year built on its foundations. I don't pine for my childhood, especially moments of mortification, but I couldn't resist revisiting a moment when sweetly sung music and ugly times coexisted, even fed off each other, in a world gone off course.

PROLOGUE: JANUARY

The new year and new decade blew in colder than expected. In Times Square, the thousands waiting to greet 1970 warded off flurries and temperatures that tumbled unapologetically below twenty degrees. Detroit and Chicago were equally frigid, and even the normally balmy Los Angeles felt the chill, the city's thermometer nose-diving to ten degrees above freezing. The cold snap then migrated across the ocean. Clouds and sleet blanketed London, and by Saturday, January 3, the cold rain and snow showers had arrived and the sun refused to materialize all day.

That morning, a cheery thirty-year-old emerged from the St. John's Wood train station and began making his way down the tree-lined Grove End Road. Sporting his usual white shirt and tie, Richard Langham strolled briskly for five minutes, finally arriving at 3 Abbey Road, a two-story building with elegant, architrave window and door frames and a small parking lot out front. As always, Langham was greeted by a security guard who flipped open a sign-in book for Langham to initial. Langham then checked the schedule and saw that today's clients, starting at 2 P.M., would be the Beatles.

Like many of his colleagues at EMI Studios, Langham wasn't necessarily thrilled at the news. A staff engineer at the studio, Langham had worked his first Beatle session in 1962, when, as a novice learning his trade, he'd helped them unload their equipment into the studio. Langham had trouble telling them apart, with their suits, ties, and nearly identical, just-over-the-ears haircuts, but was struck by their camaraderie and solidarity; he was also charmed when the drummer, Ringo Starr, kept bumming cigarettes off him. Within a few short years, though, Beatle sessions had become torturous ordeals for the studio's staff. The Beatles seemed to take forever to put new songs on tape; even when they did, they might easily return the following day and start again. They would frequently bicker, and they didn't seem to care whether they kept the studio staff long past regular hours. From the standpoint of EMI employees like Langham, working with the Beatles felt like a frustrating waste of time, and those assigned to them felt they were being punished for one infraction or another.

To Langham's relief, today's session promised a return to the band's early, bash-them-out days. From the start, they seemed like the same old Beatles, if older and more hirsute. Paul McCartney, twenty-seven, sported a bushy black beard and gave Langham his standard hug—never simply a handshake—while Starr, twenty-nine, with shaggy locks that flopped around his head, was affable as always. Few twenty-six-year-olds looked as severe as George Harrison did with his long brown hair and beard, but he too appeared in generally good spirits. The three congregated at Studio Two, the expansive room where the Beatles had recorded so much of their most indelible, groundbreaking music—"In My Life," "Yesterday," "Lucy in the Sky with Diamonds," good chunks of the White Album. In another sign that they were back to business as normal, George Martin, their longtime, straight-British-arrow producer, took a seat behind the console.

As the EMI staff learned, John Lennon wouldn't be participating today; he and Yoko Ono were supposedly somewhere in Denmark. He and McCartney hadn't spoken in several months, so no one knew for sure. Lennon's absence was duly noted: At one point, Martin pulled out a notepad and drew a rough map of Scandinavia to give everyone a general idea of where the missing Beatle was. That same morning, an interview with Lennon appeared in the latest edition of *Record Mirror*, the weekly music tabloid. "I suppose it is a lot more difficult for us to get together now because everyone is involved in different things," he commented on the state of the band. He nixed the idea of Beatle live performances in the near future; after all, he said, "For the Beatles to come back now, people would expect Jesus and Buddha." He seemed far more interested in plugging his new concert album *Live Peace in Toronto* or talking about pornography in Denmark or the avant-garde nature of his albums with Yoko Ono, *Wedding Album* and *Unfinished Music No. 2: Life with the Lions.*

Whether the other Beatles saw the interview or not was unclear, but Harrison, who had a subtly scathing sense of humor when he chose to flash it, turned Lennon's absence into a joke. "You all would have read that, uh, Dave Dee's no longer with us," he drolly remarked, referring to Dave Dee, Dozy, Beaky, Mick & Tich, a British pop band that made a handful of appearances on the charts earlier that decade. "But Mickey and Tich and I decided to carry on the good word that's always gone down in Number Two."[1]

Carry on they did, with a diligence and efficiency few had witnessed at Beatle sessions in years. The three settled in behind their instruments— Harrison on acoustic guitar, McCartney on electric bass, and Starr on drums—and went to work on "I Me Mine," a song Harrison had written about the struggles he was having with his inflated, fame-fueled ego. With Martin, Langham, and another engineer staring down at them from the control room above the studio space, the Beatles quickly laid down several basic takes of the song. To flesh it out, McCartney and Harrison added another layer of acoustic guitars; Harrison overdubbed a tense electric lead in the intro and riffy chords in the chorus. McCartney dubbed in a fu-

---

1. Harrison was also taking a potshot at that band. Dave Dee, a former cop who'd announced his departure from the group a few months before, had been critical of Lennon's decision to return his MBE in protest of Vietnam. "Every time Lennon sees things go a little bit quiet for the Beatles these days, he seems to leap to the forefront and do something silly," said Dee, who called the move "stupid."

nereal organ and a jaunty electric piano. In another moment that harked back to their formative years, the trio playfully jammed on a Buddy Holly song, "Peggy Sue Got Married." Thanks to their industriousness and the brevity of the song (which was all of one minute and thirty-four seconds long), "I Me Mine" was wrapped up shortly after midnight—an accelerated heartbeat by recent Beatle standards of working.

With its completion, another Beatle project was also nearing the finish line. Almost exactly a year before, the band had been filmed rehearsing and recording new material at Twickenham Film Studios in the London suburb of Twickenham (and later at the studio of their company, Apple Corps Ltd., on Savile Row). Between the damp, impersonal space and the forced camaraderie the band tried to exhibit as cameramen continually circled them, the experience at Twickenham was notably unpleasant, and the unedited canisters of the film had been relegated to storage ever since. But in the fall of 1969, Allen Klein, the pugnacious, proudly coarse New Jersey-born accountant who'd taken over the band's business affairs the previous spring, had done the seemingly impossible. Striking a deal with United Artists, he'd actually revived the movie everyone would rather have forgotten, and *Get Back*, as it was initially being called, was set for a spring theatrical release.

A movie meant a soundtrack album, which in turn meant today's visit to EMI Studios. During the filming at Twickenham, McCartney, Harrison, and Starr had banged out a rough take of "I Me Mine" as Lennon and his ever-present wife-to-be, Yoko Ono, waltzed hand-in-hand. The footage was considered so charming that everyone agreed it needed to be in the film. (Additional footage of Ono would also mollify Lennon, who was worried that director Michael Lindsay-Hogg was focusing too much on McCartney.) Since that rendition of "I Me Mine" was fairly raw, even by the standards of the back-to-basics *Get Back* project, the band needed a more polished version to include on the soundtrack album now being assembled.

Consisting of only two verses—and a chorus that was only played once—"I Me Mine" barely amounted to a full song. Yet even in its final, manicured version, it exposed small cracks and divisions like sunlight pouring into a white-painted room. The verses, sung by Harrison, were lugubrious and mournful, laden with a sense of weary burden that had increasingly crept into his songs. Those parts felt less like a "heavy waltz," as Harrison had described the song to his bandmates at Twickenham, and more like a dirge. On the chorus, Harrison's voice and the doleful tempo were overtaken by McCartney's frenetic, half-shouted exhortations and a faster, pushier tempo. (McCartney's piano overdubs were particularly frenzied, and his voice tapped into the manic Little Richard homages of the band's early Cavern Club days.) "I Me Mine" didn't merely feel like two songs welded together. It sounded like the mesh of two different people and personalities—one resigned to a finale, another desperate to avoid it.

The following day, January 4, the three Beatles, joined by McCartney's wife, Linda, returned to Studio Two to polish up a near-completed song, a hymn-like McCartney ballad called "Let It Be," taped a year earlier. McCartney added a new bass part; Harrison replaced his original, squishy guitar solo with a more forceful one. A brass section was tacked on, as were backing singers, including Linda. The work was businesslike and somewhat tedious; at one point, George Martin scribbled "Lettuce Be" on a pad and drew a picture of a bunny to amuse himself. When it was over, the EMI staff, including Langham, punched out and checked the schedule to see who'd be working in the studio in the days ahead. The Beatles returned to their separate homes, in some cases over an hour outside London.

For two days, the Beatles had once more been a working band, one with a hit album on the charts (*Abbey Road*, their latest LP, was still the best-selling album in America). But at one point, Geoff Emerick, an engineer who'd also spent innumerable hours in the studio with the band, stopped by to say a quick hello. He found McCartney strangely quiet and low-key. (Starr's mustache drooped around his mouth like a permanent upside-down smile.) What Emerick and others didn't know was that on December 30, 1969, EMI had informed Apple of its plans to release the soundtrack album to *Get Back*. The Beatles had reassembled at EMI a mere four days later, as if they couldn't wait to put the whole mess of a movie and record—and other, more pressing matters—behind them.

On the night of January 6, McCartney settled into his seat at the Royal Albert Hall. Along with five thousand others in the elegantly domed theater with boxed seats, he was about to witness the London debut of the band everyone was calling the "American Beatles." (One of them was actually English, but a catchy press moniker couldn't be denied.) Thirteen months earlier, George Harrison had passed on signing them to Apple, but now they were stars on a headlining tour of Europe. In one sign of their stature, their massive sound system, complete with a lighting rig specially designed for them, had arrived in London from the States by boat. They were put up in the city's five-star Dorchester Hotel—where the grand reception party for the Beatles' *A Hard Day's Night* had taken place in now far-off 1964—and the Rolling Stones lent their managers an office in town. Whatever David Crosby, Stephen Stills, Graham Nash, and Neil Young wanted, they received.

They were a little nervous, with ample reason. All the major newspaper critics and a host of celebrities—not merely McCartney but Donovan and Ahmet Ertegun, the worldly, Turkish-born head of their label, Atlantic—had assembled to scrutinize them in person. Nash, who'd grown up in Manchester, knew some of his fellow countrymen were skeptical because he'd left the beloved Hollies and his native country to join this new band in Los Angeles. Before they began the show, they calmed their nerves by indulging in one of their pre-show rituals, a shared joint. By the time Crosby, Stills & Nash took the stage—with Young to follow later—Crosby was either so high, nervous, or energized (or some combination of the three) that he didn't notice a stagehand slapping an "L" sign—the British learners permit for driving lessons—on the back of his brown fringe jacket as he walked out.

The audience guffawed as one; everyone knew Crosby, Stills, Nash & Young were hardly newcomers. The public had first become aware of them eight months earlier with the release of *Crosby, Stills & Nash*, made before Young joined up with them. The bands they'd once been members of—the Byrds, Buffalo Springfield, and the Hollies—had made some of the most dynamic, sparkling music of the '60s. Yet the public embraced the new configuration in ways it had only occasionally taken the other bands to its bosom. The California-sun-drenched embrace of their labored-over, multitracked harmonies, the three distinctive-looking men reclining on an outdoor couch on the album cover, the variety of music from the dramatic, postapocalyptic soar of "Wooden Ships" to the turbulent churn of "Long Time Gone": Whatever it was, *Crosby, Stills & Nash* quickly went gold, selling a half-million copies. As 1970 began, it remained firmly lodged in the top 10 in the States.

Starting with their name, which read more like a law firm than a rock band, they wanted everyone to know they were a paradigm for a new, more liberating era in rock and roll. The group format, they insisted, had become too restrictive, too limited, too Establishment. (To hammer that point home and tweak his former life, Crosby would sometimes play a few seconds of the chimey twelve-string lick of the Byrds' "Mr. Tambourine Man" onstage, which always drew a laugh: *The Byrds? A pop group? How quaint!*) As the Royal Albert Hall crowd witnessed, they didn't even resemble a traditionally cohesive band. Crosby, at twenty-eight the veteran, had the bushy hair, serpentine walrus mustache, and stoner-bliss smile of the hippie commune leader next door. Nash, who'd be turning twenty-eight the following month, had a head engulfed in sculpted brown hair and a wardrobe of vests and floral-print shirts that embodied modish counterculture. Stills was younger than both—he'd turned twenty-five three days earlier—yet more conservative in attire (white-button shirts, dark suit jackets) and hairstyle (sideburns and prematurely thinning dark-blond hair framing chiseled cheekbones). Young, the relative baby at twenty-four, opted for patched denim and white-lace shirts. His furrowed brow and shoulder-length locks set him apart from the others as did the way he'd lurk behind them, near the guitar amps, during their shows.

After opening with "Suite: Judy Blue Eyes," the seven-minute Stills homage to former girlfriend Judy Collins that had become one of their signature songs, their utter self-confidence kicked in. As McCartney looked on, they sang one of his own songs, "Blackbird," from the White Album. They'd tackled it before, including at Woodstock the previous summer, but tonight it was a declaration of their eminence: It practically declared that they were picking up where the Beatles had left off. (To their credit, they sang it lovingly, with Stills holding a long, raspy note in the "dark black night" line that made the song their own.) The rest of the show broke with tradition in numerous ways. For the first, acoustic half, the four sang some songs as a quartet, others separately, others with a combination of the four. Like their garb, the songs mirrored their diverse personalities and lifestyles. Crosby's "Triad" openly coaxed a girl into having a ménage à trois; Nash introduced "Our House," about the cozy, music-and-lovemaking existence he had back home in Laurel Canyon with his girlfriend Joni Mitchell. (He also told the crowd it was from a new album they'd just completed, to be called *Déjà vu*.) Young's "The Loner" seemed to be as much about himself—the way he worked on his own schedule, at his own pace, on his terms—as about the song's borderline-stalker character.

Halfway through the set, a curtain behind them parted, revealing a bowl-haired drummer, Dallas Taylor, and a very young-looking black bass player, Greg Reeves. Thus began the electric second half of the show, which shed additional light on their personalities. Stills was particularly competitive and driven, no more so than during Young's tightly wound shuffle, "Down by the River," during which the two men jabbed at each other with their lead guitars over the course of fifteen minutes. Like the group itself, the performance was both rehearsed and ragged, teetering on the brink of chaos. Just as the tangle of guitars and rhythm section was on the verge of collapse, Nash, ensconced behind an organ and waiting patiently for his moment, shouted, "All together now!" signaling a return to the song's chorus—and, at last, an end to the show.

Throughout the night, they remained anxious, and it showed: They exchanged in-jokes with each other and indulged in lengthy tune-ups between songs. Yet few seemed to mind. The Royal Albert Hall crowd laughed adoringly at their jokes and applauded every lapse, from the not-always-precise harmonies to the sight of the four professionals trying to decide what song to do next. *(Set lists! So rigid!)* They could seemingly do no wrong. Atlantic had already taken in $2 million in preorders for *Déjà vu*. At a company sales conference in Palm Springs, California, in January, label executives touted the album as one of its biggest potential earners of the year. CSNY would embody both the decade past and the decade to come: no rules, no restrictions, just as "free and easy" as "Wooden Ships" declared.

Back at the Dorchester, Ron Stone, a bearded native New Yorker who worked for CSNY band managers Elliot Roberts and David Geffen, noticed something odd. Reeves had sprinkled something outside the door of his room. When asked, he said it was witchcraft powder to ward off evil spirits. *Hmmmm*, Stone thought. *What was that about?* Reeves' behavior had begun to raise eyebrows, yet no one could tell if it had to do with this heretofore-unknown aspect of his personality or the quantity of drugs everyone was now consuming.

For the time being, no one gave Reeves' eccentricities much more thought. Introducing the bass player to the Royal Albert Hall audience a few hours before, Crosby had blissfully declared, "God smiled and sent us Greg Reeves." Amidst the intoxicating applause, plaudits from their industry, and backstage temptations, it was hard to believe God would stop beaming their way anytime soon.

The signup sheets posted on each floor of New York University's School of the Arts building—a big, blocky stucture on East 7th Street in the East Village surrounded by Polish diners, used record stores, and head shops—were almost too crude to be believed. Typed and mimeographed, each resembled a homework assignment more than a department memo. The first line, from the office of David Oppenheim, the School of the Arts' imposing, culturally connected dean, read like an April Fool's gag: "Paul Simon of Simon and Garfunkel has offered to teach a course in how to write and record a popular song." According to the flier, the course would carry no credit and meet on Tuesday evenings from February through May. "Only those who are already writing and have music or lyrics to show Mr. Simon should apply," Oppenheim's instructions added.

Both the memo and the class were so modest that the sheets took a while to fill up. Only thirteen students in the graduate film and television program jotted down their names; no one from the dance department bothered. By the deadline, January 16, sixty-nine had signed up, and the following week they began showing up at the building, around the corner from the Fillmore East, New York's leading rock theater. Cradling guitars and sheet music, they began congregating in a drab hallway in the East 7th Street building, waiting to be summoned for their auditions.

Although he'd never taught a class before, Simon, at twenty-eight, had indisputable credentials. The duo he'd formed with his schoolyard friend Art Garfunkel had had a fitful start: a hit single thirteen years earlier in 1957, followed by a series of flops, a breakup, a reunion, another flop, and finally, at last, a hit with "The Sound of Silence," a melding of English-lit-class surrealism and sullen folk chords that Simon had written in the bathroom of his parents' house in Queens, New York. This time, success stuck. Since December 1965, they'd logged eight top 20 hits, from "The Sound of Silence" through "The Boxer" the previous summer.

Physically, they resembled a high rise jutting up next to a brownstone. Almost five inches taller than his partner, Garfunkel, who was also twenty-eight, towered over Simon. Garfunkel was blue-eyed and gamin-like, Simon brown-eyed and comparatively gnomish. Garfunkel's blond Afro contrasted sharply with Simon's prematurely receding hairline, which Simon attempted to disguise by growing his hair longer on the side. But their voices, if not their looks, blended together, and their dotingly crafted, meticulously harmonized songs connected with a generation trying to remain calm during a chaotic period in America's history. A 1967 Columbia Records press release touted them as possessing "a unique understanding of the soul of the young city-dweller" who sings of "the alienation, excitement and loneliness that are peculiar to and so much a part of life in the Big Town." While flowery, the label's hype wasn't far from the truth: Simon and Garfunkel even looked like a couple of grad-school enrollees.

As soon as he saw the flier for Simon's class, Ron Maxwell, a twenty-one-year-old NYU graduate film student, called one of his high-school friends from nearby Clifton, New Jersey, a fledgling composer and pianist named Joe Turrin. The previous year, the two had written *Barricade*, a rock opera inspired by Maxwell's time in Paris during the 1968 student uprising. At the appointed audition time, Maxwell arrived at the building—the same one where he'd hung a handmade "US Out of Vietnam" banner out a window as one of his teachers looked on with head-shaking disdain.

Maxwell and Turrin were called in, and there was Simon, alone in a classroom with only an upright piano. At all of five feet four, Simon was more diminutive in person than on his album covers. The three shook hands and made some introductory small talk. Simon seemed impressed that Maxwell and Turn had written an entire show. Propping up the 150-page libretto of *Barricade*, Turrin settled in behind the piano and began playing, Maxwell singing the lyrics and acting out the plot. In the middle of one song, Turrin noticed Simon standing behind him, staring at the score. Turrin, who'd studied at the Eastman School of Music in Rochester, was instantly rattled: Paul Simon, of all people, was scrutinizing his work.

At the end of the performance, Simon looked at Turrin apologetically. "I didn't mean to bother you," he said. "I can't believe you notated all of that." To the surprise of both would-be students, Simon told them he couldn't read music. To Turrin, the admission was shocking: One of the leading songwriters of his generation, the man who managed to slip a phrase like "superficial sighs" into the chorus of a pop single, couldn't decipher sheet music?

Had Turrin and Maxwell known more about Simon, they would have been equally surprised. At that moment, he and Garfunkel were on the verge of a new and potentially colossal era. The week before the scheduled start of the course, Columbia Records would be unveiling *Bridge Over Troubled Water*, the duo's first new album in over a year. The label's radio department was hustling hard to promote the title song, which *Billboard* had already declared a "national breakout single." A tour of Europe and another headlining date at New York's Forest Hills Tennis Stadium were being planned. Yet here was Simon, committing himself to nearly three months in a classroom at NYU. Everyone assumed it was a lark—that when it ended, Simon would resume the career that had finally paid off for him after years of dues-paying. It was inconceivable to picture Simon without Garfunkel, without further luminous melodies, and without the syllable-for-syllable harmonies that made him and his partner seem less like entertainers and more like brothers.

In the ramshackle offices of the Vietnam Moratorium Committee in Washington, D.C., co-organizers Sam Brown and David Hawk knew they needed a second act for the new decade. But what, precisely? The Moratorium had begun in the spring of 1969 as a call for students to strike in opposition to the Vietnam War. Gradually, the plan mushroomed into a nationwide antiwar rally. Held October 15, it defied even Hawk and Brown's most optimistic expectations. Around the country, a million people congregated to express their disapproval. In what *Time* dubbed "a calm, measured and heavily middle-class statement of weariness with the war," one hundred thousand gathered in Boston Common, bells in small towns tolled somberly, and World War II veterans in Detroit suburbs congregated to show their solidarity. Students burned draft cards, but no one anticipated the housewives in Texas who blocked a bridge leading to a defense plant.

The new decade was already sending mixed signals. On one hand, aspects of the one before appeared to be intact. The Beatles were completing a new album and film. In the wake of Woodstock the previous August, which had lured a half-million generally peaceful music fans to New York farmland, a slew of similar multiday and multi-act festivals were being planned throughout 1970. In July and then November 1969, America had finally succeeded in dropping men onto the moon; a third mission was set for April.

Yet other events of the previous six months had been hard to comprehend. No one yet knew what to make of a series of ritualistic murders in Hollywood the previous August, supposedly led by an elfin, wild-eyed hippie named Charles Manson who looked like someone who could've been in those Woodstock throngs. In December, a free concert by the Rolling Stones at the Altamont Speedway in northern California had ended with the knifepoint murder of a young black man at the hands of a Hell's Angel. (Crosby, Stills, Nash & Young had played at that very show, hours before the murder.) The fact that the decade had begun with John Kennedy and ended with Richard Nixon, who'd been inaugurated in January 1969, didn't bode well. Even *Mad* sensed a change in the winds. In its January 1970 issue, cartoonist Sergio Aragones rolled out another of his gleeful skewerings, "Protest Demonstrations." A group of whites holding "White Supremacy" signs head toward an intersection; a band of African-Americans, holding their own "Black Power" signs, are on a collision course with them from another direction. Between them, a street preacher carries his own sign: "Prepare to Meet Thy Doom."

The future of the Moratorium was as undecided as the newly born '70s. Brown and Hawk's original plan called for a series of similar mass protests: one in October, two in November, three in December, four in January 1970, and so on, building into a continuous, nonstop display of public disgust. Yet they knew they couldn't possibly top the first October 15 event. A second gathering, this time organized by New Mobilization Committee to End the War in Vietnam, wasn't at all their planned sequel. In a letter to the *New York Times* published November 11, a Mobilization co-organizer declared plans for "legal and peaceful, totally non-violent demonstrations in Washington, San Francisco, and points in between." Unfortunately, they didn't all turn out that way. When one speaker in Washington encouraged the crowd to storm the Justice Department, Hawk, who like Brown wasn't involved in the Mobe's planning, winced. As if on schedule, marchers from the more radical fringe began running through the Washington streets and police were lobbing tear gas.

Instead of holding further Moratoriums and Mobilization events, Hawk, Brown, and their colleagues decided on the most sensible option: raising money for pro-peace candidates running in the upcoming midterm elections. Assuming they won, those officials could begin cutting off funding for the war. The plan was pragmatic and sensible—and, Hawk knew, would have zero appeal to the rising number of far-left groups. He wasn't even sure what to call one of the leading groups, since their name kept changing: Was it the Weathermen or the Days of Rage people? Whatever their moniker, Hawk knew they favored open combat in the streets over subvert-from-within tactics. The Weathermen made the Moratorium organizers promise not to denounce them publicly. Privately, though, Hawk was worried how far they were going to take their tactics and what impact they could have. Was the public intelligent enough, he wondered, to distinguish antiwar demonstrations from violent hooliganism?

While those debates ensued, a far more immediate problem needed to be addressed: paying for the expenses involved in mounting the October and November Moratoriums and replenishing the Moratorium fund. With the help of Peter Yarrow of Peter, Paul and Mary, one of pop music's most passionate antiwar advocates, a benefit—the Winter Concert for Peace—had been planned for Madison Square Garden in January.

The day of the show, January 28, Hawk, a studious-looking, bespectacled community organizer and former Cornell student, flew to New York, went to the Garden, and addressed the twenty thousand in the venue. In the minds of Hawk and Moratorium workers like Jane Barlow, the show achieved the perfect balance of political rally and quasi-Woodstock music experience. Thanks to his connections in the music business, Yarrow had assembled a wide-ranging assortment of acts: folksingers Richie Havens and Judy Collins, the Long Island blue-eyed soul band the Rascals, the big-band pop group Blood, Sweat & Tears, the cast of *Hair*, and the Edwin Hawkins Singers (who'd taken gospel to the pop charts the previous year with "Oh Happy Day"). With memories of the first Moratorium still on everyone's mind, the crowd was noticeably charged.

That is, until the arrival of the headliner, Jimi Hendrix. Two and a half years earlier, Hendrix had ignited the audience *and* his guitar at the Monterey Pop Festival. But the man who took the New York stage now was a far cry from the carnal rock and roll gypsy of Monterey. He looked and sounded prematurely careworn. Taking the stage very late with his new band, Band of Gypsys, he made it through only one song before he began muttering incoherently. "That's what happened when Earth fucks with Space," he told the crowd before sitting down. "Never forget that." Both the audience and the musicians were baffled, if not uneasy, and Hendrix soon left the stage.

No one ever quite knew what drug Hendrix was on or who gave it to him. His intake had become so notorious that few at the Fillmore East had been surprised when he consumed a large amount of cocaine backstage at a New Year's Eve show just a few weeks earlier. But as he left the stage and the Winter Concert for Peace crumbled to a close, Hawk grimaced in his seat. This wasn't the Hendrix of Monterey, Woodstock, or "All Along the Watchtower." This Hendrix, he thought, was too far gone. The concert organizers were disturbed but tried hard not to dwell on the evening's unfortunate anticlimax. They had another, similar concert to plan for the summer.

Sitting at his desk at the Warner Brothers Records office on Burbank Boulevard in Burbank, California, Stan Cornyn glanced over the list of the label's upcoming releases. As vice president of creative services,

Cornyn was responsible for the company's clever, postmodern ad copy. (A print advertisement for a new album by the Fugs, the ragged East Village folk-rock anarchists, said, "You will find the usual Fugs quota of atonal masochism . . . In spite of this, there are redeeming qualities in this album.") Physically, Cornyn embodied the new breed of music business executive. With his horn-rim glasses, Cornyn looked bookish, but he'd stopped wearing the blue suit jackets favored by Warner executives in the early '60s and had begun growing out his hair. The makeover helped him forge a bond with the younger acts on Warner and its sister label Reprise: One day, Joni Mitchell dropped by his office with a notebook of lyrics she asked Cornyn to type out for liner notes.

Of a typical batch of new albums released by Warner in any given week, two or three would be the label's big guns—Peter, Paul and Mary, Bill Cosby. As for the rest, they were nobodies—"the weirdos," Cornyn would call them. As he prepared to bang out copy for ads that would run in the music trades the first week of February, Cornyn noticed one of those oddballs on the list: James Taylor.

Cornyn knew the basics: Taylor was a twenty-one-year-old singer-songwriter, guitarist, and apparent nomad (his homes had included Martha's Vineyard, Manhattan, North Carolina, London, and currently the couch in his producer's house in town). He'd recorded an album for the Beatles' Apple label, and Joe Smith, the president of Warner, had snatched him away and was releasing Taylor's second album, *Sweet Baby James*. Cornyn also knew the Apple album had received good reviews but hadn't sold, and that Smith's enthusiasm alone didn't guarantee anything. His knowledge of Taylor pretty much ended there. Cornyn was accustomed to seeing musicians pop in and out, like Neil Young storming out of Reprise head Mo Ostin's office. But Cornyn had yet to meet Taylor or even glimpse him around the building.

Taylor had actually visited Smith's office a few weeks earlier, but Cornyn, along with most of the Warners staff, simply wasn't told. The scrappy, avuncular Smith had first caught sight of Taylor at the Newport Folk Festival the summer before. Taking in the sights during an after-show party at one of the plush estates near the festival grounds, Smith saw a tall, lanky kid taking long strides across the lawn. At times he seemed to be staggering, as if he were on one substance or another.

When they met, Smith instantly recognized Taylor's name from the Apple release. Taylor, who was performing at the festival, began complaining about the Beatles' shaky organization and indicated he was looking for a new record deal. Smith introduced Taylor to the Everly Brothers, who'd integrated Appalachian harmonies into rock and roll in the late '50s and were now struggling to look and sound contemporary. Right there on the lawn, the three began harmonizing together on one of Taylor's songs, "Carolina in My Mind." Smith took note: If two of rock's greatest singers could easily adapt to one of Taylor's songs, maybe plenty of other people could appreciate Taylor too. Smith wound up signing Taylor.

On a midwinter January day, Taylor and his manager, Peter Asher, visited Smith's office to play him what they had of *Sweet Baby James*. The two were quite the pair. Taylor was all arms and legs; his shoulder-length hair, parted in the middle, slouched down either side of his face. He had a penetrating gaze and a high forehead. Asher, though older than Taylor by four years, looked younger: With his dark-rimmed spectacles and red mop top, he could have easily passed for a polite British schoolboy.

Normally, Smith invited other label executives to sit in during listening sessions to meet the artist and get an early feel for the music they'd be marketing. But he sensed Taylor was different—that he'd be easily spooked by the presence of strangers—so Smith decided the meeting would be restricted to himself, artist, and manager.

Asher and Taylor arrived and handed Smith a tape. Smith popped it in as the two men sat on the other side of his desk. From the opening line about a young cowboy on a range, Smith was hooked. He reveled in the easygoing lull of the songs and Taylor's upright but soothing delivery. The music was gentle, melodic, and direct. It wasn't rock and roll, nor was it imbued with even a millisecond of political consciousness. But Smith related to it in ways he didn't always with other acts he'd signed, like the Grateful Dead. Smith kept hoping and praying the Dead would record something approaching a single (when they finally did a few months later, with "Uncle John's Band," he literally whooped with joy).

Throughout the playback, Smith made appreciative comments about the songs. After a while, Smith realized Asher did all the talking; Taylor said little, if anything. He mostly nodded and, once in a while, flashed a bemused expression. Smith had amicable relationships with many artists on his label, but he sensed he wasn't going to get to know Taylor very well. Later, when Smith heard about the heroin bouts, the wards with locked doors, and Taylor's stay in a psychiatric hospital only months before, Taylor's mood that day made sense. But at the moment, Taylor simply seemed shy and fragile.

Long after Taylor left the Warner compound, Stan Cornyn sat behind his typewriter and banged out copy for the ad touting the label's forthcoming releases. "Last year, James Taylor's first album, on friendly competitor Apple, was dearly loved and glowingly reviewed," he wrote. "This year the same will happen to James Taylor's second album, *Sweet Baby James*. Only much more so." Like all commercials, it was noticeably optimistic. Since the album cover wasn't finished, Cornyn opted for an in-joke: a photo of an Apple with a bite chomped out of it. Even if the record tanked, like those by so many other unknowns, he hoped everyone would at least remember the ad.

PART ONE

WINTER INTO SPRING
A Song That They Sing When They Take to the Highway

CHAPTER 1

Smack in the middle of a workweek—Wednesday, February 11—Mort Lewis took the type of call any music business manager longed to receive. A friend at Columbia Records informed him that the company had officially shipped one million copies of Simon and Garfunkel's *Bridge Over Troubled Water*. At a time when the bar for success was the gold album for sales of half a million, the figure was especially remarkable. Days later, Lewis, a tall, toothy World War II veteran who'd become Simon and Garfunkel's manager in 1965, received an honorary souvenir from Columbia commemorating the conversation: a dime mounted on a wooden plaque with the inscription, "To Mort Lewis—For Posterity."

Lewis chuckled, as he would for years afterward whenever he saw the plaque, but he was also relieved. Between the creation of the album, the constant interruptions, and that damn television special, the previous year had been a trying one for his clients.

Not that they hadn't asked for it, to some degree. Like everyone who worked with them, from Columbia president Clive Davis to the session musicians who had to repeatedly replay their parts in the studio, Lewis was painfully aware of how exacting Simon and Garfunkel could be. The creation of their fifth album stretched back to January 1969, when the duo went to Nashville to record—or, it turned out, start recording—one of Simon's new songs, "The Boxer." The track began simply, with Simon and session guitarist Fred Carter Jr. fingerpicking the gentle sway of Simon's melody on Martin guitars. Then Simon, Garfunkel, and their coproducer and recording engineer, Roy Halee—a Columbia staffer and native New Yorker who had become an intrinsic member of their tightly knit team—began layering the track to enrich the sound. Only later did Simon add lyrics—the story-song of a worn-down prize-fighter meant to be a metaphor for Simon and the criticism sometimes leveled at his work.

In the end, "The Boxer" incorporated a tuba, harmonica, drums, and a mournful, otherworldly solo that combined a pedal steel guitar cut in Nashville with a piccolo overdubbed in New York. For the "lie lie lie" fi-nale that never completely satisfied Simon, Garfunkel suggested they record at a chapel at Columbia University; the echo would be just what the song needed. Columbia Records balked at spending so much money on one song, but they had little choice in the matter. The duo's track record of hit singles gave them the latitude to take however long they wanted, and however much money it would take.

A few months later, in the summer of 1969, Simon and Garfunkel left their hometown and decamped to Los Angeles. Simon rented a house on Blue Jay Way in the Hollywood Hills, a home previously occupied by George Harrison, who'd immortalized it in a drony piece of psychedelia of the same name on the Beatles' *Magical Mystery Tour*. With the Beat-les still on his mind, Simon brought with him a new song he'd begun in New York. His lawyer Michael Tannen had first heard it when Simon showed up late at Tannen's birthday party on Manhattan's Upper West Side. "I've just written my 'Yesterday,'" said Simon, who, despite fending off a cold, sang it for the partygoers.

As with "The Boxer," "Bridge Over Troubled Waters," as it was first called, was no painless undertaking. Starting with the simple strum of an acoustic guitar, Simon's demo of the song was understated and gen-tle. "When peace is all you seek, I will be there," he sang, almost as if he were back in the British folk clubs he'd played earlier in the decade. Then, reflecting one of his newfound musical passions, his voice glided up into a falsetto inspired by Claude Jeter of the Southern gospel group the Swan Silvertones. (It was the Silvertones' "Oh, Mary Don't You Weep," with its line "I'll be a bridge over deep water if you trust my name," that inspired Simon to write his own variation.) At the Blue Jay Way house, Simon sang it for Lewis and Garfunkel. Lewis loved it right away, and Simon suggested it as a showcase for his partner. Surprisingly, Garfunkel initially demurred, not feeling the song was a perfect fit for his voice. Simon persisted, and Garfunkel eventually agreed.

To begin the process of capturing the song on tape, Simon called in Larry Knechtel. Born in southern California, the twenty-nine-year-old Knechtel had worked with them on their previous album, *Bookends*; his extensive résumé also included playing piano in the famed Wrecking Crew, a group of renowned Los Angeles session musicians featured on more hits (by the Mamas and the Papas, the Beach Boys, the Fifth Dimension, and many others) than an AM radio could handle. Knechtel, a taciturn professional with shaggy sandy-brown hair, had seen it all—or so he thought. Starting August 1, 1969, he clocked in at Columbia's basketball-court-size studio on Sunset Boulevard, joining Simon, Garfunkel, and Halee. Simon played Knechtel the new song on guitar and told him he wanted to center it around a piano instead. Once the chords were transposed with the help of arranger Jimmie Haskell, Knechtel devised an introduction and an outro, and the rehearsals began. Knechtel took a seat at the piano, and Garfunkel stood next to him, both donning headphones, microphones dangling from the ceiling to capture as full a piano sound as possible.

As Simon watched with hawkish intensity from behind the control-booth glass, Knechtel and Garfunkel began performing "Bridge Over Troubled Waters." That day alone, Knechtel worked from 10 P.M. to 4:30 A.M., with a half-hour break. Knechtel knew his bosses could be exacting, but over the days ahead, he didn't expect to play the song—two verses, totaling just under three minutes—as many times as he did. His own estimate was seventy-two takes. "Paul wanted it to be gospel, but *not* gospel," Knechtel recalled. "That was the hard part, since Art couldn't sing that stuff." Knechtel admitted he probably screwed up a few times; he wasn't used to so many replays. Meanwhile, Simon rewrote some of the verses and changed "waters" to the singular "water" in the title phrase.

Once Simon decided on a take he liked—the second, it turned out—it was then to stage two: a muted drum part by Hal Blaine, another member of the Wrecking Crew; two bass parts by Joe Osborn, also a veteran of Simon and Garfunkel sessions; vibes; drums recorded in an echo chamber; a string section. Realizing the song was too short, Simon told everyone to leave space for a third verse he'd write later. Inspired by the sight of his girlfriend Peggy Harper looking in the mirror at the Blue Jay Way house and seeing a gray hair—"silver girl" was the phrase that came to mind—Simon finished the new words, and Garfunkel sang an early draft of them on August 13.

And yet work on the song was only just beginning. When they returned to New York, Garfunkel began two painstaking weeks of vocal work at a Columbia studio. Garfunkel could be as exacting as Simon, but during the session, Simon would nonetheless get visibly angry if his partner sang a note Simon hadn't planned out beforehand. Although he'd known his collaborator for nearly fifteen years, Garfunkel was still taken aback. He'd been gone most of the previous few months, on a movie set, and had to readjust to Simon's demanding ways.

Tensions between them were nothing new; if anything, they were as much a part of their lives as their shared borough backgrounds. In Nashville during initial work on "The Boxer," the two were driving around one day with Halee and arguing about who could run the fastest. Right then, Simon demanded a race. Halee pulled over into an empty parking lot, and all three jumped out and bolted across it. Simon finished first, Halee second, and Garfunkel last. Nothing about the incident—the impromptu contest, the sprint, the results—surprised anyone who knew them.

They'd been friends and competitors as long as anyone could recall. One day in the fall of 1957, when they were both sixteen, they'd gone shopping together for sweaters. Even though they were mere Queens high-school students, they'd actually placed a song on the charts, "Hey, Schoolgirl," and needed to spruce up their wardrobes. In the store, they began arguing: Simon wanted one type of sweater, Garfunkel another. In the end, they couldn't agree on what to wear and wound up leaving with nothing. A few hours later, they laughed about it, and the cycle began again.

As children, they'd lived within three blocks of each other, in the middle-class section of Queens, New York, and went to the same elementary school, P.S. 164 in Flushing. Simon had migrated from nearby Newark, New Jersey, where his father, a bass player and bandleader named Louis Simon, had been born. The family—which also included Louis' wife Belle, who taught school, and a younger son, Eddie—moved to Kew Gardens Hills, a largely Jewish section of the borough. Garfunkel was already living there with his parents, Jack and Rose, and his two brothers, Jules and Jerry. Simon had taken note of Garfunkel's singing during a school talent show. "I saw you on that stage and I thought, 'That's how you get popular,'" Simon told him after they'd become friends. Garfunkel took note of Simon's sense of humor, and they finally met during a sixth-grade production of *Alice in Wonderland*.

From the start, rock and roll drew them together. Inheriting his father's love of music, Simon began learning guitar and playing his own type of music. At a ninth-grade dance, he and Garfunkel joined up to sing Big Joe Turner's recent hit "Flip, Flop and Fly"—"I'm a Mississippi bullfrog, sittin' on a hollow stump," went part of its rollicking lyrics. By the time they were attending Forest Hills High School, they were singing songs by the Crew Cuts and their heroes, the Everly Brothers. Once, when they were trying to learn the Everlys' "Hey Doll Baby" from memory, they inadvertently came up with a song of their own, "Hey, Schoolgirl," in half an hour.

31

While they were putting it on tape in a Manhattan studio, Sid Prosen, owner of a local indie label with the presumptuous name of Big Records, overheard them. In the immediate way in which the early rock and roll business worked, he offered to make a record out of it on the spot. Prosen spoke with their parents, cut a deal, and, two days later, shipped fifty thousand copies of "Hey, Schoolgirl" to record stores and jukeboxes. One obstacle remained to assimilating themselves into the culture: their names. They rechristened themselves Tom and Jerry: Garfunkel was now Tom Graph, a nod to his love of math and charting pop hits on graphs, while Simon rechristened himself Jerry Landis.

With its "who-bop-alook-chi-bop" hook and its tale of a smitten teen who eventually lands the girl, "Hey, Schoolgirl" recalled the Everlys enough to peak at a respectable number 49 on the charts. Before they knew it, Tom and Jerry were wearing white bucks and singing the song on Dick Clark's *American Bandstand* around Thanksgiving 1956. They were rock stars—but, it turned out, only for a moment. Tom and Jerry's second single, the less confident "Our Song," recycled the "Hey, Schoolgirl" chords and died quickly. A third single, "That's My Story," amounted to banal white doo-wop and also withered. By the time they graduated from Forest Hills High School, their career was finished.

For the next few years, they barely spoke. Mere months after "Hey, Schoolgirl," Simon had cut a single on his own—a hiccupy slice of Queens rockabilly called "True or False," under the name True Taylor. The secretive recording signaled that Simon was intent on a career in pop music—and that he suspected his partner wasn't equally driven. Garfunkel, who had such a sharp, numbers-driven mind that he was already tutoring math in high school, was miffed by Simon's side project. They went off to different colleges—Garfunkel to Columbia to study architecture, Simon to Queens College, right near his parents' home—and fell out of touch.

As "Hey, Schoolgirl" proved, Simon was a quick, savvy study when it came to pop music trends. Those skills were only sharpened in the early '60s, when he took jobs at song publishing companies during his noncollege hours, where he'd sing on demos of songs being pitched to stars. In the process, he learned about record-making—and, just as important, which pop styles were in vogue at what moment. Cutting records on his own with various pseudonyms, he tried his hand at sweet ballads with pitter-patter beats ("Just a Boy," "Shy") and Elvis imitations ("Teenage Fool"). A savvy bid at airplay, "Play Me a Sad Song," implored a disc jockey to spin something woeful to ease his angst. In "It Means a Lot to Them," he was the archetypal nice Jewish boy, concerned about receiving the consent of his girlfriend's parents. The tracks were polished and au courant, but the arrangements—syrupy backing vocals and clip-clop rhythms—sank them. His sense of humor and developing sense of rhythm only poked through on "The Lone Teen Ranger," a novelty record with a honking sax solo that tapped into the *Lone Ranger* TV show frenzy.

Like many of his peers, Simon glommed onto the folk music boom that arrived after the Kingston Trio and then Peter, Paul and Mary brought strums and hearty harmonies to the masses. Before long, he'd ditched the doo-wop affectations and was transforming himself into a socially conscious singer-songwriter, just like Bob Dylan and all the new-generation balladeers playing in nearby Greenwich Village. One night in his parents' bathroom—either 1962 or early 1964, depending on the source—he began writing a new song about the alienation his generation was starting to feel. (The opening reference to "darkness" referred to the way he'd sing in the bathroom with the lights off.) During his part-time song-plugger job, Simon would often drag along his guitar and play his own songs for publishers. One day, he played "The Sound of Silence" for Tom Wilson, a Columbia Records executive. Wilson liked the song and decided to cut it, so Simon brought along Garfunkel, with whom he'd reconciled after a chance meeting on the streets of Manhattan. Wilson, a young black producer, was impressed with Garfunkel's white Afro—it was the first he'd ever seen—and before long, the former Tom and Jerry had been signed to the same label as Dylan.

With the contract, they finally reverted to their actual names. Goddard Lieberson, Columbia's distinguished and erudite president, first thought "Simon and Garfunkel" sounded too much like a department store, and a few Columbia executives considered their moniker too Jewish-sounding. Club-goers at their earliest Village folk-club shows would approach them at intermission and ask when the jokes were coming; they assumed "Simon and Garfunkel" was a comedy duo. But the time called for authenticity over artifice, so they were, finally, Simon and Garfunkel.

Released in October 1964, their debut album, *Wednesday Morning, 3 AM*, showcased what they could bring to the folk music table. Their harmonies—Simon on the low end, Garfunkel on the high—were altogether different from the rousing three- or four-part vocal blends heard on the majority of folk records; Simon's lyrics were pensive and scholarly. "The Sound of Silence" was a snapshot of a generation colliding with conformity, mass media, and "neon gods." With its images of the homeless, poets reading by themselves, and early morning fog, "Bleecker Street" evoked Greenwich Village's main thoroughfare after the music had faded for the night. The careful intertwining of the two men's voices only added to the song's mood of predawn, empty-streets fragility. But the bare-boned production throughout the album was overly wan, and the two men weren't altogether convincing in the sturdy–sing-along department ("You Can Tell the World" and "Go Tell It on the Mountain" weren't as rousing as they wanted to be). Columbia spent all of $3,000 recording it and only sold a depressing 1,500 copies. By the end of the year, Simon had relocated to London and was singing in folk clubs and train stations, and Garfunkel was back in school. Simon and Garfunkel had capsized as quickly as they'd launched.

In the middle of 1965, with folk-rock the industry rage thanks to the Byrds' cover of "Mr. Tambourine Man" and Bob Dylan's "Like a Rolling Stone," the strangest thing happened: Without Simon or Garfunkel's knowledge, Wilson overdubbed electric guitar, bass and drums onto the original "The Sounds of Silence." The transformation made all the difference: The electric guitar made the song spooky and spectral, as if listeners were walking into a long, darkened tunnel. Simon was in England when he heard the news, and from London, he read each week, stunned, as the song began climbing the charts.

In need of a manager, the duo reached out to Lewis, then overseeing the Brothers Four, a blatantly commercial folk group. Lewis freely admitted that jazz was his preferred genre; after the war, he'd stumbled into a job in the office of a press agent for one of his heroes, jazz pianist Stan Kenton, and eventually managed Kenton and pianist Dave Brubeck. Lewis first met Simon and Garfunkel at his Manhattan apartment around Thanksgiving 1965, where Simon was visibly impressed with Lewis' personally autographed copy of a Lenny Bruce LP. ("You *know* Lenny Bruce?" Simon asked in amazement.) Still, Simon was skeptical. At a subsequent meeting with Simon and a lawyer, Lewis declared he could get Simon and Garfunkel $10,000 a week in concert earnings. Simon asked Lewis to step outside for a few minutes. When Lewis returned, Simon said they would sign with him, but only if the contract could be terminated in six months. At twenty-four, Simon had already devoured the lessons, good and bad, of the music business and didn't fully trust Lewis.

Lewis wasn't kidding; within two months, they were playing colleges on weekends and taking home thousands of dollars a night. They quickly capitalized on the hit with an album, *Sounds of Silence*, largely comprised of dour melodies Simon had written in London: songs about recluses and suicides ("Richard Cory," "A Most Peculiar Man"), isolation ("I Am a Rock"), failed romance ("April Come She Will"), and premature nostalgia ("Leaves That Are Green," in which Simon looked back wistfully at his life of a few years before). For all its rainy-day ambience, the album was meatier, in both production and material, than their debut. From the second it began, with Simon's doleful opening guitar lick, "I Am a Rock" found a middle patch between cranky isolation and record-making smarts and became their next hit.

By early 1969, when work on the *Bridge Over Troubled Water* album commenced, the two could look back on an astonishing three years. Each album had sold better than the one before and, just as important, advanced their art as well. *Sounds of Silence* gave way to late 1966's *Parsley, Sage, Rosemary and Thyme.* The album was more precious than *Sounds of Silence:* "Scarborough Fair/Canticle" and "Cloudy" twinkled like stars, and "The Dangling Conversation" worked in references to Emily Dickinson and Robert Frost amidst its pointed sketch of an erudite couple on the rocks. Simon's "A Simple Desultory Phillipic" couldn't decide whether it was a mockery of protest songs or an attempt to copy Dylan. (Likewise, bleating organs throughout *Sounds of Silence* were directly lifted from a Dylan record of the period.) But the duo's creative balance—Garfunkel's tendency toward the opulent and grand, Simon's toward reflection and sheltered intimacy—played out beautifully in "Homeward Bound," "Flowers Never Bend with the Rainfall," and a cascading Garfunkel showpiece called "To Emily, Wherever I May Find Her." Simon was loosening up as well: Featuring members of Dave Brubeck's band, "The 59th Street Bridge Song (Feelin' Groovy)" added a slice of jaunty bounce to their repertoire.

The following year, director Mike Nichols used some of their older songs—and a new, unfinished one originally called "Mrs. Roosevelt" but renamed "Mrs. Robinson"—for his film *The Graduate.* When the movie became a smash by capturing post–Kennedy assassination disaffection, complete with a Jewish leading man in Dustin Hoffman, Simon and Garfunkel were embedded even further into the mass consciousness. *Book-*

ends, from 1968, was half devoted to a suite of songs that looked at life from childhood to old age, from the urban chaos of "Save the Life of My Child" to the young couple on the road in the luminous "America" to the graying couple on a park bench in "Old Friends." The album's flip side collected a random assortment of unconnected but equally thrilling singles and B-sides like "Fakin' It" and a more polished version of "Mrs. Robinson." The often affected quality of their first records—heard even in the poetry-student tone in Simon's between-song comments during early shows—burned away, replaced by songs and singing more conversational, more direct, and less mannered; they could also be whimsical in the best way.

As rock stars, they didn't always fit the bill. Their private lives were secretive; neither Simon's London girlfriends nor he and Garfunkel's dabblings in pot and acid ever made the tabloids. (Writing to a friend from London, Garfunkel joked about not using the postal service to send them hash.) They were precise and orderly, taking vacations every December and January. After concerts, their dressing rooms would be visited not by groupies yearning to sleep with them but by girls eager to share their poetry. At one Detroit concert, a security guard stopped Simon and Garfunkel at the backstage door, thinking they were audience members. "Well, we *work* here," Simon said, calmly. Their hipness, or lack of it, was far less important than their considerable craft.

By late 1969, Simon's musical sojourns continued pressing onward. In the same way gospel had inspired "Bridge Over Troubled Water," a love for South American music drew him to "El Condor Pasa," a gently floating ballad he'd heard performed in Paris by the Peruvian band Los Incas. Another day on Blue Jay Way, his younger brother Eddie—an equally skilled guitarist as well as the eerily spitting image of Paul, down to their identical fresh-from-the-Army-barber haircuts of the mid '60s—began banging a rhythm on a piano bench. Simon and Garfunkel soon joined in, and Simon taped it for fun. It wasn't much beyond a clanky, bustling rhythm track, but Simon kept returning to it, drawn in by its mesmerizing polyrhythmic pull. Eventually he pulled out a guitar and began playing along, and out came a new, rollicking song, "Cecilia."

Simon's fastidiousness and musical-explorer tendencies weren't the only reason for the delay in completing *Bridge Over Troubled Water*. Just as the sessions were getting underway, Mike Nichols reentered their lives. After *The Graduate*, Nichols had decided to adapt Joseph Heller's absurdist World War II novel *Catch-22* to the screen. Since filming would take place in Mexico and Rome, Paramount gave Nichols a sizable budget of $15 million. Having grown friendly with both men, especially Garfunkel, Nichols offered Garfunkel a role as the naïve, idealistic Captain Nately.

From the start, Garfunkel's participation in the film was a sensitive issue. Lewis tried to talk him out of it; he and Simon both felt it would take Garfunkel out of action on the album for too long. But Nichols convinced Garfunkel, and Garfunkel himself thought the timing—a three-month shoot—would work out: While he would be filming, Simon could be working on new material. In January 1969, Garfunkel, who was paid $75,000 for the role, departed for Guaymas, a town in northwest Mexico so remote that it could only be reached from Mexico City by way of a thirty-hour train ride.

Catch-22, which entailed a fully operative airfield, freshly constructed roads, and working B-52 bombers, didn't promise to be an even remotely trouble-free production. Cast and crew were stranded in Mexico for almost five months. In order to rehearse their new songs, Simon had no choice but to fly down to Mexico himself at least once. Sequestered in Garfunkel's hotel room, the two worked on their harmonies and arrangement of "The Boxer" into the night, keeping at least one cast member, a young New York-based actor named Bob Balaban (later to find wider fame appearing in most of Christopher Guest's satirical, improvised films), awake in his room next door. Filming of *Catch-22* continued in Los Angeles in June, followed by scenes in Rome in the fall.

Returning to Los Angeles, Simon was now on his own. His central collaborator would now be Halee, a stocky, patient, and equally fastidious studio technician several years older than Simon. (His short, parted-on-the-side haircut and shirts and ties worn in the studio made his age even more aparent.) Simon began to grumble to some of his studio musicians about Garfunkel's absence or, other times, that Garfunkel was holding him back creatively. During film breaks, Garfunkel popped in when he could, Simon presenting him with new songs he thought his partner should sing or with largely completed tracks. An early point of contention became "Cuba Sí, Nixon No." Reflecting his ongoing love of early rock and roll, Simon had written a mocking song about the then-new president, set to a frisky stomp that recalled Chuck Berry's "Roll Over Beethoven." The song's recording became a barometer of each man's diverging musical tastes. During one early rehearsal, Simon, reveling in a groove and rhythm unlike anything the two had done on their first four albums, sang and played the half-finished song with a smile. Leaning in to harmonize, Garfunkel struggled to find the right vocal blend to match the song's tone.

When a near-complete take was ready, they and Halee gathered in the Columbia control room for a playback. As the song boomed out of the speakers, Simon was animated, playing air guitar and bouncing on his heels. Garfunkel, hands tucked into pockets, stood silently, nodding ever so slightly. As much as Simon loved it, Garfunkel wasn't feeling it, and later they argued over whether or not it fit in with the rest of the album. The song was ultimately dropped.

Although the album should have been wrapped up by fall, other commitments intruded. In October, Simon and Garfunkel went on the road for the first time in over a year, playing ten concerts between New York and Los Angeles. To beef up their sound onstage, they brought along a band—Knechtel, Blaine, Osborn, and Carter—who joined them for several songs each night. Also along for a good portion of the tour was a two-man film crew.

With an incomplete album hanging over their heads and Columbia growing more impatient with each week—a Christmas release was now out of the question—the last thing Simon and Garfunkel needed was an additional project. But earlier in the year, they'd committed to a television special sponsored by AT&T, a company so desperate to appear hip that it doled out over $600,000 for the rights to the show. Hired to oversee the project was Robert Drew, a former *Life* magazine correspondent who'd produced well-regarded documentaries (or "candid films," as he called them) on JFK, firefighters, farmhands, and heroin addicts.

On the set of *Catch-22*, Garfunkel had befriended Charles Grodin, a thirty-four-year-old Pittsburgh-born actor with a slew of TV and Broadway credits to his name. Grodin had blandly handsome features that disguised a subversive side and a dry, off-kilter sense of humor (and his Orthodox Jewish background as well). Before long, Grodin began joining Garfunkel on visits to Simon's Blue Jay Way house. After Simon had had unsatisfying meetings with potential directors for the film, he asked Grodin, who had some stage directorial experience on his résumé. Grodin helped Simon flesh out the framework for the special and agreed to direct and work with Drew.

Shortly before the scheduled airdate of November 30, 1969, executives from AT&T gathered in a screening room at Drew's Fifth Avenue offices to watch the finished product, *Songs of America*, for the first time. They expected to see a music special and did—half the time, anyway. Cameras caught Simon and Garfunkel onstage and in hotel rooms, arriving at airports, and rehearsing for their tour. The concert footage made it clear that all they needed was Simon's resonant, agile guitar chords as accompaniment; despite the caliber of their musicianship, the rock band behind them often felt intrusive. The AT&T types watched as one hit after another—"America," "Homeward Bound," "The Boxer"—tumbled out. As always, Garfunkel stood rigidly as he sang, as if preparing to read a term paper in front of a class, while Simon had a tendency to casually gyrate in time with the rhythm.

During the first half of the hour-long special, though, the phone executives began shifting in their seats. In preliminary meetings, Simon told Drew he wanted to make "a home movie about where he thought the nation was," as Drew recalled. In Simon's mind, the country was split in two and unraveling at every turn. (He'd broken down in tears the night Nixon had been elected.) To the discomfort of the AT&T executives, half of the hour-long special adhered unwaveringly to Simon's vision. As their music played in the background, the phone company reps watched footage of decaying housing projects, burning buildings, and bloodied antiwar protesters hurling rocks at police. A montage of John Kennedy, Martin Luther King Jr., and Robert Kennedy was set to the just-finished but still-unreleased "Bridge Over Troubled Water," which never sounded more mournful. "Scarborough Fair/Canticle" accompanied a pastiche of Vietnam soldiers and hand-holding hippies. "Punky's Dilemma," a slice of subtly anxious draft-dodger whimsy from *Bookends*, was heard over footage of congressional hearings and Lyndon Johnson. Both Simon and Garfunkel were seen questioning the country's role in Vietnam ("It's . . . *crap*," said Garfunkel, disgustedly). In one outtake, the duo sang a birthday song to the country, on the verge of its bicentennial, then broke into an imitation of an exploding atomic bomb.

The AT&T men watched in silence and left. Later, an executive from its ad agency called Grodin and yelled at him: "You're using *our* money to sell *your* ideology," he barked. Someone else from AT&T told Drew

41

they'd never air it. At the very least, the company demanded that Coretta Scott King's speech during footage of a civil rights rally be lowered in volume. "This is not what we contracted for," an AT&T executive told *Advertising Age*. "We bought an entertainment show, and they delivered their own personal social and political views." The *Washington Post* devoted an op-ed to the controversy, but AT&T wasn't swayed: The company dumped the special, selling the rights to Alberto-Culver, maker of hair products like VO5 and Noxzema, for $50,000 and taking a considerable financial loss in the process.

When the show eventually aired on CBS, it was massacred in the ratings by its competition, a Peggy Fleming dancing-on-ice special. By then, it hardly mattered to its two stars. Taken aback by AT&T's qualms, Simon and Garfunkel wound up spending most of their earnings on lawyers who fought to keep the show on the air. Little about the partnership felt effortless anymore.

Arriving at Columbia's studio on East 52nd Street in early January, Clive Davis was both elated and curious. After a year of waiting, he was finally going to hear a new Simon and Garfunkel album. Davis, who'd taken the reins at Columbia in 1967 after rising from a job in the label's legal department, was both old and new school. With his thinning head of hair and omnipresent suits and ties, Davis looked his thirty-seven years. Yet his fan-boy enthusiasm for pop—even the corporate-psychedelic patterns of his suits—set him apart from previous label heads. With his ingratiating manner (if not his own formidable ego), Davis knew how to relate to bands like Santana and Big Brother and the Holding Company, both of whom he'd signed to Columbia early in his tenure.

Simon and Garfunkel were another matter, and Davis knew it. By the time he became head of Columbia, they were already stars unafraid to demonstrate their clout—by, among other things, negotiating a higher royalty rate (an inordinately high fifty cents an album and two cents per side on singles) and demanding an extension of their contract. He also realized they were complicated men: When Davis wanted to price *Bookends* higher than their previous albums, they resisted, not wanting to gouge fans.

Yet Davis knew how to work with and flatter his acts. He knew that bohemians like Janis Joplin would claim not to care about sales figures, then call him after-hours to ask how their records were doing. Simon initially nixed the idea of using their music on a soundtrack album for *The Graduate*, thinking it would be asking fans too much to buy a collection recycling older material—until Davis went to a screening of the film, heard the judicious use of their music in it, and called Simon directly. He told Simon he'd make their name smaller on the cover to avoid any whiff of exploitation, and Simon eventually agreed

Davis' power of persuasion came in handy when he arrived at the studio, where Simon and Garfunkel had been joined by members of their families. When the album playback finished, Davis announced that he loved what he'd heard, and the duo asked him to pick the album's all-important first single. They were expecting him to say "Cecilia," but instead he told them it had to be "Bridge Over Troubled Water." Simon and Garfunkel balked—a nearly five-minute ballad wouldn't have a chance on the radio, they argued. Yet Davis pressed his case: "You can't play everything according to the book," he told them. The fans who'd heard a preview of it onstage during their fall tour—and often gave it a standing ovation—were also a reliable gauge. After much discussion, they agreed.

Davis' populist instincts—his love for the big ballad aimed at the heart of middle America—were again proven right. When "Bridge Over Troubled Water" was released in late January, *Billboard* was nothing less than ecstatic: "They are going straight to the top with this beautiful, almost religious-oriented ballad," wrote their unnamed reviewer. "Performance and arrangement are perfect." Almost as soon as their version was out, the Ray Conniff Singers, the Beatles of elevator music, covered it. "Not just a number one record, but an instant classic," read Columbia's trade ads for "Bridge Over Troubled Water." True to the hype, the song became the best-selling single in the States within weeks. Without meaning to, Simon had finally managed to do something he'd never done before: write a song, like "Yesterday," that wasn't merely a hit but a standard.

"Bridge Over Troubled Water" sounded like nothing he and Garfunkel had done before. Knechtel's comforting opening chords—as florid as a Vegas lounge player yet grounded in the gospel feel Simon required—set the tone, followed by Garfunkel's muted vocal entrance and lyrics about a devout friendship that built on Simon's original opening lines. The arrangement was mathematically precise; strings and other instruments arrived gradually, in calm waves. As the last verse built to a crescendo, Blaine's drums crashed in the distance and the orchestra surged to match Garfunkel's shiver-inducing climactic high note. Given that the musicians on it had once worked with Phil Spector, "Bridge Over Troubled Water" felt like a distant cousin of one of Spector's Wall of Sound productions.

In this case, though, the song was nothing less than a Wall of Balm. The two years leading up to its release had been brutalizing ones: a succession of Vietnam bombings and casualties, urban riots, and assassinations of beloved political figures like King and both Kennedys. Had it been released earlier, "Bridge Over Troubled Water" might not have had the same impact. But arriving after a numbing period in the country's history, it became a much-needed respite from one piece of bad news after another. It was a perfectly written and produced song that had arrived at exactly the right time.

The song became the leadoff track on the most eclectic and expan-

sive album of their career. The most immediately striking aspect of
Bridge Over Troubled Water was its sonic warmth and richness. Although
Simon and Garfunkel records had always had their share of aural beauty,
the album took that aspect to often breathtaking new levels. The haunting Andean quena flutes that engulfed "El Condor Pasa" were the genuine article: Rather than copy the original Los Incas arrangement, Simon
chose to license the group's original recording, over which he and Garfunkel added new vocals. "So Long, Frank Lloyd Wright" couched one
of Garfunkel's sweetest performances in crisp bossa nova guitar and congas. With its honking saxophones and layers of street-corner harmonies,
"Baby Driver" evoked the hamburger stands of post-Elvis America. For
all the hard labor that went into its creation, "The Boxer" flowed like
the gentlest winding river. The sonorous, strummed guitar chords that
opened "The Only Living Boy in New York" were merely the start of
one of their most magnificent creations. The music—a sustained, hushed
murmur, with Knechtel's organ and Osborn's bass adding the occasional
splash of color—evoked send-offs and loneliness, as did Simon's unusually melancholy solo vocal. When he and Garfunkel's voices converged
in the song's coda—with the help of an echo chamber at Columbia's studio—the melancholy burned away, as if the sun had finally, gloriously,
risen over the city.

Beneath its crisp surface, the album told two separate, if converging,
stories. The first was the tale of one person, Simon, following his newfound world-music muse, whether to South America or Jamaica (a gawky
crack at reggae, "Why Don't You Write Me"). Its stately title ballad aside,
Bridge Over Troubled Water was looser and more playful than anything
the two had done since their Tom and Jerry days. Whether "Cecilia" was
about a particular girl or possibly Saint Cecilia, the patron saint of music
from ancient Rome, the frisky sexuality of its lyrics and rhythms was
hard to deny or resist. Even as a teenager, Simon hadn't written a line as
bluntly sexy as "making love in the afternoon," and the song's thwacking,

thumping battery of percussion felt like an ad-hoc group of street-musician drummers pounding away in Central Park. The pageantry blare of horns that concluded "Keep the Customer Satisfied," Simon's intentionally overstated lament about the rigors of the road, was also rare for a Simon and Garfunkel album.

In terms both personal and veiled, the album also laid out another story, nothing less than the rise and fall of a friendship. The two men's shared mutual love of the Everly Brothers emerged in a version of "Bye Bye Love." (In another sign of the way Simon was toying with record-making rules, they turned the ebullient clapping of an audience at one of their 1969 shows into a rhythm track, which was tacked onto a studio-sung cover of the oldie.) "The Only Living Boy in New York" described Simon's ambivalent feelings about Garfunkel leaving for Mexico to film *Catch-22*. (Calling Garfunkel "Tom" was a furtive nod to their Tom and Jerry days, but few made the connection, since the duo excluded any references to those days and records from press releases.) "So Long, Frank Lloyd Wright" referred to another of Garfunkel's outside-music passions, architecture. In a telling moment, Simon and Halee were heard shouting "So long, Artie!" during the song's fade-out.

Throughout the album, the two were heard together as often as not. "Baby Driver" was all Simon, as was almost all of "The Only Living Boy in New York." When the two men performed "Song for the Asking" during their fall 1969 tour, Garfunkel harmonized along with Simon's lead vocal. But on the record, the song—an exquisite lullaby that found Simon at his most vulnerable and conciliatory—was sung by Simon alone.

On March 7, *Bridge Over Troubled Water* became the best-selling album in America, overtaking the Beatles' *Abbey Road*. It was the number one seller from the student record store at UCLA to a Sam Goody in Stony Brook, New York. Although it was impossible to verify, Columbia claimed it had moved 1.7 million copies of the album in its first three weeks. The fact that as much as a third of it didn't feature the voices of

Simon and Garfunkel in tandem was barely noticed by anyone other than Simon, Garfunkel, and Halee.

On a chilly late-winter afternoon, Maggie Roche clutched her guitar and watched nervously as one stranger after another strode in and out of the NYU arts building. Finally, after three hours, the person she'd been patiently scoping for—Paul Simon—walked in.

An eighteen-year-old Bard College student, Roche was already an accomplished songwriter and guitarist. On weekends, her father would drive her and her younger sister Terre, who was still in high school, from their home in Park Ridge, New Jersey, into Manhattan. Working the Village folk clubs, they'd met local legend Dave Van Ronk and his then-wife Terry Thal, who mentioned that Simon, one of Roche's songwriting heroes, would be teaching a songwriting class nearby. Although she was small and shy, Roche was confident in her abilities and determined to join Simon's class.

To her surprise, Simon was alone—no entourage, no handlers—and even more surprisingly, he didn't brush her off when she approached him. She told him she and her sister were singers and songwriters, and he replied by saying she should come back a week later—which she did, this time with Terre, the most conventionally pretty of the Roche sisters. Simon led them into an empty classroom upstairs. "Go ahead—play something," he said.

The two started on Maggie's "War Song": "Set your eyes upon the greatest soldier in the war/His battlefield is strewn with corpses of his dreams," went part of it, complete with counterpart harmonies. Halfway through the first verse, Simon stopped them. "Okay, play something else," he said.

The two were jarred by his response: Did that mean he liked it or not? Although momentarily discombobulated, they sang another of Maggie's songs, and Simon again halted them midway through and asked them to move on. Finally, several half-sung songs later, he said, "Okay, you can come to the class." They wouldn't even have to pay.

The two sisters followed him upstairs to another classroom, where they saw for themselves what a Paul Simon songwriting course looked like. Desks were askew, papers piled high in one corner, a large, eraser-faded blackboard on the wall. Astounded that they were actually in the room with their hero, along with a dozen or so other students, the Roche sisters were in such a daze that the night was a blur. The evening grew even more surreal when class broke and Simon asked if the two needed a ride home. When they said they had to get to the George Washington Bridge to catch a bus to New Jersey, Simon offered them a ride, and all three piled into his blue sports car parked outside: Maggie upfront with Simon, Terre scrunched into the small backseat with her guitar case.

As Garfunkel had learned many years before, his partner was a particularly exacting taskmaster. Tonight it would be the Roche sisters' turn. As Simon navigated the Manhattan streets uptown, the sisters thought his generous offer to join the class, for free, was a sign: Maybe he was so impressed with them that he was about to offer to help them land a record deal or produce their music. At one point, "Bridge Over Troubled Water" came on the radio, but Simon paid it little mind. Instead, he took them to task: They had a gift, maybe enough to win local talent shows in their hometown, he told them, but they weren't ready for a professional career.

"Do you think you're as good a songwriter as Paul McCartney?" he asked Maggie. Confident in her abilities, she replied yes; Simon was silent.

After he'd deposited them at their stop, Simon told them he'd see them again next week. Awaiting their bus home, the sisters tried to make sense of the encounter. Simon had clearly been generous in offering them a free slot in an NYU class, alongside students who seemed more technically advanced than they were. Yet his blunt assessment shocked them. "It was such a powerful experience, that ride," Terre Roche recalled. "On one hand, we'd be coming back next week. But on the other hand, we'd been dealt with rather harshly. He was very critical. He was like a surgeon."

Returning the following Tuesday, the Roche sisters took their seats. A fellow student announced he'd just seen an impressive new singer and songwriter at a Village club. He asked Simon if he'd heard of him—someone named James Taylor. Simon replied no, he hadn't.

CHAPTER 2

By the early afternoon of December 8, 1969, James Taylor's limbs had finally healed. Three months earlier, he'd stumbled across a stolen motorcycle held in storage by the police department on Martha's Vineyard, where his family had been spending summers the previous sixteen years. Jumping on the bike, Taylor ripped through the backwoods and promptly smashed into a tree so hard he broke both his hands and feet. When his friend and fellow guitar player Danny Kortchmar heard about it, he groaned and thought, "What a fucking asshole," but part of him wasn't surprised. Taylor had had a less traumatic motorcycle accident not long before, and Kortchmar—Kootch to his friends—heard Taylor had almost cut his hands off with a chainsaw and wood chipper. Taylor always seemed to be living a bit on the edge. "If he hadn't done that, he would have jumped off a cliff," Kortchmar recalled. "He was always trying to kill himself."

When he first heard about the accident, Peter Asher wasn't merely concerned; he was terrified. Although Asher knew his way around showbiz, first as part of the British Invasion duo Peter and Gordon and then as a talent scout at the Beatles' Apple label, Taylor was Asher's first client as a manager—and was proving to be more of a handful than first imagined. In some regards, Taylor, whose maternal grandfather was a boat builder, was a strong sort—six feet three and projecting a brawny but cerebral new style of American masculinity. Yet his physique masked an inner fragility. At the very least, the accident meant the recording of Taylor's second album would be delayed, not the best of news for Warner

Brothers Records. Later, Taylor would show his manager the chunk of tree that had been taken out by one of his clenched fists.

By the first week of December, Taylor was over three thousand miles away from the Vineyard at Sunset Sound, a studio on Sunset Boulevard in Los Angeles. The casts were off his feet and hands, and he was eager to put his new batch of songs to tape. Joining him were Kortchmar—who, at twenty-three, was two years older than his friend—and, on piano, a twenty-seven-year-old Brooklyn-raised songwriter named Carole King Goffin. Each was experienced at making music, from the string of Brill Building hits King had cowritten to Kortchmar's tenure in underground bands in New York as well as one with King in L.A. The drummer was Russell Kunkel, a lanky kid from Pittsburgh only three years out of high school. Between two and six P.M. on December 8, the three of them—augmented by Randy Meisner, a bass player who'd briefly been a member of Poco, the country-leaning offshoot of Buffalo Springfield—efficiently cut three songs: "Blossom," "Country Road," and "Lo and Behold." When the work was done, Taylor was paid $170, with $13.60 deducted for his musicians' union pension.

As both Asher and the musicians discovered, reading Taylor wasn't always easy. Asher had to look for the smallest signs of any dissatisfaction, like the way Taylor might look grumpy at the end of a take but never articulate what he didn't like. "It would take a little digging to find out what should or could be changed," Asher recalled. "You had to extract information from him." Asher found Taylor a jumble of contradictions: quick-witted and intelligent, yet so gawky and nervous he didn't always look people in the eye when he spoke to them. At least Taylor wasn't spending prolonged, unexplained periods of time in the bathroom, as he had during the making of his first album. Given what Taylor had been through already, that alone felt like a significant victory to Asher.

Anyone who knew James Taylor knew he was a product, in equal doses, of music and isolation. When Taylor was three, in 1951, his family—led by his father, Isaac, a doctor educated in Boston, and his mother, Trudy—had returned to the state where Isaac was born, North Carolina. Isaac had accepted a job as an assistant professor at the University of North Carolina School of Medicine.

On the surface, their new home in Chapel Hill was idyllic: eight rooms, twenty-five acres, a hammock in the backyard. Music was everywhere. An upright piano took up residence in the living room; in the kitchen, the Taylor kids—oldest brother Alex, followed by James, Livingston, Hugh, and Kate—would pull out cans from the cupboards and break spontaneously into the jingles for each product. The children would sing sea shanties, Woody Guthrie songs, and sing-along favorites like "On Top of Old Smoky." Thanks to Trudy, who'd studied voice at the New York Conservatory and had once trained with Aaron Copland at Harvard, the concept of a professional career in music wasn't unthinkable. James himself—born in Boston in 1948—took cello lessons, briefly played in Chapel Hill's first Young People's Orchestra, and performed once with the North Carolina Symphony, playing the ballad "Blue Bells of Scotland." Alex brought home Ray Charles and Bobby Blue Band records and joined a local bar band, the Corsairs.

The family summered on Martha's Vineyard in Gay Head and Chilmark, where James befriended Kortchmar. Hailing from Larchmont in Westchester County, just north of New York City, Kortchmar couldn't have been more different from Taylor: He was shorter, more extroverted, and gregarious, a born rock and roller even in his youth. During their first summer hanging out on the Vineyard, they realized they shared a mutual love of soul, R&B, and blues records. "That was so heavy to find someone else who was into that kind of music," Kortchmar recalled. Kortchmar also learned his friend could sing when Taylor broke into a Ray Charles song while they were hitchhiking. Before long, the two were playing at hootenannies on the Vineyard.

The tranquil settings masked a sense of unease and anxiety. Isaac had a drinking problem and was prone to go off on extended work trips, like the voyage to Antarctica that took him away from the family for nearly two years in the mid '50s. Trudy Taylor had to fend for herself, with sometimes unpleasant results (once she was stung by a swarm of bees while protecting her family). Isaac's isolation impacted on the family in deeper ways. Although Kate remained bubbly, Alex grew into the family rebel, the one always fighting with his parents. James was, according to his younger brother Livingston, "observant and fairly quiet, always held his cards close." He could often be seen taking walks alone in the nearby woods. The sense that they were in the South but "of the North," as James recalled, led him to feel isolated early; summers in Massachusetts only intensified those feelings. Even a hundred years after the Civil War, Taylor felt in his bones the difference between Southerners and, he recalled, "Yankees and outsiders," and he was caught between them.

The mounting sense of disconnection inside him only grew after the family enrolled him in Milton Academy, a strict boarding school ten miles south of Boston, in the fall of 1961. Although he was returning to the state where his family had once lived, Taylor wasn't comforted by Milton's wide-open yards and brick buildings. As a teacher once recalled, he was hardly an "activist." He tended to stay in his room and practice his new instrument, the guitar. When a rowdy classmate broke it, Taylor was fairly traumatized—"a bad moment for me," he would later say. Although it was repaired, it never sounded the same.

When a depression set in around Thanksgiving of his senior year, the family pulled him out. "I had a shattered brain," he recalled, leading to a stint at McLean Hospital, a $36,400-a-year Boston-suburb infirmary that, with its cottages and lawns, resembled a college campus. The sight of her older brother living in a locked ward so upset Kate that she broke down during a visit. One day at dinner in an adjoining ward, he looked over and saw—or thought he saw—Ray Charles. "I thought I was hallucinating," he recalled. "It scared the shit out of me." But his eyes didn't deceive him; Charles, who'd been sent to McLean after a heroin bust, was actually there. The sight of one of his heroes in the ward haunted him for decades.

After graduating from McLean's affiliated school, Taylor gravitated to New York City and its folk and blues clubs. His parents put up the money for his first apartment, on the Upper West Side, where he had only a mattress and a radio. With Kortchmar and another friend, drummer Joel O'Brien, he formed a band, the Flying Machine; later, he and O'Brien relocated to the Hotel Albert on East 10th Street, home base of Tim Buckley, the Lovin' Spoonful, and others whose music spilled out of Village clubs nearly every night. The band landed gigs at some of those spots, particularly the Night Owl, and Taylor's songwriting began to blossom with songs like "Night Owl," which alluded to his dark side. Like his physique, his singing voice was sturdy and stoic, with an underlying ruggedness.

Although the Flying Machine recorded a few of its songs, the band struggled, barely taking in $10 a night at clubs. By then, Taylor had discovered heroin. "My family has a history of addiction," he recalled, "and I'm probably genetically predisposed to substance abuse. So I didn't stand a chance. Those drugs, powerful drugs, were as available as a beer at the bar. The places I was living, the people I was spending time with—everybody was experimenting with everything all the time. So it was just a matter of time. There wasn't as much information available about what it meant to be getting high and how addictive things were. You still thought you could take some drugs and not get addicted to them."

Taylor was wrong, of course. Once again, his body crashed, and Isaac drove up to New York to haul his drug-addled son back home to North Carolina. "Sort of to lick my wounds a little bit," James later said. He was only home about nine months before he left again—this time for London, again with funding from his parents. Only nineteen, Taylor arrived in the city in late 1967. At first he lived with a friend of the family's from the Vineyard who had a place in Manhattan; later, his duffel bag became his home. By coincidence, Kortchmar had a contact in London. Several years before, one of Kortchmar's bands, the King Bees, had played behind Peter and Gordon. Kortchmar heard Asher was now working at Apple and was in charge of signing acts. Kortchmar didn't think Taylor would actually call Asher; his friend already seemed battered by his experiences in life and the music business. But Kortchmar also knew Taylor was capable of doing the unexpected.

Wearing a black suit with a yellow tie, Paul McCartney arrived at the Apple office on Baker Street in the early months of 1968 to chair a meeting. The Beatles' attempt to control their destiny after the death of their manager, Brian Epstein, Apple was a multi-legged beast—part record company, boutique, film studio, electronics company, and any other whim that came to mind. Also in the meeting was Asher, newly appointed as Apple's A&R man. Asher's connections with McCartney ran deep. Although he'd begun by singing protest songs in clubs at fifteen, he made a name for himself as one half of Peter and Gordon with his friend Gordon Waller. By chance, Asher's sister Jane was dating McCartney, and when another British act, Billy J. Kramer, rejected a new McCartney song called "A World Without Love," Peter and Gordon eagerly recorded it and turned a reject into a number one American hit.

Although the duo crashed the charts a few more times, Asher tired of touring and making too little money. When the Apple offer came along, Asher, a courtly and friendly type, was more than ready to make the switch to talent scout. At this particular meeting, he brought with him a tall, gangly man who sat in a chair against the wall, saying nothing and cracking his knuckles. When the meeting broke, McCartney, Asher, the stranger, and a few employees adjourned to a nearby pub, where Asher finally told everyone who the kid was—James Taylor, an American musician whom Asher wanted to sign to the label.

"Peter says your songs are very good," McCartney told him.

"Well, uh, I don't know," Taylor stammered. "I hope they are."

Asher had met Taylor only a month or two before, when Taylor called him at his apartment on Marylebone High Street and asked if he could drop off his demo tape, which included songs like "Something in the Way She Moves" (which inspired George Harrison's "Something") and "Knocking 'Round the Zoo." When Taylor showed up, Asher welcomed him into the apartment he shared with his girlfriend Betsy and played Taylor's acetate, which impressed him. To Taylor's relief, Asher allowed him to live at the apartment for a while—and, even better, told him McCartney had liked his songs and had received permission from the other Beatles to make Taylor Apple's first signed artist. Despite his own self-destructive tendencies, Taylor was suddenly the proud owner of a three-year record deal with the most talked-about new label in the business. "I was signed before I knew what was happening," he recalled. "It was really a remarkable turn of events. I was this huge Beatles fan and I definitely landed on my feet in a great position."

Like so many situations before in his life, this one began with nothing but promise. While awaiting the chance to begin making his record, he became friendly enough with the Beatles to be able to drop by and hear the first playback of "Hey Jude" and watch them work on "Revolution." At Asher's house in the Surrey countryside, he'd sit alone in an empty pool and play and sing. He'd claim he wanted to be alone, but in doing so, drew attention to himself anyway. In July 1968, Taylor and Asher began Taylor's album, using Trident Studio whenever the Beatles weren't working there; McCartney dropped by to play bass and sing harmonies on one song, "Carolina in My Mind," and Harrison also, according to Taylor, sang an uncredited part on the same song. (The "holy host of others standing around me" in the lyric was Taylor's nod to the Beatles.)

Released in the U.K. first, in 1968, *James Taylor* revealed a songwriter with a graceful gift for melody and musicality. The best of its songs—"Carolina in My Mind," "Rainy Day Man," "Brighten Your Night with My Day"—felt instantly familiar and ingratiating, not unlike McCartney's sharpest moments. Taylor's skills as a guitarist—the crisp-air, pulled-string fingerpicking style that would become his trademark—announced themselves on a version of the traditional ballad "Greensleeves"; typical singer-songwriters normally couldn't play with such jazz-influenced syncopation.

At the same time, anyone who scoured the lyric sheet also noticed a songwriter grappling with multiple issues. "Something's Wrong" hinted at his aimless life, while "Knocking 'Round the Zoo," which dated back to the Flying Machine days, detailed Taylor's stay at McLean. ("There's bars on the windows and they're counting up the spoons," he sang, if somewhat drolly.) The songs mentioned pain and sadness and, far less convincingly, sunshine and solace. *James Taylor* was the sound of a man grappling with something—and Asher's production couldn't seem to figure it out either. Sometimes, as on "Something in the Way She Moves," Asher was savvy enough to know Taylor's voice and guitar would suffice. Other songs were unnecessarily gussied up with bassoons, harpsichords, string sections, and horns. In the way the arrangements worked hard to liven up the songs, Asher's production, which was designed to draw attention to his act, was a study in denial.

The album's launch was less than auspicious. In America, Capitol mounted a billboard of the album cover on Sunset Boulevard, but the record, released there in February 1969, didn't even make the charts. In the U.K., it sold only eight thousand copies. As quickly as it began, Taylor's career was in danger of running off the rails. Taylor was frustrated that

Apple seemed to ignore the album, just as it did with too many other Apple releases that didn't have the word "Beatle" on the cover. When Taylor went to London in the summer of 1969 to begin recording a follow-up, no one at the label was organized enough to book studio time. Asher too was frustrated: Although he'd been given enormous freedom to sign up new talent, Apple didn't seem to know how to promote most of it.

Taylor himself wasn't completely satisfied with the record. "It took months to make, and it was catch-as-catch-can," he said. "It seems so half-baked, like I didn't have enough focus to bring the songs home the way I wanted them to be." The reason for the fuzziness was again chemical. In London, Taylor's addiction returned; he was able to buy heroin from legal junkies who were registered users with London's maintenance treatment program. As a result, Taylor found himself unraveling once more. "Again, I found people to hang out with who were also getting in trouble and had bad habits," he recalled, "and I ended up with another habit and sorta crashed and burned." In the summer, he flew back to the States, wearing a velvet suit he'd worn to the premiere of the Beatles' movie *Yellow Submarine* the previous summer. (He was such a part of the Apple family that company tailors had made the suit especially for him.) Suspicious of his looks, airport officials strip-searched him, which didn't relieve his fragile state of mind.

For Asher, Apple changed dramatically after the arrival of Allen Klein, and he resigned soon after Taylor's album was out. He briefly landed a job at MGM Records in New York, but when the head of the label was fired, various employees, including Asher, were let go. No matter. Asher already had a new idea: He wanted to manage Taylor and produce his next album for a new record company. When Asher decided to talk to Taylor about his plan, he found himself heading for the Austin Riggs Center, a psychiatric hospital in Stockbridge, Massachusetts. Taylor had committed himself once more, this time to a different hospital.

Asher flew to Boston and planned to drive to Austin Riggs. There was only one problem: Asher didn't have a credit card to pay for a rental car. He told the car rental employees he was visiting a local client on business, and the company said it would approve the rental if a nearby resident would vouch for him. Asher did the only thing he could—he called Taylor at Austin Riggs. "He was probably on Thorazine or something," Asher recalled. "He was no doubt brought to the phone by a white-coated attendant." Though addled, Taylor backed up Asher's story, and Asher was able to rent a car. As Asher had already discovered, Taylor was neither a typical client nor a standard potential pop star.

After he'd checked out of Austin Riggs, Taylor, at Asher's instigation, began performing. It was already apparent to those around him that playing in front of crowds fulfilled something in him, what his brother Livingston would describe as "a deep personal need to connect to an audience, to speak with them and to tell them he loves them and hear from them that they love *him*." He was well received during his afternoon set at the Newport Folk Festival, where he later met Warner's Joe Smith. At other showcases, he played so softly that audiences talked through his set or thought he was merely the opening act. Whatever the situation, Taylor went along with few complaints. "Perhaps because of McLean, I got used to not having any expectations about what would happen—or even that I would *have* a future," he recalled. "I went in the loosest sort of way from one situation to another, without any strategy."

Asher, though, adhered to his original idea. He already knew about Warner Brothers and its sister label Reprise; any label home to singer-songwriters like Neil Young, Joni Mitchell, and Gordon Lightfoot, and hyped with Stan Cornyn's hip ad copy, felt like a good fit for Taylor. Asher called Smith, and over breakfast at the Hyatt House hotel in Los Angeles in October 1969, the two talked business. Their goals were mutual; Taylor wanted out of Apple, and Smith, who wanted in on Taylor's career, offered a modest $20,000 advance and a recording budget of the same amount for the first album. (Stock options in Warner Brothers were also on the table.) The Grateful Dead had received a slightly bigger advance from the label—$25,000—but Asher was nonetheless happy. As an added incentive, Asher made Smith agree to indemnify him and Taylor, since Asher suspected Apple might sue Taylor if he left his contract a year early. Smith agreed (the other Beatles eventually went along with McCartney's request to release Taylor from his Apple obligations), and they had a deal.

After Taylor arrived in Los Angeles that December, his motorcycle injuries healed, he moved in with Asher and Betsy at their spacious, Spanish-style rental at 956 Longwood Avenue, on the corner of Olympic Boulevard. The location wasn't ideal for a sensitive artist—public buses loudly rumbled by on Olympic, shaking parts of the house—but the spacious living room, complete with sun pouring through the windows, was a perfect rehearsal space. Asher began assembling a band to back Taylor. Kortchmar, who'd already moved to Los Angeles, was called in, along with Carole King, who'd met Taylor during his Flying Machine days in New York four years earlier. To her, he was "the tall one with the guitar," but otherwise she hadn't remembered that much about him.

King herself was starting over. After writing a string of hits with her husband, Gerry Goffin—"Will You Love Me Tomorrow" for the Shirelles, "The Loco-Motion" for Little Eva, "One Fine Day" for the Chiffons, "Up on the Roof" for the Drifters, and so many other songs that defined pop radio in the first half of the '60s—King had separated from Goffin and relocated with their two children to Laurel Canyon in 1967. She and Taylor became reacquainted when Taylor visited L.A. to promote the Apple album early in 1969, and he ended up jamming with her, Kootch, and Joel O'Brien, who'd formed a band called the City. Taylor was so self-effacing that King was pleasantly surprised by the quality of his guitar work; for a folkie type, he played so dexterously and intricately that his guitar sounded like a bell. Asher had overheard Taylor and King playing guitar and piano together and thought King would make an ideal accompanist for Taylor's second album.

At a recording session for former Kingston Trio member John Stewart, Asher had heard Kunkel, who'd logged time in a local band, Things to Come. Asher now had a skeletal band, all of whom gathered in Asher's living room to practice in early December. The room was so devoid of furniture, the acoustics so loud, and Taylor's approach so muted that Kunkel, who was accustomed to playing rock and roll, resorted to brushes instead of sticks for his drum kit. He didn't want to overpower the tall, quiet guy at the center. "Everyone had to walk on eggshells in order to get the dynamics to work," Kortchmar recalled. "James was a very quiet singer."

During the making of *James Taylor*, Asher had noticed Taylor disappearing into the lavatory for long stretches and looking tired. At the time, he wasn't aware of Taylor's drug history. Asher knew all about it now, but he noticed Taylor was far more focused. With Taylor's passel of new songs—including one called "Sunny Skies," written, ironically, at Austin Riggs—the musicians, augmented by several different bass players, shifted to Sunset Sound. Starting December 8, they methodically began working their way through the material.

From the start, Kunkel saw Taylor as more than just another sulky folkie: "James could go from completely sober to completely silly in the snap of a finger," he recalled. So it was at the sessions. Taylor's sense of humor emerged when he and Kortchmar sat down at the end of one night and, with just their two guitars, knocked out a blues parody, "Oh Baby, Don't You Loose Your Lip on Me." During the Flying Machine days in the Village, Taylor had heard one too many pretentious white blues bands and wrote "Steamroller" to mock them. Again, he and Kortchmar laid it down in one night, Taylor singing intentionally exaggerated metaphors to the accompaniment of their two electric guitars. (A rhythm section and horns were added later.) Both the schedule and the funds were so tight that when Taylor showed up with a head cold, they had no choice but to record the song anyway; his congestion could be heard in the final take.

Taylor had begun writing another new song, "Fire and Rain," in London, under less than pleasant circumstances. During the making of *James Taylor*, a friend from McLean and the Manhattan druggy period, Susan Schnerr, had intentionally overdosed on pills. "We had never been that tight, but I really liked her," Taylor recalled. Afraid of upsetting him or distracting him from his work, friends like O'Brien kept the news from Taylor for months. When he finally heard, Taylor was shaken and started sketching out the first verse in his London apartment. "It just found its way into the first verse of the song," he recalled. "It was easy to write." The second verse, which came later, detailed his heroin problems and methadone treatment and was written in a New York psychiatric ward he'd checked into just before committing full-time to Austin Riggs. The third verse, with its references to "sweet dreams and Flying Machines in pieces on the ground," detailed his breakdown just before and after his short-lived band.

Taylor had written overcast songs before, but "Fire and Rain" took that intensity to a new, almost frighteningly stark level—and, ironically, was greeted by his friends as a potential breakthrough. "When I played it for Joel O'Brien, he said, 'You know, that could be a very commercial, big song for you,'" Taylor recalled. "Peter thought that, too." In Los Angeles in January 1969, Taylor, Kortchmar, and bass player Charles Larkey, King's boyfriend and new collaborator, put an early version of the song on tape, but it didn't feel right. Back in Los Angeles almost a year later, they tried again and cut it, efficiently, on December 9. Initially Kunkel played his part with drumsticks, until Asher, recalling their rehearsals, suggested the softer, swishier sound of brushes. The revised rhythm became a signature part of the arrangement, an emotional sputter and touch of drama at the end of each chorus. Meanwhile, King added spare piano chords, as if tiptoeing around Taylor's melancholy.

At the end of the third day, Taylor told Asher that was it. Even though they'd only recorded nine songs, he didn't have any more. "Well, we should really finish this and deliver it and get it down and get the money," Asher told him. The two came up with an idea to combine three half-finished songs into a brand-new one. Everyone returned to Sunset Sound on December 17 and quickly cut "Suite for 20G," named in honor of the amount of money they'd receive once they handed in the completed album. "Twenty thousand dollars was a lot of money back then," Kunkel recalled. "It meant Peter could buy some furniture." Adding up the costs of studio time and musicians, Asher realized they'd spent $7,600 recording the entire album. He was so green he felt he'd be in trouble with Smith for not spending enough of the label's money.

Taylor was pleased with the results but unsure of where the record might take him. "We were just making another record," Taylor recalled. "We were better at it. Peter was a better producer. We had a more focused idea and the players on it were good. We were in Los Angeles in a professional recording studio doing professional work. It's always good to make an album quickly and in a concise way, because it makes it have a cohesion and makes it hang together in a natural way. But I had no idea if it was any good or not."

Everyone, including Taylor, agreed on one thing: The cover was striking. Four days before the "Suite for 20G" session, Henry Diltz—an affable thirty-one-year-old photographer and folk musician who'd taken the photo used for the iconic cover of *Crosby, Stills & Nash*—had arrived at Asher's Longwood Avenue home. Sitting on the living-room floor beneath a large window, his back against the wall and his legs spread out before him, Taylor sat quietly, picking out the notes of Stephen Foster's "Oh, Susannah" on guitar. He, Diltz, and Asher then drove out to an isolated farm off Bonham Boulevard in the Lake Hollywood section and veered down a dirt road, finally arriving at a hippie commune in the woods. Given how unvarnished Taylor's music was, the sheds and barns in sight felt like the right setting.

Diltz snapped away as Taylor, in a blue denim work shirt, walked around the property. At one point, he leaned against a post and stared straight ahead. Frowning beneath a King Arthur shag and a stoic, Gary Cooper-as-folksinger gaze, he suddenly looked like a star. "Hold that a minute," Diltz said, grabbing his color camera to snap off a few frames. Diltz hadn't intended the color shots to be for more than a slide show for friends, but after developing the shot, he saw its potential.

After a few hours, Diltz stopped clicking and went off on a more glamorous assignment: hanging out with Jim Morrison to examine the skid-row photos Diltz had taken for the cover of the upcoming Doors album, *Morrison Hotel*. Morrison, along with the likes of David Crosby and Stephen Stills, was the sort of charismatic pop star Diltz was accustomed to shooting. Taylor had talent, but he wasn't part of any particular scene; if anything, he seemed like an apolitical loner. To Diltz, he was just another guy with a guitar, one of many coming up around then.

To John Fischbach, Taylor was simply a stoner buddy. A few years older than Taylor, Fischbach had, like many of his friends, left the East Coast for the West, in his case by way of Colorado. A record producer and engineer, he was in the midst of setting up a studio in town and lived with his girlfriend, Stephanie Magrino, in Laurel Canyon, the tightly—incestuously—knit musical community in the hills. Through Magrino, who'd befriended King, Fischbach met Taylor.

His new acquaintance's predilection for hard drugs wasn't a secret. "For God's sake, everybody was high," Fischbach recalled. "He was just one of us." On those occasions when Taylor dropped by Fischbach's home, the two would ingest whatever substances were available, grab fistfuls of rocks, jam them in their pockets, and jump in the pool. After sinking to the bottom, they'd sit on the floor for as long as their lungs would allow. Neither knew why they did it; they just did. At that point in their lives, there wasn't much else to do, anyway.

The Fischbach-Magrino home was one of many where Taylor crashed in the early months of 1970 as he awaited the release of his just-finished record. Essentially homeless, Taylor would alternate between Asher's home, a couch in Kortchmar's house on Hollywood Boulevard, and the habitat of any friend who'd have him. The situation was loose and care-free, especially when it came to relationships. On Martha's Vineyard, Kortchmar had noticed Taylor's effect on girls, and Chapel Hill lore had it that when Taylor was in high school, he and one girl had sex in the nearby woods in a poison ivy patch. Both wound up in the hospital, Taylor showing a friend the somewhat embarrassing place where he'd made contact with the plant.

In Chapel Hill, Taylor had been dubbed "lady-killer" by friends, and the same nickname could have also applied in Los Angeles. Although Taylor had a girlfriend he'd met in London—Margaret Corey, daughter of comic Professor Irwin Corey—plenty of other women in his new community, including Magrino, had crushes on him. "It was from a time when nothing much was expected of me," Taylor recalled. "So I didn't have the expectations, the *burden* of expectations, of coming up with something that was going to be commercially successful. It was a relatively free and easy time. I had a sort of group, a family in Los Angeles, that I was managed by, living with, *loving* with. And making music with. And that was a nice thing." Taylor had a new home and community, both fairly insular and disconnected from any turmoil outside Los Angeles. Vietnam was not a concern: Given his earlier stay at McLean, the Selective Service deemed him unacceptable for the army.

On the other side of the country, in Martha's Vineyard, Taylor's younger brother Livingston, a developing singer-songwriter about to sign a record contract of his own, played an early copy of his brother's LP for acquaintances. "I could see they thought it was nice, but they didn't know how good it was," Livingston recalled. "And I looked at them and said, 'No, you don't understand. This is a truly great record and it's going to be *enormously* popular.'" To the friends, the idea still seemed fairly preposterous.

CHAPTER 3

"We try not to make plans," John Lennon emphasized to the newest group of reporters gathered around him. He was referring to himself and Yoko Ono, who sat quietly beside him, flashing a retiring smile. In his almost singsongy Liverpool lilt, Lennon continued: "I don't really like knowing what I'm gonna do for the next eight months."

Even for someone who preferred to live life on the fly, it's doubtful Lennon had planned on being where he was now, on the chilly afternoon of January 5. A few weeks earlier, he'd been in Toronto, talking up a festival he was helping organize and meeting with Prime Minister Pierre Trudeau. Now, on the fifth day of the new decade, he was giving a hastily organized press conference in what felt like the most remote locale possible, a college in the remote northeast of Denmark.

For anyone who'd kept up with the Beatles' changes in wardrobe and hairstyles, he looked and sounded like the revamped modern John: wire-rimmed glasses, shoulder-length waterfall of brown hair, full beard. Ono flanked him on one side; on the other was her six-year-old daughter Kyoko from her first marriage, to Tony Cox. Cox himself, sporting sunglasses and a smirk, sat next to Kyoko, along with Cox's new, stern-looking wife, Melinda Kendall. When the local press had heard Lennon was in town and wanted to know why, Lennon agreed to the press conference.

As soon as it began, he still flashed a bit of his familiar combination of wit and sneer. "All right, you rumor mongers, let's get going!" he cracked. To the reporters, he denied reports he'd bought land there, said he loved the snow, and addressed rumors about the Beatles' finances. "The people around us made more money than the Beatles ever did, I'll tell you that," he said bluntly. "None of the Beatles are millionaires. But there's a lot of millionaires who became millionaires around the Beatles."

Although he wouldn't dwell on it that afternoon, the past year had been a particularly turbulent one for the Beatles and Lennon. The filming sessions at Twickenham almost a year before had been unpleasant enough. Then they'd reconvened in July to make a new album, *Abbey Road*, the old-fangled, studio-produced way, but the four were rarely in the same room together. One reporter who visited during the sessions witnessed McCartney giving Harrison a particularly hard time over a guitar solo—and that was when a journalist was around. The days when they were together, all for one—in Liverpool and Hamburg, on *The Ed Sullivan Show*, having pillow fights for the press in hotel rooms—now felt as distant as Lennon's childhood. Factor in a sometimes hostile press, heroin, and intragroup business friction, and no wonder Lennon—who'd turned twenty-nine three months before—had removed himself, even temporarily, from it all.

As 1969 receded, Ono grew desperate to reconnect with her daughter, whom she hadn't seen in years. Cox, who'd been given custody of Kyoko, was temporarily living in Denmark. Shortly before Christmas, the Lennons had flown to Aalborg and been driven to Cox's rented farmhouse outside the small town of Vust.

From the start, Lennon went along with Cox's lifestyle requests, like undergoing hypnosis to stop smoking. Few were surprised he was agreeing to all this for Ono's sake. Wearing matching black turtleneck sweaters at the Danish press conference, the couple came across as a hairier, countercultural version of the Bobbsey Twins. In a recording studio in London that winter, they sat together in a control room, listening to a new track and chewing gum in time. "They breathed the same air and completed each other's sentences," recalled Dan Richter, a friend who was house-sitting at their home outside London that winter. "They were like Romeo and Juliet, only older."

Lennon remained his seat-of-the-pants self, as John Brower, a young Canadian promoter and club owner, had witnessed in the fall. One September day, Brower had phoned the Apple offices to ask if Lennon would be willing to participate in a multi-act festival, the Toronto Rock & Roll Revival, that Brower was organizing. To his surprise, Lennon took the call and agreed—and then almost missed the chaotic flight over. On the plane, Lennon and the band he'd thrown together for the show—Ono; Eric Clapton; artist, bass player, and longtime friend Klaus Voormann; and Alan White, a twenty-year-old drummer between bands—rehearsed in seats at the back of the plane. (When Lennon called to offer him the gig, White thought it was a joke and hung up; luckily, Lennon called back.) Before the show, Lennon took heroin and wound up leading the band through a bedraggled, under-rehearsed set. But the rawness and electricity of the event inspired him. He hadn't received a rush like that from his regular band in what felt like years.

Brower, a dough-faced twenty-three-year-old with sunken eyes, had been inspired too. After the festival, he approached Lennon with a far more grandiose, almost fantastical plan: a "music and peace conference" to be held outside Toronto over the July 4 weekend. Brower and Ritchie Yorke—a Canadian journalist who'd come to know Lennon during the Toronto Rock & Roll Revival—would organize it, and Lennon would recruit the talent. Everyone was hoping for a turnout of two million— an event that would dwarf Woodstock and announce to the world that a new era of peace and harmony had descended on the planet in the year 1970.

Brower and Yorke were the next to arrive in Denmark, even though, like Lennon, they hadn't planned on it. Lennon had summoned them by phone in order to discuss plans for the festival, and they had no choice but to take the long flight from Canada. On the morning of January 15, the day after they'd arrived, the two of them—along with Anthony Fawcett, the Lennons' personal assistant—found themselves sharing a taxi from their hotel in Aalborg to Vust. As rain turned what been a foot of snow into dreary slush, they stared out the windows at the desolate landscape until the cab pulled up at what looked like a deserted farmhouse. At the door, Cox asked them all to remove their shoes, leave any drugs behind, and step inside.

The sight that greeted them was like nothing they'd expected. Yes, upon his arrival Brower had met with a mysterious, bug-eyed "doctor" Lennon had also flown out to Denmark and who was talking about extraterrestrials visiting the festival. Sure, they'd heard the story the night before from a local hairdresser, who told them she'd been summoned to a farm to trim John Lennon's hair. Before she began, Lennon had shown her a copy of his passport photo, from the *Sgt. Pepper's Lonely Hearts Club Band* days, and asked her to cut it even shorter. Ono cried as her husband's locks fell to the floor. When it was over, Lennon asked the haircutter to move on to Ono and then Kyoko. It was as if Lennon was both returning to his past and simultaneously cutting his ties from it. Adding to the strangeness, all the shorn hair was collected into bags and carted away.

Despite these stories, neither Brower nor Yorke expected to be so taken aback by a gaunt Lennon, his hair buzz-cut short, staring at them from the kitchen table. He looked less like a Beatle and more like a Vietnam POW after months in the Hanoi Hilton. "That was a shock," Yorke recalled. "It was a pretty dramatic moment." Seemingly confused by all the adults around, Kyoko ran up to Brower and said, "I don't like my hair, I want my old hair back."

From that point, the meeting took a dramatic turn akin to Lennon's makeover. In no uncertain terms, Lennon announced the festival should be free. Brower was stunned by the comment: How would they be able to pay for such a thing if that were the case? Lennon didn't want to hear it. "It was all a bit dismaying," Yorke recalled. "There were conflicting agendas. What we hoped to start with John was certainly not turning out the way we'd hoped." To Brower and Yorke's surprise and chagrin, Allen Klein popped into the kitchen—despite the fact that Lennon had asked them to compile a dossier on Klein's reputation in the music business.

Less than an hour later, Brower, Yorke, and Fawcett were back in a taxi, returning to the Aalborg hotel. What had just happened? Having digested a mysterious tarry black substance on toast in the Cox kitchen— probably hashish, although he never knew for certain—Brower was doubly befuddled. Where was the Lennon that Brower and Yorke had met with a few months before—even the funny, animated man at the press conference for the festival in Toronto just before Christmas? "Fawcett said, 'They love their hair,'" Brower recalled. "So cutting it was like embarking on this new path." But what was that path, and where would it lead? No one, perhaps even Lennon, was sure at the moment.

On January 25, Lennon and Ono finally returned to London; the next day, Ringo Starr left. By then, Starr had two comfortable homes: a house with a garden in Highgate, a hilly London suburb, and a centuries-old Tudor mansion in Elstead in county Surrey that he'd purchased in 1968 from his friend, actor Peter Sellers. With its oak-beamed rooms, wandering packs of ducks and geese, and separate movie theater, Brookfield House, as the Elstead home was called, was a welcome retreat from the pressure of Beatlemania.

Still, Starr had to leave, even for a bit. As unappealing as the thought of inquisitive reporters was—he dreaded the inevitable questions about how the Beatles were getting along—he had a movie to promote and a career of his own to map out. With Maureen, his low-key wife of nearly five years, and Apple administrative director Peter Brown, he boarded a plane for Los Angeles.

The oldest Beatle and the last to join, Starr had been a drowsy-eyed but amiable child growing up in Liverpool. To everyone around him, he still was. He'd been the first to say he was leaving: After a tense 1968 recording session, he stayed home and didn't return for several days (when he was welcomed back with a drum kit enshrined in roses). They knew he would come back: More than the others, Starr was always happy with his job, so why change anything? According to one former Apple employee, Richard DiLello, Starr's presence was especially welcome the day Lauren Bacall called and said she wanted to swing by with her daughter to meet a Beatle. Starr, the only Beatle available on short notice, charmed them so much that Bacall felt as if they were *all* in the offices. Starr's interest in the business of the Beatles, while never as intense as McCartney's, rose in the new decade: Now it was he, not McCartney, who was the most visible at 3 Savile Row and most passionate about the idea of the Beatles. As the four pulled away from each other, Starr steered closer to home base.

The previous October, Starr had launched a project of his own, an album of standards from the pre-rock era—purposefully cornball but guileless songs like "Bye Bye Blackbird," "Love Is a Many-Splendored Thing," and "Stardust," with big-band arrangements courtesy of Quincy Jones and McCartney. "The idea of Ringo doing his own album made us all think, 'Oh, *really?*'" remembered Paul Watts, an EMI marketing executive at the time. Plenty of others, including Starr himself, didn't see the project as more than a way to pass the time and record long-ago pop songs his mother would enjoy hearing him sing. Over the course of four months, with the Beatles on an extended hiatus of some sort, Starr worked on the album at his leisure.

Since he'd been such a natural, unaffected screen presence in *A Hard Day's Night* and *Help!* a career in acting became another way to pass the time between Beatle projects. He'd already played a Mexican gardener in 1968's *Candy*, a warped sex comedy based on a novel coauthored by

Terry Southern and Mason Hoffenberg, and he'd just wrapped up a larger, costarring role in *The Magic Christian*, also based on a Southern novel, in which he was cast as the adopted son of a rich cynic (played by Sellers) who bribes unsuspecting people to do outrageous things for cash. The film had already opened in the U.K. to mixed reviews, but a U.S. premiere was set for the middle of February.

Arriving in Los Angeles for the film's opening, Starr made nice at a press conference. With his usual nonchalance, he deflected most of the Beatle questions, only saying the group would most likely be recording together soon. Hardly anyone seemed to care about the movie; most of the non-Beatle questions had to do with working with his busty costar Raquel Welch.

Starr couldn't have been happier to leave the next day for Las Vegas to see Elvis Presley. The previous summer, Presley had returned to live performance with a string of triumphant and inordinately profitable shows at the International Hotel. Coming on the heels of his 1968 comeback TV special, the Vegas shows marked the concert debut of a different Elvis. His voice revealing new layers of emotional depth and velvety richness, he was still undeniably sexual, a prowling cougar on-stage. But he was singing far more contemporary pop tunes, he was sur-rounded by a choir and orchestra, and he was wearing a newly designed one-piece jumpsuit that made his karate stage moves easier to pull off. Before long, Presley would be taking a nearly identical version of the show on the road.

After being sneaked in through the kitchen entrance at the Interna-tional, Starr, Maureen, and Brown were escorted to their table. Halfway through the show, Presley introduced the visiting Beatle from the stage and Starr, good-natured as always, took a bow. Afterward, he and Brown were hustled backstage for a quick meeting with Presley. Despite the presence of more beefy security types than he'd ever seen, Brown was pleasantly surprised by how chatty, courteous, and charming Presley was.

Six years before, the Beatles had visited Presley at his Bel Air home, a meeting notorious for Presley's indifference to their presence. Now, as the new decade arrived, Presley and Starr were on equal ground: two well-compensated, beloved pop aristocrats, each searching for something new in their lives and work.

○ ○ ○ ○

Two weeks after John Brower left Denmark, Lennon's assistant Anthony Fawcett tracked him down at a hotel in Los Angeles, where Brower was being interviewed about his grandiose festival by a writer from the Los Angeles *Free Press*. Still scrambling to turn his idea into reality, Brower had changed the name of his festival company to Karma Productions. Now, here was Fawcett on the line, telling him Lennon had written and recorded a new song, "Instant Karma!," and offering to play it for him over the phone.

On January 26, just before the call, American gossip columnist Earl Wilson had written a syndicated column, "Beatles May Not Record Together," in which he noted there was "increasing conviction among their intimates that they may never record again as a whole." The following day, Lennon unintentionally backed up Wilson's story. Having just returned from his Scandinavian trek, he'd woken up with a lyric in his head, written a rudimentary melody on a piano, and then, with the help of Apple employees Mal Evans and Bill Oakes, rounded up a quick cast of musicians (including Harrison and White, substituting for the now-departed Starr) to help him put it to tape. To oversee the session, Lennon suggested Phil Spector.

In rock and roll circles, the diminutive but intense Spector was a controversial and mythical figure. After a flush of early success, he'd retreated into seclusion. Starting with a cameo as a drug dealer in *Easy Rider* the year before, he'd emerged from semiretirement. He was strong-willed and strident, yet he and Lennon shared a caustic sense of humor right from the start: The two men joked about starting and finishing the song in a day. As Spector scurried around the studio hooking up tape machines and setting up microphones, the band began rehearsing the tune. "John played the song and we all started playing and it sounded good and was very swinging and came together fast," recalled Voormann, a German artist and musician who'd met the Beatles in Hamburg and was playing bass at the session. Evans corralled a bunch of locals from a nearby pub to join in on the background vocals in the chorus. By 4 A.M. it was done—recorded, mixed, and ready to roll off a vinyl assembly line. Again, Lennon was elated: The Beatles would never have bashed out a song so fast. "There was a simplicity in the way he did it that I don't think he would have been able to get across with the Beatles," recalled Voormann. "He felt much freer than before."

In the L.A. hotel room, Brower and the *Free Press'* John Carpenter picked up separate phone lines and prepared to hear the results. "Instant Karma!" roared out; even over a Transatlantic connection, Brower could hear its massive, reverberating piano chords and White's loud, pushy shuffle beat, which put a massive exclamation mark at the end of each line in the chorus. But those lyrics . . . "Who on earth do you think you are—a superstar? Well, right you are!" taunted Lennon with a rasp that stung like scalding water.

When it was over, Carpenter looked at Brower and brought up the use of the word "karma" in the song. "Isn't that the name of your company?" he asked. "I don't know if that's a song for your festival. It doesn't sound very positive."

Brower had to admit that, yes, it *was* the name of his production company, and no, he didn't know what to make of its message. Similarly, plenty of Beatle fans scratched their heads when copies of "Instant Karma!" arrived in stores ten days later: The sleeve credited the song to "John Ono Lennon." Although Lennon had had his middle name officially changed from Winston to Ono when he wed Ono the previous March, "Instant Karma!" marked the first time he used the name on a record. Even in the world of John Lennon, it was hard to imagine a more puzzling month than the one just ended.

Both everyone and no one knew where Paul McCartney was. Certainly, the other Beatles and Apple employees knew he'd spent a good deal of the winter holidays at his bare-boned farmhouse outside Campbeltown in the remote southwest of Scotland. He'd purchased it several years before, during his relationship with Peter Asher's sister Jane. In the fall of 1969, when a new degree of tension enveloped the Beatles, McCartney had retreated to the house with Linda, her seven-year-old daughter Heather from her previous marriage, and her and McCartney's new baby Mary. Aside from a *Life* magazine photographer and journalist who tracked him down that fall, looking to prove he was actually alive during the "Paul Is Dead" uproar, McCartney was guaranteed isolation.

None of the Beatles ever made the trip to the house, and in February, Lennon gave an interview—one of many at the time, sometimes to promote his peace causes, sometimes to simply keep his name in the papers—saying he and McCartney hadn't spoken in two months and only communicated by postcard. Even Peter Brown, Apple's dapper and unflappable administrative director and one of the few in close touch with McCartney, didn't bother making the trek to the farm, knowing he'd have to hike from a main road to reach it. McCartney told everyone the house didn't have a phone, even though it did; Brown, who'd more or less taken over the duties of handling the Beatles after Brian Epstein's death in 1967, would often receive calls at Apple from Scotland.

With McCartney's exact whereabouts up in the air and communication among the Beatles fractured, Klaus Voormann was particularly stunned to receive a call one winter afternoon from McCartney himself. Would Voormann be up for a visit to McCartney's home in London?

In Hamburg a decade before, Voormann, then a young Berlin-born artist with male-model cheekbones, chanced upon the Beatles when they were blasting out sweaty rock and roll at the Kaiserkeller Club during their residence there. With his friends Astrid Kirchherr and Jürgen Vollmer, Voormann became an immediate Beatle follower and friend. When he moved to London a few years later, he remained close with Lennon, Harrison, and Starr; it was Lennon who suggested Voormann illustrate the cover for *Revolver*, and Voormann at various times crashed at Harrison's and Starr's homes.

No sooner had Voormann said yes to McCartney's invitation than the Beatle himself pulled up to Voormann's apartment on Heath Street. McCartney was driving a Mini, one of Europe's fashionably small cars, complete with dark-tinted windows. In the car on the way to McCartney's home in St. John's Wood, Voormann noticed the collar of his friend's blue shirt: scruffy and worn down, not quite the sartorial garb everyone associated with McCartney. Like others, Voormann had heard McCartney's fashion sense had taken a funkier, more downscale turn with his new wife.

In less than ten minutes, they arrived at 7 Cavendish Avenue, a cozy three-story home behind a black security gate that McCartney had purchased five years earlier. Voormann stepped inside and came upon keyboards, drums, and guitars: a veritable one-man band scattered about the living room. Voormann picked up a guitar and the two men jammed a bit together. Then, to Voormann's added wonder, McCartney cued up a tape machine and played him a few songs he'd been creating on his own.

Upon his return to London in the new year, McCartney had bought a home recording unit and had it delivered to Cavendish Avenue. There, he began putting on tape some of the songs and fragments he'd been playing at the farm. He started with a trifle, strumming lazy chords and singing about the way Linda looked "with the lovely flowers in her hair." It wasn't much of a song, but it was a start. Over the next month and a half—at home and then in Morgan, a studio just north of London—more songs began taking shape, with McCartney playing all the instruments himself. Some, like a modest rocker called "That Would Be Something" built around a coiled-up guitar line, were cut in his living room. (In that song and others, he'd hum when he didn't have enough words written down.) He tossed off "Valentine's Day," an instrumental, and resurrected "Junk," a wispy, lullaby-style leftover from the White Album sessions. With its bumpy rock and roll feel, "Oo You" recalled "Why Don't We Do It in the Road," from the White Album. "Momma Miss America," another instrumental, was fueled by a rumbling piano and drumbeat that were, by his standards, experimental and ambient. Like a few other songs, it devolved into random strums and giggles, as if McCartney wanted to make it explicitly clear that he wasn't taking it all terribly seriously.

In late February, McCartney returned to EMI Studio, the Beatles' home base, bringing the tapes with him. John Kurlander, a young EMI employee who'd worked as an assistant on the *Abbey Road* sessions, couldn't help but notice the difference in McCartney's mood. McCartney was now relaxed and productive, playing one instrument at a time as he constructed or finalized his new songs, only Linda and their children his companions. Inspired by the plight of a South American tribe he'd seen on TV, he recorded "Kreen-Akore," essentially a drum solo, then played every instrument and sang every note on two truly fully realized songs, "Every Night" and "Maybe I'm Amazed," both odes to Linda.

To Peter Brown, one of the few told of the work in progress, the unassuming project hardly felt out of the ordinary. After all, Brown thought, the Beatles were always working on one thing or another, albeit increasingly on their own. As McCartney well knew, Lennon had just finished

"Instant Karma!," Harrison had already put out an album of instrumental film music, *Wonderwall Music*, and Starr was at work on his album of oldies. Brown also knew McCartney had a particularly strong work ethic and, far more than the others, a deep-seated need to entertain.

On February 25, one of McCartney's last days at the studio, he began and finished an entire song, "Man We Was Lonely." The music—a gentle sway led by an acoustic guitar, with mild bass and drum parts that hinted at polka oom-pah—was determinedly casual. Starting with the ungrammatical use of "was" instead of "were," the song was consciously hammy, and the repetitive lyrics, with their references to his former city life and his new wife, were his most direct comment on his state of mind. "But now we're fine all the while," he and Linda sang at the end—three times in a row, as if to ensure the point was made. "After all the tension with the Beatles, spending several weeks up at the farm with Linda put him in a state of relaxation he hadn't been in for a while," Kurlander recalled. "There was no one else to answer to at all."

In part, that was because few knew he was there. Following an earlier session, on February 22, Kurlander jotted down McCartney's name in his logbook—then scratched it out and wrote "Ssssh." Starting the following day, McCartney was referred to in Kurlander's journal as "Billy Martin," his *nom de studio*. For reasons Kurlander couldn't discern, the sessions were suddenly clandestine.

The silver film canisters squirreled away in an office at Apple Corps told their whole story, or at least the early part of it. Footage of them, young and ebullient, at the Cavern Club. Clips from their early days on tour, playing to swaying stadiums of weeping female fans. Film of Brian Epstein, youthful, alive, talking of his plans for the group. The canisters sat in a small room with no windows located next to the second-floor office of Neil Aspinall, the Beatles' longtime and loyal friend. Despite all the changes in the band and at Apple, Aspinall remained a valuable, rock-steady presence. He'd gone from working as their first road manager—putting up posters of their club gigs, among other tasks —to helping run Apple from its launch. A movie projector sat in the middle of the room, with a projection screen nearby. All that was needed was someone to cat-alogue the contents of each canister, and for that job, Aspinall turned to Chris O'Dell.

O'Dell, a vivacious brunette born and raised in Oklahoma, was on her second tour of duty at Apple. She'd been living in Los Angeles in 1968 when she'd met Derek Taylor, Brian Epstein's former assistant and a dap-per hippie aristocrat in his own right. After a falling-out with Epstein, Tay-lor moved to southern California to become a rock publicist—for, among others, the Byrds, who then included David Crosby. When Taylor met O'Dell, he told her he was returning to London to work for the Beatles' new business, Apple. A few months later, at Taylor's invitation, O'Dell was at Apple herself, working random jobs like answering the switchboard, until Peter Asher asked her to be his personal assistant. In the fall of 1969, O'Dell left Apple and returned to Los Angeles to be with her new boyfriend, singer and pianist Leon Russell. But when their relationship soured, O'Dell was back in London, this time at the dawn of 1970.

A year and a half after its launch, Apple Corps at 3 Savile Row looked unchanged in many ways. The five-story building tucked away on the modest central London street, alongside a string of upper-crust tailoring shops, retained its reddish-brown brick exterior; the Apple Scruffs, the loyal female fans, still gathered outside, just beyond the black iron front gate. Peter Brown was still reporting to work, handling the band's social engagements, helping organize wedding plans, and juggling innumer-able Beatle details. His office at Apple was on the second floor, right across from the one the Beatles shared, and Brown, in the old days, would see McCartney there almost every day.

But that was before Epstein's death, before the fractious making of the White Album, before the Twickenham Studio filming, before Lennon and Ono had held that meeting with Allen Klein. It was before their marriages and house purchases, and it was certainly before the meeting in Brown's office the prior September, when McCartney had argued for future concerts and a TV special and Lennon had called him "daft," told everyone he wanted a divorce from the band, and stormed out. "Well, that's that, then," said one Apple employee glumly afterward.

Apple was different now. Inside, the whirlwind of activity O'Dell had witnessed in 1968—the constantly *brrrring* phones, the sight of McCartney, Lennon, Harrison, or Starr whipping in and out, the secretaries brewing tea and making sandwiches—was largely gone, as was her old boss Peter Asher. Everything was so quiet now, the mood so much less freewheeling. O'Dell heard from the outset that McCartney, once the most business-focused, never came into the office anymore.

Apple was hardly in a position to hire, especially now that Klein was pruning its budgets and attempting to rein in its out-of-control finances. But Aspinall needed an assistant, so O'Dell had a new job helping him dig through the film canisters. For several weeks, O'Dell diligently scribbled down the contents of each reel. Aspinall never talked about his assignment in detail, but after a while O'Dell assumed he was putting together a documentary on the history of the Beatles. It felt odd to compile what amounted to a chronicle of a band that still existed, but O'Dell didn't question the project.

Nor did she see it through to completion. To O'Dell's surprise, Harrison called her one late winter day and asked her to work for him at his new home. By 1970, rock and roll was roughly fifteen years old and ready for royalty of its own. The Beatles fit the bill, and as O'Dell saw for herself on a late-night drive to the house, so did Harrison's new home. In early March, he and wife Pattie Boyd had left their bungalow in Esher, Surrey, and moved into Friar Park, a Gothic mansion in Henley-on-Thames, Oxfordshire, over an hour west of London. Once visitors drove past the entrance house and onto the main property, they saw a mansion a far cry from the drab, two-floor Upton Green, Speke, council house in which Harrison had lived with his family as a teenager. Surrounded by thirty acres, Friar Park had two dozen rooms, stained-glass windows, multiple gardens, oak-paneled rooms, a library, and pointed turrets outside. If Harrison wasn't able to place many of his own songs on Beatle albums, he'd at least show them up with the grandest of all Beatle residences.

Although now a devout student of Hinduism, Harrison could also be unpredictably moody, sullen, or sarcastic. Part of him stewed over the way the others, McCartney especially, were dismissive of his songs and still treated him as if he were simply the lead guitarist. He'd gritted his teeth through the *Get Back* and *Abbey Road* sessions. At Friar Park, Harrison was finally in control of at least one aspect of his life. He could work on his songs in solitude, without feeling the scrutinizing eye of McCartney. When he so desired, he even had his own bass player. Shortly after moving in, he heard Voormann's marriage was breaking up. "Come on, stay here," he told Voormann, who took his friend up on his invitation to move into one of the cottages on the estate. The two would play or talk about music, apart from the others and in Harrison's own enclosed world. At one point, O'Dell overheard Ono remark that O'Dell was now in "George's camp." "*We're in* camps *now?*" O'Dell thought.

Lennon had his own luxurious camp by then. The previous May, he and Ono had bought Tittenhurst Park, an estate thirty miles outside London. Starting in the fall of 1969 and continuing into the new year, their friend Dan Richter had been overseeing its renovation. A thirty-year-old actor from the American Northeast, Richter had made his name with mime performances throughout Europe. While doing street theater in Tokyo in the early '60s, he'd met Ono and Tony Cox. After moving to London in 1965, Richter reconnected with the couple and rented an apartment right next to theirs; the two homes shared a common balcony. Before long, Richter noticed all wasn't well with the Ono and Cox marriage. Looking out his window, he'd see Lennon's white limousine pull up and Ono rush in.

By the summer of 1969, Richter achieved a level of fame. He'd been hired by director Stanley Kubrick to choreograph the enigmatic opening sequence of *2001: A Space Odyssey*, in which a group of prehistoric, manlike apes fight with another tribe and come across a mysterious black monolith. Richter wound up playing the head ape in the scene. But he was also addicted to heroin, and at the Lennons' invitation, he and his wife Jill moved into two of the back cottages at Tittenhurst.

Like O'Dell at Friar Park, they were overwhelmed by the grandeur of the place and its surroundings: seventy-two acres surrounding a massive white house with huge bay windows. Since he needed something to do, Richter was hired (albeit for no pay, at his request) to oversee the makeover of the home. A white marble fireplace was installed on the first floor. A round bed—resembling a turntable, at Lennon's request—had been built for the Lennons' bedroom (for which Richter had to search for custom-made circular sheets). The floors were covered with off-white carpets made of unbleached wool specially woven in China; a green Queen Anne desk was installed in the bedroom. Since Lennon wanted to wake up each morning and see water, a lake was dug where once had lain an empty field. Everyone darted around the estate on golf carts. "The money kept coming in," said Richter, who signed off on all the work charges without ever looking at the bills. "It was like a waterfall."

By the time Lennon and Ono returned to Tittenhurst from Denmark, their hair still far from grown in, the work was dragging on; a planned recording studio off the kitchen remained under construction. Unde-

terred, Lennon and Ono went about their many varied plans. While they
were in Denmark, a gallery exhibit of their partly nude lithographs, "Bag
One," had opened in London. (A tweedy Upper East Side gallery in New
York City also displayed them, complete with ads that read, "Over 18
only.") The British police raided the London gallery, confiscating a number of the prints on grounds of obscenity, although the charges were ultimately dropped. Later, at a press gathering in London, they publicly
donated their shaved locks to Michael X, an incendiary, Trinidad-born
radical who spearheaded the Black Power movement in the U.K. X was
planning to auction off the hair to raise money for his commune, Black
House. To some, their string of controversial media events were fun and
charming, while others, like Brown, weren't sure how seriously to take
any of it.

In contrast to the Lennons' public joviality, the atmosphere around
Tittenhurst grew as gloomy as the English winter. After the creative out-
burst that resulted in "Instant Karma!," Lennon seemed creatively adrift.
Few other new songs emerged, and his main hobby became watching
television in his bedroom. Lennon was clearly depressed, and he and
Ono were squabbling more than they had. In March, Ono had a mis-
carriage. In his back cottage, Richter was trying to kick his heroin addiction with low doses of methadone; a doctor visited him daily. Lennon
and Ono, who were talking about having a child, were trying to do the
same. Richter never asked them about why they'd shaved their heads in
Denmark but assumed it was connected to their desire to get clean. "We
were all holed up," he recalled. "They were up in their bedroom and I
was over in mine. We all decided it was time to stop. You don't have a
good future if you use heroin. Both of them had their careers, and it was
clear it was time to stop."

By then, Lennon's other planned activity, the Music and Peace Conference, had been discarded. In the middle of March, John Brower told
Billboard it had been canceled because he "didn't want another Alta-

mont." But he was just saving face. Earlier, Lennon had sent Brower a telegram declaring he wanted nothing to do with it anymore. The entire project collapsed of its own naïveté, poor planning, and Lennon's requirement that the shows have free admission. The first major cultural event of 1970 was finished before it started.

On March 17, about two weeks after Harrison and Boyd moved into Friar Park, the Beatles nearly reunited. Harrison threw a twenty-sixth birthday party for his wife on the grounds, and Lennon, Ono, and the Starrs showed up and took their first private tours of the estate. All were impressed with the imposing grandeur of Friar Park. Afterward, everyone gathered in the main hall, smoking pot and casually chatting. The McCartneys were invited, but few remember seeing them there.

Even Starr began to realize he needed something to do—a plan, both creatively and financially. After all, he wasn't the one receiving all those checks for publishing royalties from Beatle albums. He began doing something he'd rarely done before—writing a song, this one with the working title "You Gotta Pay Your Dues." In the basement studio of his Highgate home, he sang what he had for Voormann: a "nah nah nah nah *nah*" melody and little more. "He had a few nice starts for songs and then didn't know how to carry on," Voormann recalled. "George or I would say, 'Well, you could play another chord there.' He always did things with the help of his friends. Like that song."

Harrison, always eager to help his ally, started to shape and trim the many words Starr began jotting down for the lyrics. In late winter, Starr bore down on what would be his first genuine statement as a recording artist in his own right. Lending a hand in the studio over the course of many days were Harrison, Voormann, George Martin, and on piano, one of Starr's new friends, Stephen Stills.

CHAPTER 4

Hold *still*, thought photographer Tom Gundelfinger as he aimed his antique camera at the men gathered in David Crosby's backyard. A few more seconds and Gundelfinger could snap the ideal photo for the cover of the new album by Crosby, Stills, Nash & Young. Using a hundred-year-old camera that required his subjects not to move was challenging enough. That they'd snorted up a line of cocaine right before the shoot began wasn't helping: No wonder they all seemed so *jittery*.

They'd begun arriving at Crosby's house in Novato, just north of San Francisco, one late morning in November 1969. After a group breakfast and shared snort, the costumes and props rented in Los Angeles—a Confederate uniform, a buffalo hunter's jacket, a white frilly shirt, pistols, rifles, bullet belts—were disbursed. Down to the smallest detail, everything was precisely the way they wanted it for an album everyone knew would be one of the biggest of the following year.

How far and how fast they'd come. Just a year before, in the winter of 1968, Crosby, Stills & Nash had had the dubious distinction of being rejected by the Beatles. The three had joined forces months before and left their home base in Los Angeles to woodshed material in an apartment on London's Moscow Road. Dropping by to hear them sing, George Harrison and Apple A&R man Peter Asher politely listened and left. Later, the three were told Apple had passed for unspecified reasons. Maybe the Beatles didn't want competition, or perhaps Harrison remembered the feud he'd had in 1965 with the Hollies, the Manchester pop band that showcased Nash's high, keening harmonies. Harrison had dismissed their cover of "If I Needed Someone," his contribution to *Rubber Soul*. "You can't please everyone," a peeved Nash fired back at the time, adding, "The Beatles are always having a go at us quietly. But I'd back any of our boys against any of the Beatles musically anytime."

One year, one gold album, and a tsunami of accolades later, it was Crosby, Stills, Nash & Young—not the Hollies—who had a shot at unseating the Beatles. Even before it was completed, *Déjà vu* was being treated as an event; *Rolling Stone* used that very term in an article published during its recording. In January, two months before its release, Atlantic began advertising the album in music trade magazines.

To make its significance as unambiguous as possible, an equally momentous package was required. In the late summer of 1969, Gundelfinger (who later changed his surname to O'Neal) received a call from art director Gary Burden: CSNY, Stills in particular, wanted the jacket of its next album to resemble an old leather-bound book (or, Stills said, "a hymnal"), and the band wanted to be photographed in Old West garb. They hadn't yet decided to call the album *Déjà vu*, but the image played off one of Crosby's two contributions to the album, a spacey, tempo-shifting song with the refrain "we have all been here before." Could Gundelfinger devise a way to make the photo look as if it were a hundred years old?

Gundelfinger checked in with Stills, who had a simple message: "He said, 'I want the real deal,'" Gundelfinger recalled. "End of story. End of conversation." For a few hundred dollars, Gundelfinger found a store in Hollywood that rented him a well-preserved wooden-box camera from the Mathew Brady era. Using it would be tricky: It had an exposure time of two and a half minutes, and the pictures would have to be developed immediately.

On the day of the shoot, Gundelfinger found himself in Crosby's backyard watching the four of them, along with Dallas Taylor and Greg Reeves, suit up. Since their album was being recorded in the Bay Area, the photo session had to be shifted up north. Crosby became a hippie version of Buffalo Bill, Nash a farmer, Stills a soldier, Young something close to an aristocrat. Somehow, they remained still enough for Gundelfinger to take two shots. The task completed, the four of them whooped it up.

Ultimately, the photos didn't have enough contrast in them, forcing Gundelfinger to use a shot from a modern camera he'd set up as a backup next to the antique box. (In the one they ultimately chose, a dog wandered into the shoot seconds before he snapped.) To make the newly taken photo look like a relic from the days of Gettysburg, Gundelfinger soaked the negative in a chemical solution and let it dry in the sun, a method used by Civil War photographers. If Stills wanted the real deal, he now had it—or something as close to it as possible.

The photograph was merely phase one of several torturous steps in the album's packaging. The faux-vintage band photo had to be placed in precisely the right spot on each imitation-leather (actually hard-cardboard) cover—and it had to be done by hand, since record-plant machinery hadn't yet been invented to do it automatically. For Ron Stone of Lookout Management, the process was "an absolute fucking nightmare. The band looked at it and said, 'That's fucking great.' I looked at it and said, 'How the fuck are we going to *do* this?'" At seven pressing plants around the country, hundreds of thousands of CSNY photos had to be hand-glued onto the embossed cover. When the label learned four of the plants were gluing the photo the wrong way, production was switched at the last minute to the remaining three. No one could, or would, say no to Crosby, Stills, Nash & Young.

As rock and roll bands went, they were especially complicated—and seemingly incompatible from the start. Crosby had been a handful from the day he was born in 1941. The son of Hollywood cinematographer

Floyd Crosby, who'd won an Oscar for his work on the 1931 film *Tabu*, he'd been raised in seeming comfort, and from an early age, his singing voice was disarmingly sweet and honeyed. A chubby kid who never lost a recurring roundness in face and body, Crosby had a naughty twinkle in his eye that shaped what came next in his life. His back story included jail time for burglary, a roaming life as a folksinger that took him from Los Angeles to New York to Florida to San Francisco to, finally, Los Angeles again, during which he impregnated (and left) one woman and befriended songwriter Fred Neil and future Jefferson Airplane cofounder Paul Kantner.

Finally, in 1964, Crosby found the musical combination he'd yearned for when he met two fellow folkies, Roger McGuinn and Gene Clark, at the Troubadour. Inspired by the Beatles and their way with electric guitars and harmonies, they, along with Chris Hillman and Michael Clarke, became the Jet Set, then the Byrds. From the start, McGuinn heard about Crosby's bad-boy reputation, but couldn't deny his talents as a harmony singer. The Byrds' shimmering 1965 cover of Dylan's "Mr. Tambourine Man" was merely the starting point for music that came to encompass folk, country, and Beatle-influenced sonic adventures that the Beatles themselves admired. Crosby eagerly devoured the pop-star life, swooping into Sunset Strip nightclubs with his green cape and mischievous grin, joints in each hand.

One of the many musicians Crosby met on the scene was Stills; in fact, Buffalo Springfield had once opened for the Byrds. Stills' family had called Illinois, Louisiana, and Florida home at various points; during his high-school years, they were living in San Jose, Costa Rica. Stills' musical palette came to encompass the blues he'd heard down South, the Latin music he'd loved in Costa Rica—and, finally, the folk music of the Village, where he relocated in 1964 after graduating from high school in Costa Rica. Determined and musically dexterous, Stills was already adept at playing guitar, drums, and numerous other instruments, and in New York, he'd joined a large-scale folk band, the Au Go Go Singers. Yet it was only after he relocated yet again, to Los Angeles in 1965, that his career jelled. With his Au Go Go bandmate Richie Furay and an elusive and inscrutable Canadian named Neil Young, Stills formed Buffalo Springfield. By then Stills had a reputation for being talented, self-assured, and obsessed with moving his career forward as fast as possible. Everything about him—his prematurely hardened and wary expressions, his aggressive body language, even the way he sometimes wore suits to photo shoots—set him apart from the hippie crowd around him.

Crosby had met Nash when the Hollies made their first trip to Los Angeles in 1966, the same year they cracked the American top 10 with "Bus Stop" and "Stop Stop Stop," two exceptionally vibrant examples of the Hollies' crisp, ebullient harmonies and hooks—merry-go-round Merseybeat pop. With his Manchester childhood friend Allan Clarke, Nash had put that band together around 1962. Their earliest English hits were white-British-boy covers of R&B songs like "Stay" and "Searchin'," but they soon forged their own identity. Crosby and Nash had been introduced to each other by Cass Elliot, the beloved member of the Mamas and the Papas who'd known Crosby from their days in folk groups.

In different ways, all three felt stymied by the middle of 1968. Stills had tasted success when Buffalo Springfield hit the top 10 with "For What It's Worth," his eerily calm song about the Sunset Strip "hippie riot" of 1966. But thanks in part to Young, whose thirst for fame never equaled Stills', the Springfield had fallen apart. The previous fall, Crosby had been fired from the Byrds for his motormouth personality and risqué material. Nash, longing to be taken seriously as an artist of the rock era, was encountering resistance to his new songs from the Hollies. Hard as it was to believe, an effervescent new song he'd written about trendy hippies traveling to the Middle East, "Marrakesh Express," was deemed too experimental.

Stills and Crosby, who hooked up first, were an unlikely duo. Stills' voice was a croon with a twist of leathery raspiness, while Crosby's was nothing but sweet. Stills preferred liquor over Crosby's favorite indulgence, pot. Crosby was brash and unafraid to share his opinions at any moment; Stills tended to simmer and struggle between bouts of self-assurance and self-doubt. Stills was almost tyrannically regimented; Crosby wasn't. But both were unemployed, low on cash, and desperate for a new career break, and their voices proved to be a better blend than anyone would have thought. Depending on the source, all three first sang together at either Joni Mitchell's or Cass Elliot's house, but the vocal blend they achieved was inarguable. "I'd heard that golden sound that me and David and Stephen created, and I wanted it," Nash recalled. "As a musician I had no choice. I knew what harmony was, and the Springfield and the Byrds were known for their harmonies, but this was different."

The months that followed—in Los Angeles, London, and Sag Harbor, New York—were ambrosial for them. The songs were pouring out; Stills alone knocked out almost two dozen between the spring and fall of 1968, songs about his former lover Judy Collins like "Suite: Judy Blue Eyes" and "So Begins the Task." With Crosby and Kantner, he wrote "Wooden Ships." Confident in the sound they created, with three disparate voices that blended in ways that previous harmony groups like the Beach Boys and the Four Seasons hadn't, they'd break into their songs for anyone who'd listen. Nash took the high parts, Stills the low, and Crosby was the warm middle—and each man's voice, unlike harmony groups of the past, was also very distinct in the mix. To better understand record deals, Crosby and Nash took a Manhattan restaurant meeting with Paul Simon, whom Nash had met during his Hollies days. (The Hollies had done a cover of Simon's "I Am a Rock.") By early 1969, they'd worked out their contractual mess (each was on a different label) and wound up on Atlantic, the Springfield's home; Atlantic head Ahmet Ertegun was a passionate fan of Stills'.

In many ways, Crosby, Stills & Nash was a corporate merger, a business deal. Yet from all accounts, the atmosphere at Wally Heider's studio in Los Angeles, where their first album was constructed, was half work and half bromance. "We were in love with each other," Nash recalled. "They were funny and world-wise, and I loved them." Writers like Ellen Sander and *Rolling Stone*'s Ben Fong-Torres dropped by and found the three huddled around microphones, ecstatic over the music they were making. Stills was on all burners: In one night, he played the entire backing track to "Suite: Judy Blue Eyes," then stayed up for days to work on the other songs. Along for the ride was Dallas Taylor. Although only twenty-one, Taylor, whose face was squashed beneath a bowl-shaped haircut, had met Crosby, Stills & Nash by way of their friend John Sebastian of the Lovin' Spoonful. Taylor and Stills had gotten off to a rocky start: Stills didn't pay Taylor for an early session, leading Taylor to file a complaint with the musicians' union. But he and Stills had nonetheless clicked as musicians; Taylor was like Stills' sidekick younger brother, and he wound up playing all the drum parts of their first album.

The group the Beatles didn't want was all anyone heard about in and around Laurel Canyon. Waiting for his friend James Taylor to mend from his motorcycle accident, Danny Kortchmar began hearing the whispers about Crosby, Stills & Nash. "That was the most happening thing in Los Angeles," he recalled. "That was all anyone talked about." Months before meeting Taylor, drummer Russ Kunkel was in the Canyon living room of his friend Gary Burden when Crosby and Nash stopped by with a test pressing of the record. Joints were lit and the LP was put on Burden's stereo. "When I heard *that*, I knew, 'Okay, this is huge,'" Kunkel recalled. "There was never anything like it. It was completely unique."

Released in late May 1969, *Crosby, Stills & Nash* had its dark undercurrents: Stills' songs about his painful breakup with Collins, "You Don't Have to Cry" and "Helplessly Hoping," and Crosby's Bobby Kennedy-inspired "Long Time Gone," its harmonies groping for a way out of the darkness. But it was also a sunnier record than anything any of them had made before, and the joy that went into its creation was heard in every rapturous harmony or crystalline guitar. In July, the album peaked at number 6 on the charts and remained there for a total of forty weeks.

Although their personalities were volatile from the start, the group immediately messed with its own chemistry. Realizing they had to flesh out their band in order to play their songs onstage, they could have opted for a session musician who'd toil away in the background. Instead, they began asking their well-known musician friends—Eric Clapton, Stevie Winwood, even, according to Taylor, Harrison—to join. Everyone turned them down. With a tour in the making, Ertegun suggested Young.

Stills knew all about Young, of course. They'd been born the same year, 1945, but in different countries—Young kicked around Canada for all his youth—and had first met in Ontario in 1965 when Young's band, the Squires, wound up on the same bill as the Company, an offshoot of the Au Go Go Singers. They'd bonded from the start and eventually crossed paths again, far more fatefully, a year later. Young and Bruce Palmer, his scarecrow-like bass-playing friend, had driven to Los Angeles in Young's hearse. By happenstance, Furay and Stills saw the car, Stills remembered his eccentric friend Young with the funeral-mobile, and the result was Buffalo Springfield.

Given the way the two of them had butted guitars and heads in the Springfield, Stills was resistant at first to Ertegun's idea. "I went, 'Why would we *do* that?'" he recalled. "'You know him—he has control issues. He'll tell you himself.' As a trio we worked pretty well." But Ertegun insisted, and the deal was sealed after Nash met Young over breakfast in New York and was sold on his humor and sensibility. According to Taylor, "Stephen asked me one night, 'What do you think of Neil maybe joining the band again?' And I said, 'Isn't that the reason Buffalo Springfield broke up? You never got along?' And he said, 'Yeah, it'll be different now.' Famous last words."

Young and Crosby, Stills & Nash did share one common bond: a manager. A Brooklyn hippie who'd relocated to California, Elliot Roberts, born Elliot Rabinowitz, was by then managing both acts with his partner, a tough, forever-hustling former William Morris agent named David Geffen. Everyone knew Young's first album, 1969's lushly produced *Neil Young*, sold poorly next to *Crosby, Stills & Nash*. "That was not lost on Elliot and Neil," said Stone. "I'm not sure Neil wanted to do it, but he clearly saw it as an opportunity to raise the profile of his solo career." Soon enough, Young was in the band, playing guitar alongside Stills at the Woodstock Music and Arts Festival in August 1969 as their peers stood behind them and watched approvingly. "Neil saw himself with a solo career even before CSNY," Crosby reflected. "CSNY was a vehicle to establish himself."

Back home, the same people who'd heard so much in advance about the new trio were left pondering the idea of Stills and Young working together again. "I was surprised," recalled Nurit Wilde, a photographer who'd known both men during the Springfield days. "I thought, 'I wonder how *that* will go?'"

How it would go became evident soon enough. In the fall and early winter of 1969, work shifted from Los Angeles to San Francisco for the making of their first album as a quartet. On paper, the scenario looked promising. They'd be cutting tracks at Wally Heider's studio, favored by their friends in the Grateful Dead and Jefferson Airplane. Crosby had already relocated to the Bay Area, and Stills, Nash, and Young would be living a five-minute walk away at the Caravan Lodge Motel in the seamy Tenderloin district. Each arrived with a satchel of new or half-completed songs.

On the first album, Stills had been very much in charge, playing most of the guitars and all the bass and organ and shaping the textures and contours of the music. Sometimes the only ones in the studio with him were Dallas Taylor and engineer Bill Halverson. Barely a year later, their lives had taken so many different turns it was sometimes hard to think straight. Stills was no longer the dominant force in the band. After Young had joined, CSNY had also added a bass player, Greg Reeves, a sixteen-year-old recommended by Young's friend Rick James. (Young and James had, strangely enough, played together in the short-lived Mynah Birds in Detroit.) "Stephen had previously done whatever he wanted," said Ron Stone. "All of a sudden, Stephen's space was invaded." Stills grew frustrated when his bandmates began writing songs in the studio, wasting time and money. "*Déjà vu* was very miserable," Stills recalled. "It was bedlam, everybody doing whatever they wanted."

Young's formidable gifts—the Canadian high-lonesome spookiness in his voice, the penetrating sting of his electric guitar leads, and the unassuming poetic flow of his lyrics—were clear, but so were his aloofness and inability to commit to the others. Young first cut "Helpless" with Crazy Horse, the band he was now working with on his own music, but when it didn't sound right, he tried it again, with Crosby, Stills & Nash. This time, thanks to Crosby-arranged harmonies that rose behind Young from a muted murmur to a vocal blanket, it clicked. Other times, like on the near-symphonic three-part suite "Country Girl," he worked on his own terms, venturing by himself to a studio in Los Angeles to overdub a massive pipe organ. "Neil pretty much did his stuff on his own and brought it finished to us and said, 'You want to put some vocals on this?'" Crosby recalled. To Nash's annoyance, Young didn't play on his two contributions, "Our House" and "Teach Your Children"—songs Nash was confident would be the hit singles the group would need to continue. "I knew what a hit was," Nash recalled. "We wanted to *sell* this bloody thing. Neil was being a little weird and selfish." (Young also had a pair of bush babies—tiny, night-vision monkeys—running around his hotel room, which enhanced the craziness.)

Given the limitations of the twenty-minutes-a-side LP format, they'd be lucky to land two songs apiece on the album, so they argued over who placed more material (and received more royalties) on the record. "Everyone was powerless watching this freight train of resentment and anger and 'I want more of my songs on the record,'" Taylor said. "The whole vibe from the first album was gone." Among the casualties—songs recorded or attempted—were Young's "Sea of Madness" and a multitude of Stills numbers. Whenever they seemed to be on a roll, someone from management would come by the studio with a contract to sign, leading to someone or another in the band being unhappy and the mood being wrecked for days. To everyone's surprise, the normally reserved Nash broke down in tears one night at the studio. They had something special, he told them, but they were messing it up, bad. "We were in a different space," Nash recalled. "The bloom had gone off the rose. We'd been to-gether for a while and the novelty had worn off a little."

Drugs, never in short supply to begin with since the days they'd jok-ingly dubbed themselves the Frozen Noses, were omnipresent. "By the time we got to *Déjà vu* and we'd snorted eighty pounds of cocaine, things were a little different," Nash remembered. The drugs helped fuel their creativity—or so they thought—and made it possible to keep working in the studio day after day. But it also fueled the insanity. One night, Nash stayed until three in the morning to finish a final mix of one of his songs. When he returned later that day, he replayed the tape and found it didn't sound anything like he remembered. At first, he thought he was losing his mind—*why does it sound like this?* He learned Stills had stayed even later and remixed it without telling him.

Nash himself wasn't immune to pickiness. He was so unhappy with the last note on "Our House" that Halverson had to fly down to L.A.

and find a Steinway piano to re-record that one concluding, sustained piano note. "They were second-guessing themselves," Halverson said. "They had so much to live up to. It was, 'Now what do we do?'" After a bunch of other distractions, like the midwinter European tour that had taken them to London's Royal Albert Hall and Scandinavia, Crosby, Stills, Nash, and now Young completed the album by the end of January. The most important year of their careers had just begun, and already they were weary of one another.

Crosby didn't know what was more surreal: the daytime darkness or the elephant bustling down the street. Was he *that* high? At that moment, all he knew was that he and Nash had set sail from Florida on Crosby's boat, the *Mayan*, sometime in February. They'd just anchored in the seaport town of Salina Cruz, on the southwestern coast of Mexico. Otherwise, nothing about that moment made any sense.

The last few months had been rough ones for Crosby. In October 1969, just before the *Déjà vu* sessions had commenced, his girlfriend, Christine Gail Hinton, had been killed in a car accident near their re- cently purchased home in Novato. As she was taking their pet cats to the vet, one leapt onto her lap, causing her to swerve into an oncoming bus. "We were at the pool in David's house and she brings out three joints and says, 'I'm going to take the cats to the vet, so smoke these,' " Nash re- called. "I never saw her again." Given the carefree, responsibility-free life adventures he'd had before, Crosby wasn't remotely prepared to deal with the loss. The man who was so often the band's cheerleader was now reduced to sobbing on the floor of Heider's studio. A metal Halliburton case stashed away in the Novato home held his only remaining memen- tos of their relationship—photos and embroidered shirts Hinton had made for him. At the *Déjà vu* photo shoot, Gundelfinger noticed Crosby

wasn't the same jubilant self he'd once been: "You could see he was carrying around a lot of pain."

After the Royal Albert Hall show, the Crosby, Stills, Nash & Young tour
of Europe played two more shows, in Copenhagen and Stockholm, before
it wrapped up. (Road manager Leo Makota later told author Dave Zimmer
the band donated its unused drugs to American draft dodgers in Denmark.)
With his obligations temporarily fulfilled, Crosby asked Nash to join him
on a boat ride. Even though he'd never been on a ship before, Nash liked
the idea; Crosby had been an avid sailor since his teen years, after all. Nash
assumed they'd be taking a quick day trip to the Catalina Islands from Los
Angeles. Not quite, Crosby told him: He'd decided to fulfill his dream of
burying Hinton at sea by depositing her ashes in San Francisco Bay, near
the Golden Gate Bridge. The *Mayan*, the fifty-foot schooner he'd bought
after leaving the Byrds, would take him there. Since it was docked in
Florida, they'd fly down and then sail from there to San Francisco.

Nash hesitated, then agreed. At first shocked by and angry over Hinton's death, Crosby was now being confronted by the reality of her absence. During a getaway trip to London after the accident, Nash noticed
Crosby sitting beneath an exit sign in a hotel ("I knew what he was thinking," Nash said, implying suicide). Nash decided it was best to keep a
close eye on his relatively new friend. With only a few others joining
them on and off—Makota, fledgling actress and singer Ronee Blakely,
and Bobby Ingram, one of Crosby's folk-circuit buddies—they set sail
in mid February, far from the music business and the bad aftertaste of
the stressful *Déjà vu* sessions.

In many ways, the trip fulfilled its mission. During the six-week ride,
they ate, drank, sang, toked up, and played music; Nash began working
on a new song, "Wind on the Water," after seeing enormous, house-size
whales swim past them. Sure, Crosby threw Blakely's typewriter over-
board when her *clickety-clacking* began to drive him insane. "In a fit of irritation, I tossed it," Crosby recalled. "I regretted it later." But with only

a ship-to-shore radio aboard to communicate with those on land, the trip took them away from it all.

They couldn't entirely escape reminders of their lives back home. From Jamaica to the Panama Canal, they were joined by Joni Mitchell. Only twenty-six, Mitchell had by then a lifetime of experience, both personal and musical. When she was a young Canadian named Roberta Anderson, she'd studied art in college in Calgary, after which she'd lived in Toronto and Detroit. In New York, she met her future manager, Elliot Roberts, and, in Florida, her future producer and (briefly) boyfriend, Crosby. Crosby oversaw her first album, *Song to a Seagull,* in 1968—the same year Judy Collins had a hit with a twinkling, radio-friendly version of Mitchell's "Both Sides Now." By then Mitchell also been through one marriage and had a child she'd given up for adoption. She and Nash had met at a party for the Hollies in Ottawa. Instantly smitten by the woman with the stately cheekbones and penetratingly observed songs, he moved into her home on Lookout Mountain after he'd deserted the Hollies (and divorced his first wife, Rose Eccles) and relocated to Los Angeles.

By the time of the *Déjà vu* sessions, Nash and Mitchell were living a hippie-domestic life at Mitchell's house, a life Nash immortalized in "Our House," a song on the new album. "Lady of the Island," from *Crosby, Stills & Nash*, had also been about Mitchell, and everyone was so nonchalant about the intermingling relationships that Nash and Crosby sang it together in the studio while looking at each other knowingly.

But when Mitchell hooked up with the *Mayan* and its crew, her romance with Nash was beginning to fray. Mitchell kept thinking of her grandmother, who wanted to be a dancer but instead had to take care of her children; Mitchell thought Nash would thwart her dreams in the same way. Nash kept insisting that wasn't the case. "For some reason, she thought my idea of marriage was that she'd stay home cooking," he recalled, "and there's no *fucking* way, knowing Joni's music and knowing her and loving her like I did, that I would have ever asked her to stray from that beautiful path she was on. But that's what she thought." Mitchell flew to meet him, watched the canal open and close, and then returned to Los Angeles. Nash began to feel as if something was coming to an end. Their talk of marriage stalled.

Meanwhile, the *Mayan* crew continued on its semi-merry way. When the boat docked at Salina Cruz, Crosby and Ingram went into a bank to exchange some money. In their own country, the sight of two bedraggled, slightly stoned longhairs could lead to wisecracks or, at worst, menacing, I-want-you-dead glares. In the Mexican bank, a security guard took notice of two scraggly hippies and unsnapped the gun from his holster, and Crosby's American dollars were carefully scrutinized.

After the transaction was completed, Crosby stepped outside as afternoon darkness descended and the elephant strolled by. He quickly realized he wasn't that stoned after all: An eclipse was enveloping the town, and the elephant was part of a parade to promote a local circus. Once he realized he didn't have to freak out, he laughed. At least it was a moment of welcome relief from the last few emotionally wrenching months.

While Crosby and Nash were sailing and Young was back in Los Angeles working with Crazy Horse, Stills was, to his relief, thousands of miles away from them all.

When the others returned to the States after the European tour finished, Stills decided to stay in London a while longer. He now had the time, opportunity, and money to do it. Just before he'd left Los Angeles, he'd been handed a check for over $450,000 for sales of *Crosby, Stills & Nash*, along with his first American Express card. Between his financial windfall and newfound rock star status, the London nightlife was his for the taking, and Stills hardly shied away.

At one nightclub, a mutual friend introduced him to Ringo Starr. Before long, Stills was at Starr's house in Highgate, sipping tea and shooting pool with the Beatle and Klaus Voormann. Starting February 18, he found himself alongside Starr, Harrison, and Voormann as they helped Starr mold the song initially called "You Gotta Pay Your Dues," eventually renamed "It Don't Come Easy." The song would endure many retakes and permutations in the months ahead; parts were recut, horn sections and background singers were added. When it was finally released about a year later, it was a small wonder of a pop single: From Starr's cymbal-wash intro to the delightfully pushy clatter it became, "It Don't Come Easy" was a relentless, almost desperate plea for unity and togetherness: "Use a little love, and we will make it work out better," Starr sang. Beneath all the instrumental parts and overdubs, Stills' chunky piano could still be heard in the final version.

Just a few years earlier, Stills had seen *A Hard Day's Night* in New York's Greenwich Village during his months as a struggling folkie. (Crosby and his fellow Byrds saw the same movie at the same time, three thousand miles way in Los Angeles.) Now, here he was, making music with half the Beatles and their producer. In contrast, the thought of returning to Los Angeles—and Crosby, Nash, and Young—was far less appealing. "I basically smelled a lot of trouble," he recalled. "Everyone was getting very high. Being a rock star in the States with those guys—they were all becoming *icons*." With that, Stills made a decision: "I said, 'Well, this is great, this is it—I'm stayin'.' I decided to become a really annoying groupie and meet all the British guys." Before long, he, Starr, and Harrison were together contributing to sessions for an album by the transplanted American R&B singer Doris Troy.

At first, Stills was intimidated by his surroundings and the notorious aloofness of British musicians. "He was very focused on Ringo, that's for sure," Voormann recalled of their first meeting. "I think he was overwhelmed by being in Ringo's house." Stills' phlegmy, good-old-boy guffaw—"I was brash and obnoxious," he admitted—was also a far cry from British reserve. But thanks to his father's variety of jobs—working tract homes, tool designs, lumber, and real estate, among other vocations—he'd grown accustomed to being the new kid, the stranger in town.

Even before *Déjà vu* was released, Stills had made the decision to make an album under his own name, and one by one, his new acquaintances began arriving at Island Studios. One night, Starr showed up earlier than everyone else; he and his drum kit were ready to go when Stills arrived. Eric Clapton popped in several times, once to add a box-cutter-sharp guitar solo to "Go Back Home," one of Stills' new songs, and another to get drunk with his new friend on tequila. Clapton had first jammed with Stills and Buffalo Springfield in Los Angeles two years before—the infamous April 1968 day when Clapton and everyone in the band except Stills (who managed a quick escape) was busted for dope while rehearsing at Stills' home in Topanga. When they grew reacquainted in London, Stills helped Clapton finish one of his own new tracks, "Let It Rain," adding harmony vocals and a bit of bass guitar to its coda. Another evening, Clapton popped in unexpectedly, saying he'd been driving around with a new song in his head and wanted to put it on tape before he forgot it. Stills ended up pitching in on that one, "Easy Now," as well. (He wanted to overdub guitars and drums, but Clapton demurred, saying he wanted to keep the song simple. To engineer Bill Halverson's surprise, Stills deferred to Clapton—and, Halverson noted, Stills rarely deferred to *anyone*.)

At one of the many parties Stills attended, he met Billy Preston, the American soul-gospel singer and organ player now part of the Beatles' circle (a year earlier, he'd played the electric piano solo on "Get Back"). When Preston cracked, "If you can't be with the one you love, love the one you're with," Stills took notice. Preston thought nothing of the remark, but to Stills, it could be "the key line of a song," and Preston let him keep it. Before long, it became the basis for a new melody that, like some of Crosby's, encouraged everyone to get it on with whomever was available at the time.

Stills also spent more time with Jimi Hendrix. The two had met at the Monterey Pop Festival three years before, and they'd been guitar-jam buddies ever since in Hollywood and New York. They'd talked about making a record together, and Hendrix stopped by the studio where Stills was working and, in a half hour, added a slithering guitar part to "Old Times, Good Times," an appropriately swampy track about Stills' youth. The interplay between Hendrix's six-string and Stills' organ, each humping up against each other, was a promising start to a collaboration. The two became nightclub companions, jamming at the Speakeasy Club and living the pop star life. Although Stills had already been introduced to cocaine and had been fond of alcohol since his teen years, even he was disturbed by the sight of Hendrix popping whatever pills and drinking what liquids anyone gave him. "I would say, 'Wait, those don't *go* together,'" Stills recalled. But Hendrix was too big, his massive hands too eager to grab it all, to convince otherwise.

Nonetheless, Stills was happy to be in London, where he could run his own show and share the spotlight with no one. Few things in life made him happier than spending hours, sometimes days, toying with new guitar parts, arrangements, rhythm changes, and melodies, the very aspects of record-making that drove Young to distraction. To Halverson, Stills always seemed more comfortable in that situation than in social ones. When Maureen Starr drove him out to the Brookfield estate she and her husband were thinking about renting, Stills was even more entranced. Although he knew he'd eventually have to return to his band and country, he made the decision to put it all off as long as possible. He told the Starrs he would either rent or buy the house.

When friends saw the photograph for the *Déjà vu* cover, they assumed it was inspired by Stills' time in military school in St. Petersburg, Florida. But another reason for evoking North versus South was simple. "We felt," Stills recalled, "like we were in the Civil War."

At that moment, everyone did. The country had been ripped apart politically and culturally during the past few years, and the shell-shocked results were now coming in. In February, one nationwide poll concluded six out of ten Americans were tired of hearing about Vietnam and considered the entire mission a blunder; another survey, by Gallup, indicated the country was moving in a more conservative direction. Which one was it? Nixon himself was a polarizing figure. "The '70s will be a time of new beginnings, a time of exploring both on earth and in the heavens, a time of discovery," he told Congress during his first State of the Union Address on January 22. Yet judging by poll numbers that had lurched up and down over the months leading up to the speech, the country still seemed unsure of *him* after his first year in office. Not only was unemployment high (four percent, an alarming figure at the time), but for the first time, a higher percentage of whites than before was collecting unemployment checks.

Everyone's nerves were frayed, nowhere more so than on campuses. At the University of California at Santa Barbara—ninety miles northwest of Laurel Canyon, which Nash and Stills still called home—tensions had been building for months after a well-liked anthropology professor was denied tenure. Given his outspoken antiwar views and kinship with the campus, a majority of the student body concluded he'd been punished for his beliefs.

At shortly after 8 P.M. on February 25, something snapped. Maybe it was a rally speech by William Kuntsler, who was representing the Chicago Seven—Jerry Rubin, Abbie Hoffman, Tom Hayden, Lee Weiner, John Froines, Rennie Davis, and David Dellinger, all charged with conspiracy to "incite, organize, promote, encourage, participate in and carry on a riot" at the 1968 Chicago Democratic convention. The trial was a postmodern media circus that seemed hard to take seriously, yet five days earlier, the defendants had been found guilty of crossing state lines to incite a riot; each faced up to five years in prison. Kunstler's presence at the rally didn't alone whip the nearly three thousand students into a frenzy. That moment arrived shortly after the gathering began, when, in plain sight of students, police questioned a black student activist in connection with a local robbery. The crowd taunted the police, and when someone threw a firebomb under the patrol car, everything went haywire.

Before anyone knew it, as many as a thousand students living in Isla Vista, a placid Santa Barbara suburb, vented their rage. A real estate office was ransacked; windows in a Bank of America branch were smashed. The bank began burning when wood planks covering the broken windows, along with tables and chairs set against the building, were torched. By midnight, the police captain overseeing several hundred officers had to admit the situation was "not in control." More police, complete with tear-gas grenades, began to arrive. Calm prevailed, but only briefly. The cops would retreat, and the demonstrators, scurrying back out from alleys, would eventually return, hurling rocks, expletives, and firebombs. To protect themselves against the various projectiles, the kids used garbage can lids; the cops wore plastic eye patches.

Once a shopping district, the streets around the bank were now a battle zone. Police were so outnumbered that a squad car was abandoned and promptly set on fire. On the third day, Ronald Reagan, the state's might-is-right governor, called the demonstrators "cowardly little bums" and sent in six hundred National Guard troops to restore something close to calm. "We have two choices as to which way we can go," Bank of America chairman Louis Lundborg announced. "We can divide into camps and shoot it out. Or we can try to find common ground so that we can grow together again." The latter course, he said, was one that "can bring peace and with it a hope for the rekindling of the American Dream." At that point, no one knew what the American Dream was anymore.

The tension also extended to the other side of the Atlantic, to England, albeit in a somewhat gentler manner. Hearing that dossiers were being compiled on them—files that would include their political interests and activities—students at the University of Manchester organized what became the largest protest to that point in Britain. Carrying placards that read, "No to dossiers, yes to freedom," eight thousand students took over the school's administration building in February. After they'd settled in, they added a very European touch, ordering tea for themselves.

On the morning of March 9, WBCR, Brooklyn College's student-run radio station, became the first outlet in the country to premiere *Déjà vu*. WBCR didn't just debut it; they played it start to finish all morning long.

Over and over, the students heard the opening, buffalo-herd rumble of Stills' acoustic guitars on "Carry On," his amalgam of a post-Collins-breakup song and his Springfield song "Questions." As if warding off Stills' blues, its massed group harmonies—layer upon layer, a sound they could only achieve in a studio—barreled out of the airwaves. The Brooklyn students then heard "Teach Your Children," a folksy Nash track inspired by his relationship with his father, who died when his son was in his late teens; a spry pedal steel track, courtesy of the Dead's Jerry Garcia, added the requisite back-to-nature ambience. Next came "Almost Cut My Hair," which Crosby had insisted the band record live in the studio, everyone playing and singing at once. (After flying up to San Francisco to work on the album, engineer Bill Halverson had to scramble to devise a way to cut the song that way, knowing the previous recording engineer had been fired when Crosby hadn't gotten his way.) Crosby was the first to admit that its lyrics, a litany of hippie pride and paranoia, were far less sophisticated than those for his other songs—"juvenile," he later called them. But Crosby's raw, nearly hoarse delivery (which Stills disliked) was the sound of someone who meant every word he sang, and the way Stills and Young made electric-guitar mincemeat behind Crosby's voice was the first indication on *Déjà vu* of what Young could add to the band.

"Helpless" was another sign: an exquisite dirge, Young's frail-sounding vocal encompassed by the Crosby, Stills, and Nash vocal massage and a Stills tremolo-heavy lead guitar that sounded like a forlorn fiddle. Joni Mitchell's version of "Woodstock," about to be released on her own *Ladies of the Canyon*, was somber and intimate. The CSNY version opened in a very different manner, Young wrenching notes out of his guitar and the carefully sculpted CSN harmonies vaulting over the chorus.

Flipping the record to side two, the WBCR disc jockey was greeted with Crosby's "Déjà vu." With its shifting time signatures and Crosby's jazz-influenced modal chords, the song was among the most difficult to record for the album. But by the time they'd finished laboring over it, it felt seamless; the moment when each of the Crosby, Stills, and Nash voices came in separately before converging was one of the album's highlights. The students listening on WBCR then heard "Our House," Nash's harpsichord-enhanced serenade about his and Mitchell's home life, all flowers, vases, and fireplaces. Stills' "4 + 20," an unexpectedly vulnerable tale of a normally macho man embracing the "many-colored beast" of despair, featured only him and his guitar. (The group attempted a harmonized version but felt his solo take was better.) Young finally reappeared with "Country Girl," three songs sewn together. For all his love of Crazy Horse's funky, bare-boned stomp, Young had a fondness for symphonic pop, starting with Buffalo Springfield's "Expecting to Fly." "Country Girl," the album's most elaborately produced and arranged piece, all churchly organs and intertwining group vocals, was the next stage in that development. The album wound up the way it started, rousingly: "Everybody I Love You," a harried adrenaline rush of electric guitars and stacked harmonies, combined two separately recorded songs edited into one.

On songs like that and "Woodstock," Crosby, Stills, Nash & Young never sounded more like a band; even Taylor's drums were more prominent in the mix than on *Crosby, Stills & Nash*. But in other ways they were less of one. The general public had no idea Young played on only five of its ten songs. Supposed band tracks like "Carry On" were mostly played by Stills (and brilliantly so—few musicians could make themselves sound like one-man bands so effectively, as the layers of electric and acoustic guitars, celestial organ, and rumbly bass in "Carry On" attested). *Déjà vu* was a sonically enveloping and powerful illusion, but it was an illusion nonetheless. The group hug of *Crosby, Stills & Nash* was replaced by the sound of four men each in his own space.

The industry received a taste of their fractiousness on March 11. On the same day *Déjà vu* went on sale, Crosby, Stills & Nash won Best New Artist at the annual Grammy Awards, beating out Led Zeppelin and Chicago. Held in the banquet room of the Century Plaza Hotel in Los Angeles and not yet televised, the evening was a low-key affair. Even so, none of CSNY attended. Stills remained in London. Young, who'd made his disdain for showbiz trappings clear, was in Topanga Canyon, about to begin recording further songs for his third album, *After the Gold Rush*. Ahmet Ertegun had to accept the award on their behalf.

By then, Crosby and Nash were on the western side of Mexico, awaiting a visit from Elliot Roberts. Roberts wasn't thrilled that two of his star clients had hightailed it out of California for over a month, but he also knew there was little he could do to control them. Bearing contracts for them to sign, he flew into the Punta Graham jungles with Gary Burden, their plane touching down on a cow pasture that doubled as an airfield. On the *Mayan*, Roberts pulled out paperwork for Crosby and Nash to look over; he and Geffen had lined up a major tour for Crosby, Stills, Nash & Young. Nash signed the contracts dutifully, but part of him wasn't looking forward to the roadwork at all.

PART TWO

SPRING INTO SUMMER
A Feeling I Can't Hide

CHAPTER 5

When it came time to name the album, Peter Asher thought the answer was obvious: *Sweet Baby James*. Asher felt it was the perfect title, clever and attention getting. Taylor wasn't taken with the idea; after all, he pointed out, the song with that title was about his older brother Alex's son. He didn't want anyone to think he was referring to himself. But a deadline loomed for the record's early-March release, and besides, Warners head Joe Smith thought the title track could be Taylor's first hit. *Sweet Baby James* it would be.

As potential hits went, "Sweet Baby James" hardly fit the bill when it arrived as a 45-rpm single in late February. An idly strummed waltz, it loped rather than bolted; Carole King's piano and Russ Kunkel's drums clomped along agreeably, and the pedal steel guitar of Red Rhodes, the player of choice for L.A. acts like the Byrds and the Monkees' Mike Nesmith, gently curlicued around Taylor's voice. To Warners executive Stan Cornyn, the music wasn't all that different from crooners of a previous generation—it just sported longer hair. "If someone who you could say was today's version of Steve and Eydie and Vic Damone—that good voice you liked to hear, that your mother would not say 'Turn that down'—James was certainly there," Cornyn recalled.

From the plaintive sound of Taylor's voice to the crisp, woodsy crackle of his fingerpicked guitar, *Sweet Baby James* was undeniably old-fashioned—pre- rather than post-hippie. The songs referenced country roads, the Berkshires, and highways. A version of Stephen Foster's "Oh, Susannah," a song the Taylor family had tackled together back in the

Carolinas, evoked the traditional folk songs Taylor had grown up with, as did his own "Lo and Behold," whose chorus, a choir of overdubbed Taylors, harked back to work-song spirituals. "Anywhere Like Heaven" was Bakersfield country music after a long drought. Even Taylor's phrasing—like *"dough*-gies" for "doggies" on "Sweet Baby James"—felt more Midwestern than southern Californian.

Asher and Taylor knew they'd overplayed their hand on his first album, which was too ornate and fussy. The comparatively uncomplicated arrangements worked out in Asher's living room for *Sweet Baby James* were intended to ensure that Taylor would now be the focus. *Sweet Baby James* shared several things in common with its predecessor. Each contained songs that focused mostly on voice and guitar, each had infusions of brass and horns, and each alluded to inner pain. But if *James Taylor* was the musical equivalent of a British tea parlor, its follow-up was an unvarnished log cabin. "Sunny Skies" was nudged along by arm-in-arm acoustic guitars and a temperate drum tap. "Fire and Rain" was a masterpiece of production accents, from the dramatic tumble of Kunkel's drums before the final verse to the use of a cello (played by another session man, Bobby West) instead of an electric bass to underscore the melancholy on the song. Asher only let loose as a producer on the album's last track, "Suite for 20G," which piled on horns, Kunkel's toughest beat on the record, and Kortchmar's sputtering electric leads.

Much like the man at the center of it, *Sweet Baby James* could be droll and loose, as if the quasi-redneck Carolina kid in Taylor's upbringing would peek out from time to time. "Oh Baby, Don't You Loose Your Lip on Me" mocked misogynistic white blues, even if some in Taylor's inner circle thought there was a hint of truth to its machismo. (Kortchmar, who tossed off the song in the studio one night with Taylor between takes, considered it such a throwaway that he was surprised to find it on the finished album.) "Steamroller" was a brassier, hammier update of "The Blues Are Just a Bad Dream" from the debut album.

In the year and a half since the making of *James Taylor*, rock and roll had gone through another of its seismic shifts. By early 1970, the music's unplugged kick—instigated in part by Dylan's *John Wesley Harding* and some of the Beatles' White Album, both from 1968—no longer seemed like merely one of its periodic makeovers. Everyone wanted in, the more denim jackets the better. Thanks to acts like Crosby, Stills, Nash & Young, acoustic guitar sales were surging for the first time since the mid '60s folk boom. "Many groups are completely abandoning amplification," *Billboard* noted in January, quoting instrument store owners who were grappling with boxes of unsold electric guitars and amplifiers. Egged on by their friend Crosby, even the Grateful Dead were trying their hand at rustic melodies and harmonies, recording (in just nine cost-efficient days) an album that would eventually be called *Workingman's Dead*. The movement was a perfect musical-cultural storm, rooted partly in the "back to the land" scene that begat books like the *Whole Earth Catalog* and in the rock and roll fans now pushing thirty and wanting less aggressive soundtracks for their lives.

Still, even *Workingman's Dead* and Dylan's 1969 *Nashville Skyline*, a proudly corny celebration of Music Row bonhomie, connoted a communal experience between the musicians and their fans. *Sweet Baby James* was the awkward loner in the corner. "Lately, I've been lonesome/It seems my dreams have frozen," Taylor sang in "Blossom," King's piano following his voice and guitar like a companion walking alongside a friend down a country lane. Even when Taylor sang of the open road, he never sounded like someone who'd be particularly happy there. In its quietly determined way, *Sweet Baby James* made disconnection sound like a natural, comforting state of mind. Taylor allowed himself a rare "whoo!" during "Country Road," but only as the song faded out.

The reviews were largely kind: "Taylor seems to have found the ideal musical vehicle to say what he has to say," nodded *Rolling Stone*. Few, other than the *Village Voice*'s Robert Christgau (who gave it a C plus), were put off. Yet the album's restrained nature led to an equally low-key response. In the same issue that noted *Bridge Over Troubled Water* was the top-selling album in the country, *Billboard* called *Sweet Baby James* "the finest folk effort of the year and should bring his ever-widening audience to chart proportions." That the album was relegated to a tiny review—not a prominent one like those accorded to releases that week by the Doors, Joan Baez, and Van Morrison—implied it was destined to be a cult item, "a must for folk-blues buffs," as the review declared. A week later, *Sweet Baby James* debuted on the *Billboard* album chart at number 90 and only inched up a few spots in the weeks ahead.

Before the album was even for sale, Taylor began gearing up for his first tour to promote it, warming up with six nights at the Troubadour on Santa Monica Boulevard in Hollywood. Heavy on cozy ambience and music-business types, the club was an entry point for new acts and a place for established names to be seen and hang out. Taylor's shows attracted a few pop names, including Cass Elliot of the Mamas and the Papas, thereby confirming Taylor's status within his community. Whether or not it translated beyond the Canyon wasn't anyone's leading concern. "We were living in our own world," John Fischbach recalled. "We were having our own Woodstock every day."

Beyond Laurel Canyon, the country felt like it was exploding, often literally. Despite a rash of nonviolent protests that included the October Moratorium in Washington, the pro-peace movement's growing frustration over Vietnam was turning into a depression. That depression was turning into anger and desperation, and the desperation was turning to destruction.

The exact number of bombs set off by a variety of radical offshoots depended on the source. CBS News placed the nationwide tally between January 1969 and the spring of 1970 at 4,330, about twenty a week in

California alone. The U.S. Treasury estimated forty a week. In Manhattan, between August and October 1969, explosive devices had gone off in three buildings on Wall Street and in Macy's, followed by bombs at the Chase Manhattan Bank, the RCA Building, and General Motors in November. A letter sent by the bombers to UPI stated their motives: The enemy was the "giant corporations . . . Spiro Agnew may be a household word, but it [the public] has rarely seen men like David Rockefeller of Chase Manhattan, James Roche of General Motors and Michael Haider of Standard Oil, who run the system behind the scenes." Eventually implicated were employees of the *Rat*, an underground newspaper, and a man *Time* described as a "health faddist." In February 1970, the detonations in the New York area continued—at a GE center in Queens and outside the home of State Supreme Court justice John Murtagh, who presided at a pretrial hearing involving Black Panthers accused of trying to blow up public spaces.

Obtaining the materials to make a bomb was, one network news report said, "ridiculously simple." Dynamite came from anywhere, swiped from construction sites or military bases or, in some cases, purchased over the counter. (Where *did* those seven thousand dynamite blasting caps swiped from a Maryland plant in March go, exactly?) The laws for selling dynamite varied from state to state. In Oregon, all anyone needed was a name, address, and license-plate number. Other states required a blasting permit, making the process more difficult. "The underground promises more bombings," said one CBS reporter, "and it is clear that existing controls are totally inadequate to stop them." Working on the script for his second film, *Bananas*, that spring—it would begin filming in May—Woody Allen acknowledged the prosaic ordinariness of the explosions. When his character asks out a New York leftie played by Allen's ex-wife Louise Lasser, she replies, "Call me Saturday . . . I may be bombing an office building, but I'll know later."

In New York City, the relative ease with which explosives could be obtained and detonated by anyone determined or crazy enough to do it was slammed home at noon on Friday, March 6. One moment, 18 West 11th Street was a ten-room brownstone that dated back to the 1840s. The next moment it was a roof and a stairwell, a massive, gaping, flame-spewing hole in between. After neighbors and nearby drivers heard a massive explosion, the roof collapsed, along with all four floors; the two-foot-thick walls were scarred with holes that ascended twenty feet. The first to scurry from the building were rats, along with a few cats, followed by two girls—one nude, another just wearing a T-shirt—who were discovered by rescue workers and led to a building across the street. Dustin Hoffman, who lived next door, at 16 West 11th, joined the gawkers on the street. Clutching a Tiffany lamp and several paintings he'd taken with him, he noticed that his desk, which shared a wall with number 18, had fallen through the wall and into the burning rubble.

When police and firemen began sifting through the wreckage of the explosion, they found the body of one man beneath the debris, followed by an even grislier discovery. A large power shovel cleaning debris out of the basement scooped up a body with two missing hands, one leg, and a mangled head, nails jutting out of the torso's flesh. At first, the fire department assumed a gas leak caused the blast, but when an intact gas furnace was unearthed in the basement rubble on Monday morning, suspicions that bombs were involved were confirmed. The dead turned out to be three members of the radical group the Weathermen. One of them, Terry Robbins, had accidentally set off the bombs as he was assembling them. (The other dead were Theodore Gold and Diana Oughton, while Kathy Boudin and Cathy Wilkerson, whose father owned the building, escaped, at least for a while; they were the two young women seen fleeing.) Along with body parts, police discovered sixty sticks of unexploded dynamite, caps to set them off, primitive nail bombs, and a map of the tunnels beneath Columbia University, one of the Weathermen's intended targets.

Both the city and the country barely had time to digest what had happened when, five days later, explosions detonated in three office buildings in midtown Manhattan, in roughly the same area—42nd Street between Lexington and Third; Park Avenue and 55th; and Third Avenue at 46th. The targets were Mobil, IBM, and General Telephone and Electronics, respectively. In each case, no one was hurt; police had been tipped to the pending explosions and their precise times by an anonymous caller a half hour before. Streets were strewn with glass, elevators were deluged with water, and the buildings sustained structural damage. Over the next two days, six hundred bomb threats were called in to the city. On March 15, the *Times* reported, with no sense of sarcasm, that "the number of bomb threats in the city declined sharply for the first time since Thursday." An anonymous caller to the New York Police Department credited the Mobil, IBM, and General Telephone bombings to a previously unknown group called the Revolutionary Force 9.

Before the brownstone explosion, the Weathermen were something of underground culture heroes; they weren't succeeding at much, but they knew how to get publicity. The accidental bombing—along with their intended targets—cast a pall over the group that never dissipated. No one expected Richard Nixon to be supportive, and he wasn't. On March 12, a report called "Subject: Revolutionary Violence" was dropped onto his desk; when asked to reach out to the disgruntled younger generation, he shot back, "Forget them." But Abbie Hoffman, who had once championed the Weathermen, even helping some members escape the clutches of the law, was having his doubts. Realizing that killing innocent civilians wouldn't help the cause, he later wrote that the 11th Street incident was "the great tragedy of the underground's development," although he admitted it was "a blessing in disguise" in the way it obliterated dangerous tendencies in the group. Reading about the explosion in a Washington newspaper the next day, Moratorium co-organizer David Hawk was disgusted and thanked God no innocent bystanders had been killed.

After seeing photos of the destroyed building on the front page of the *Times* the following day, Susan Braudy, a young writer and Bryn Mawr and Yale graduate who'd attended school with Boudin and Oughton, went to see the site for herself. The block was engulfed in smoke, water, and plainclothes cops. "I just thought, 'This isn't going to work,'" she remembered. Maybe her generation wasn't going to bring about the change they hoped. Maybe all the political sloganeering amounted to nothing. Confused and upset, she began rethinking everything positive she'd presumed about the group and other radical organizations.

A month later, Braudy saw Boudin running down a street, bare-legged and wearing a winter coat. The sight seemed to make as much sense as anything else at that moment.

Early in the afternoon of March 7, the day after the brownstone explosion, a line began forming outside 116 MacDougal Street, eight blocks south of 11th Street and on the other side of Washington Square Park. The crowd was preparing for the first of James Taylor's three nights at the Village Gaslight, a tiny space crammed in the midst of the Village's club strip.

The Greenwich Village folk music scene wasn't as bustling as it had been in the early to mid '60s, when Simon and Garfunkel and Stephen Stills—not to mention Bob Dylan, Peter, Paul and Mary, Judy Collins, Ramblin' Jack Elliott, and so many others—had worked on their craft on cramped coffeehouse stages. Dylan had just relocated back to the Village after several years in Woodstock, but he and his peers had long since moved on to bigger, more prestigious venues, and folk music itself, especially the political type, no longer had the cultural impact it once had. Of the coffeehouses and clubs that had survived, the Village Gaslight held all of 130 people wedged behind its angled wooden tables; the stage was next to the kitchen. To compensate for the lack of a liquor license, the bartenders would add a bit of rum flavoring to the soda.

Taylor's first tour to promote *Sweet Baby James* had nothing approaching a budget. From town to town, Taylor traveled with just his guitar and his mother's small canvas suitcase for whatever clothes he wanted to bring along. Asher sensed Taylor would be able to attract more than one hundred people to a New York show; surely some must have remembered the Flying Machine, who'd played at the nearby Night Owl just a few years before. But Asher was savvy enough to realize that an overpacked house was far better for buzz than a half-filled one, so he'd booked Taylor into the Gaslight for three nights. On opening night, hundreds began lining up in the frigid temperatures, even for the late show, which started at 2 A.M. Someone glimpsed Dylan in the crowd.

Asher knew good publicity when he saw it. Grabbing a few dimes, he ran to a pay phone up the street and called local newspaper and TV outlets to tell them about the long line extending from 116 MacDougal all the way down to Bleecker. Afterward the *New York Post* reported that the Gaslight had turned away two thousand people. The club's owners had no idea where that figure came from, but it sounded impressive.

Ambling onto the compact Gaslight stage and taking a seat on a wooden chair, Taylor could have been mistaken for a roadie rather than the headlining act. He began singing, his gaze downward, eyes sometimes closed, his long, slightly greasy brown hair occasionally obscuring what few expressions he had. He seemed pained and didn't work hard to hide it. "Lord knows you got to take enough time to think these days," he told the crowd. Then he added, "If you feel like singing along . . . don't."

Yet Taylor also knew how to charm the Gaslight crowd. At moments, he made mild fun of rock star convention. Toward the end of the set he would do "Steamroller," picking out a few rough-hewn notes on the guitar and deadpanning, "Pick it, Big Jim." (Asher had suggested Taylor actually stand up while performing that song, for an added bit of showmanship, but Taylor declined.) When water from a steam pipe on the ceiling began to drip on him, he joked, "My guitar is gently weeping." "He was painfully shy onstage, but he knew how to make his painful shyness work for him," recalled Danny Kortchmar. "Every woman in the audience was in love with him. It wasn't a premeditated thing. Even when he was sitting in a chair, people would lean forward to hear what he had to say. It worked like a champ."

"I can feel it happening," Taylor told *New York Post* writer Al Aronowitz before the show. "I'm starting to feel good about it." Taylor's feeling was borne out in the post-show press. "Is James Taylor going to be the next public phenomenon?" wrote the widely read Aronowitz. *Cashbox*, the music trade magazine, noted, "They can smell a legend going to happen—the crowd, the 'knowing' crowd, had really gotten James Taylor's scent." Coming only a few days after the brownstone explosion, Taylor's stint at the club, his nonthreatening songs rolling out effortlessly, must have felt especially consoling.

Murmurs in Greenwich Village weren't yet translating to record sales. As the spring deepened, *Sweet Baby James* remained under the radar. In the April 25 issue of *Billboard*, it zipped up to number 25, then dropped and kept falling, until it remained stuck in the lower echelons of the top 100. At one humiliating point, it was one notch below the soundtrack to *Paint Your Wagon*, a hokey film adaptation of a '50s Broadway musical—everything Taylor's music, much less rock and roll, was supposed to have abolished. Right then, the radio was teeming with music that whooped and soared, like the Jackson Five's "The Love You Save" or Crosby, Stills, Nash & Young's "Woodstock," or ripped and roared, like Creedence Clearwater Revival's "Up Around the Bend" and John Lennon's "Instant Karma!" Next to them, "Sweet Baby James," a modest shrug, failed to chart.

The campus circuit was another, more welcoming matter. By the spring of 1970, more kids in their late teens and early twenties were attending colleges and universities than ever—over seven million, a 30 percent increase from 1965. Young, confused, and disillusioned, they began responding, albeit slowly, to *Sweet Baby James*. At a record store at the Madison branch of the University of Wisconsin, the album went top 10, just behind juggernauts like *Bridge Over Troubled Water* and *Déjà vu*. Realizing the importance of this market, Asher began booking Taylor into a string of college dates, including Harvard on April 25 and Cornell on May 2.

The turnouts varied: After the Cornell show, sponsored by Volkswagen, one of the students who organized it cracked, "It's probably the only thing Volkswagen ever lost money on." The accommodations varied as well. To save money, Taylor would often crash in student dorms. But his May 29 performance at a high-school theater—the Berkeley Community Theatre, part of Berkeley High School just north of San Francisco—demonstrated how he was beginning to connect with an audience of his own. Judging from their warm response, the hundreds gathered were clearly already familiar with "Fire and Rain" and "Country Road" from the new album, and "Carolina in My Mind" from the first. They chortled, as they always did, when he rolled out the self-deprecating "Big Jim" line in "Steamroller." "My my my," he ad-libbed that night during that song, "I don't know nothin' but the blues." The line was half joke and half branding act.

Even the outside material Taylor picked for his set built on his apolitical, lonely-guy persona. In Berkeley, he sang a muted version of Joni Mitchell's "For Free," about a pop star who sees a street musician and pines for those early, pre-pressure days. His younger brother Livingston's plainspoken, lilting "In My Reply" was a parable of people corrupted by their lust for power and money. In the hands of the Drifters eight years before, Carole King and Gerry Goffin's "Up on the Roof" was a wondrous and jubilant exaltation of city life; Taylor transformed it into a doleful lament. Later in the show, with a modest, "Hello, Carole," he even introduced King, who was joining him at select shows as his piano player. (Just before hitting the road, Taylor played guitar and harmonized on King's first album as a solo artist, *Writer*, cut that spring.) Whether he sang his songs or others', Taylor was becoming an entry point for a new generation of songwriters eager to analyze their mental states in song; community and politics were far from the agenda.

During interviews he began doing to promote the album, Taylor seemed uncomfortable discussing his stays at McLean and Austin Riggs. But neither did he completely run from that part of his past. In a press release that accompanied *Sweet Baby James*, he wrote, "In the fall of 1965 I entered a state of what must have been intense adolescence . . . and spent nine months of voluntary commitment at McLean Psychiatric Hospital in Massachusetts." At early club shows, he would turn his stay there into a quizzical in-joke: "McLean, that's a mental hospital," he told one audience. "Okay, anybody here from McLean? Let's hear it for McLean." Eager to discuss money matters, Taylor called Warners head Joe Smith one day. Taylor was distraught, and Smith said he should go to Smith's house and wait for him. There, Taylor and Smith's wife sat waiting for Smith to come home, Taylor barely saying a word for nearly a half hour. "My wife can make a conversation with a wall, but he sat there and said nothing," Smith recalled. "She finally called me and said, 'Get home!'"

The sense that Taylor had been damaged by drugs or mental instability only added to his mystique. When a reporter interviewed college students about Taylor's appeal, one answered, astutely, "The fact that he was in a mental hospital colors people emotionally before they even hear the songs. They all feel sorry for him. The girls, especially." By then, even Taylor understood that playing up his flaws wasn't such a bad idea. "I feel fine just to know you're around," he began plucking and crooning at Berkeley. At first it sounded like a love song, but soon the crowd started realizing what was happening. *Wait, what* is *this song?* Then Taylor hit the chorus: "Things go better with Coke," he sang, and the audience whooped at both the not-very-veiled drug reference and Taylor semi-mocking a corporate ad jingle.

"*Yeah!*" yelled a man in the crowd, with evident approval.

Whether he wanted it to or not, Taylor's life was growing more complicated by the day. He was still attached in some way to Margaret Corey, but he was also spending time in the Laurel Canyon cottage of Toni Stern, a native Californian and friend of King's. Stern joined him during the East Coast leg of his tour, even meeting his family in Boston. Stern brought along her dog, who often ate his way through the wooden storage racks in the airplanes.

Driving along the Sunset Strip in Hollywood, Monte Hellman looked up at one of the ubiquitous, towering billboards advertising new albums and was instantly drawn to the face on it. Hellman had never heard of James Taylor before, but the handsome face looking down at him was all that the director needed to see. At twenty-eight, the frizzy-haired Hellman was already a veteran of Roger Corman productions (*Beast from Haunted Cave*) and surrealistic westerns starring Jack Nicholson (*Ride in the Whirlwind, The Shooting*). He was considering directing a script for *Two-Lane Blacktop*, about two car-racing hustlers making their way across the country, and the man on the billboard had the perfect face for the role of the unnamed Driver.

When Asher received a call from Hellman's casting director that Hellman was interested in his client, he was torn. Asher heard Hellman was a reputable, up-and-coming director, but Taylor had never acted, and Asher, despite a background that included working as a child actor in London, knew little about dealing with the film business. Asher reached out to Mike Medavoy, an agent who represented the new breed of anti-establishment directors, including Steven Spielberg, Francis Ford Coppola, and John Milius. By coincidence, Hellman was also one of Medavoy's clients. Before long, Taylor was taking a meeting with Hellman in the director's Los Angeles office. Hellman sensed Taylor was "up for the adventure" of making a film. Hellman wanted realism, not slick actors, and Medavoy was also sold on Taylor. "James had an amazing presence," said Medavoy. "It was the presence of a guy people wanted to hug. Very likable and warm. That's rare."

By then, Hellman had already hired novelist Rudy Wurlitzer to rewrite scriptwriter Will Corry's screenplay. Wurlitzer, who'd published the cult novel *Nog*, rewrote the part of the Driver. Although he had no inkling Taylor was up for the part, Wurlitzer sketched out a character who could have passed for him. The working script described the Driver as "age 23 . . . his face is lean and angular. There is a perplexed and detached look in his eyes. His movements are graceful and yet tense, nervous." Without meaning to, Wurlitzer had carved out Taylor's next career move.

In early April, Hellman shot Taylor's screen test on a sunny day at a house in Los Angeles. Taylor had shown up with a mustache, which Hellman had him shave off as part of the test. Alternately staring down the camera or looking away as if too shy to respond, Taylor—in a V-neck T-shirt, his hair in a shag cut like that on *Sweet Baby James*—exuded a blend of irritation and amusement. More than one person, including the cautious Wurlitzer, thought he was stoned on one substance or other. "It was very awkward," Wurlitzer remembered. "He was very uncomfortable. It was very disorienting. Drugs will do that to you. You go in and out of various levels of focus."

Hellman tried to warm Taylor up, asking him about Martha's Vineyard and how many people lived there in the winter and summer. As if barely tolerating the questions being thrown at him, Taylor curtly replied he liked his place on the Vineyard because the nearest neighbor was "a quarter mile away."

At one point, Hellman mentioned the Beatles, wondering whether "Helter Skelter" was a parody of hard rock or the real thing.

Taylor managed a shrug. "The Beatles aren't, anymore."

"I just heard that," Hellman replied.

"Unfortunately," Taylor said, with a typically understated combination of sadness and irritation.

CHAPTER 6

On the first day of March, the Beatles returned, more or less, to *The Ed Sullivan Show*. Six years before, their first appearance on television's most insanely eclectic variety series had been viewed by seventy-three million people—a colossal number then and later—and transformed the culture and a generation. Now, for one of his recurring thematic shows, Sullivan decided to dedicate a full hour to their music.

This time, though, there would be no actual Beatles present. Instead, viewers witnessed an oddball, largely non-rock parade of entertainers interpreting their songs: Dionne Warwick sang "We Can Work It Out," Peggy Lee crooned "Something," ballet star Edward Villella leapt to "Lucy in the Sky with Diamonds." The lounge-lizard duo of Steve Lawrence and Eydie Gorme, two of Allen Klein's first clients, popped up as well. The show was a testament to the ways in which the Beatles, and rock itself, had become mainstream culture. But the Beatles themselves appeared only on film, performing "Two of Us" and "Let It Be" in a preview of their in-the-works movie, now retitled *Let It Be*. Even on their own show, they were a spectral presence.

No one seemed to notice, and to most of the world beyond the Apple Corps building on Savile Row, Beatle business continued as usual. In February, Klein had announced the imminent arrival of two movies: *Let It Be* and another called *The Long and Winding Road*, which he described as a documentary about their travels and escapades over the previous two years. With dreams of a financial windfall no doubt dancing in his brain, he confidently announced both would arrive in spring. By the penultimate day of spring, ads for "Let It Be," their new single, were spotted in the States and the U.K. The Beatles were on their way back.

The Sullivan show even coincided with the release of a new Beatles album—but it too felt half-hearted, perhaps even quarter-hearted. *Hey Jude* was entirely given over to songs and singles that hadn't made it onto previous Beatle albums, like the title hit and "The Ballad of John and Yoko." Originally titled *The Beatles Again*, it had been spearheaded by Klein, who was eager to ship as much new Beatle product to stores as possible after he'd renegotiated their contract with EMI the previous fall. For a grab bag, the album was still exceptional—any record that contained both "Paperback Writer" and "Lady Madonna" couldn't be anything but. Yet even the cover photo, taken the previous August at Lennon's Tittenhurst estate, was dated. Dan Richter, Lennon and Ono's friend, had accidentally walked in on the shoot and was surprised not only by their presence but their mood; they all seemed glum and morose.

Shortly after the Sullivan telecast, the Chicago chapter of the Beatle fan club—125 diehards, mostly women—congregated in a room at the Executive House Hotel on the Chicago River. They traded souvenirs and made contests out of remembering the dates of Brian Epstein's death and the premiere of *Help!*

As hard as everyone tried to revive the spirit of 1964, the general mood was less than festive. One club member pulled out a photo of Lennon and Ono in their prisoner-of-war haircuts, which led to gaping, eye-rolling, and arguments. The original Beatlemaniacs, the ones who'd first watched them on Sullivan, dismissed Ono, while the new fans at the meeting, the twelve-year-olds, were more accepting of her quirks. As the meeting wound down, the club's secretary, twenty-four-year-old Vikki Paradiso, called off plans for any further gatherings. Across the ocean, *Beatles Monthly Book*, a monthly London fanzine, announced it would be shutting down; circulation had plunged from 330,000 copies an issue to a mere 26,000.

O O O O

In Apple's Press Office, tucked away on the third floor of the Savile Row building, the newspaper clippings were beginning to pile up. When Richard DiLello was hired in the spring of 1968, the twenty-three-year-old American—who'd landed the job after meeting press department head Derek Taylor in Los Angeles, much like his coworker Chris O'Dell—was told to wade through the stacks of periodicals with articles on the Beatles. For a salary of ten pounds a week, DiLello cut them out and sorted them into piles: negative articles in one stack, positive in another, Apple Corps articles over there. When the frizzy-haired, freak-flag-flying DiLello wasn't slogging through those stacks, he'd roll joints for Taylor or make one of his weekly hash runs for the office.

New clippings arrived every day, but by now, no one was tending to them, and stacks began to sit uncollected in forlorn piles around the four desks in the office. Calls from the media kept coming in: What were John and Yoko up to now? Was the band available for a photo shoot? Taylor would gamely set up chats when he could, but few in the office knew what the individuals in the band were doing. Every so often, DiLello would look up from his desk and see a thickset, turtlenecked man with a dark pompadour of hair, staring at him as if he were an alien. The man's colleagues—men who always seemed to be sporting brown suits with brown shoes—would be trailing right behind him. Like O'Dell and anyone else still gainfully employed at Apple, DiLello was plenty aware that the man everyone simply called "Klein" was in the house.

At thirty-eight, roughly a decade older than any of the Beatles, Allen Klein was a man of voracious appetites, whether he was wolfing down a steak at his desk or going after a record company that had failed to pay royalties to one of his clients. Around Apple, everyone knew he'd managed Sam Cooke, was now handling the Rolling Stones, and was financially entangled with the Who, the Animals, and the Kinks. They also knew McCartney didn't like him very much and that the others did. And they knew that, at any moment, they could all lose their jobs.

Had they known he'd spent nearly five years in an orphanage after his mother died (his father couldn't handle raising a son alone until he remarried), they would have known Klein always felt he had something to prove to himself and the world. He hated being known as an "orphan" and saw himself instead as both underdog and their champion. After college and a stint in the Army, Klein, born in Newark, New Jersey, had first worked as an accountant for small businesses in the New York City area—a paint store here, a health club there. When his college friend Don Kirshner, who'd started as a songwriter but moved into the far more lucrative business of song publishing, asked him to audit a client's record company, Klein was off and running—or, rather, barking. By scouring the receipts of labels, Klein was able to find unclaimed sums of money for pop acts like Cooke and Bobby Darin. Klein then set his sights on the British Invasion bands. Eric Burdon, lead singer of the Animals, was walking down the street in New York when a man with a swirl of dark hair stuck his head out of a limo. "I'll give you seventeen thousand dollars for your rights to the Animals catalog right now!" he yelled, holding a pen in his thumb and index finger. The traffic was moving so slowly that Burdon could have easily signed right there and then, but he kept on walking; he'd heard about Klein.

After Cooke was shot to death in 1964, Klein moved on to manage other acts—luring the Rolling Stones away from Andrew Loog Oldham—and negotiate record or publishing contracts for the Kinks, the Who, and the Dave Clark Five. Kirshner instilled in Klein the idea that the key to wealth in the music business was owning song copyrights, and Klein, a quick study, understood. In the fall of 1968, after purchasing the Stones' catalog, he went hunting for an even bigger prize.

Beginning with his days as a clerk at the *Essex County News* in New Jersey, Klein wasn't just savvy with numbers; he knew how to ingratiate himself with musicians using a combination of tough talk (the record companies were the Man!), an intimate knowledge of pop songs, and ego massaging. When he set up a meeting with Lennon and Ono at a London hotel in January 1969, the first of many steps in his plan to work his way into the Beatles' fold, Klein ordered their favorite macrobiotic food and impressed Lennon by knowing precisely which Beatles songs he'd written and sung. Klein sensed how important it was for Lennon to differentiate himself from the others, especially now that he and Ono had become the butt of jokes and hostility. In one of his frequent snap decisions, Lennon knew Klein was his man. Wanting to maintain their own lifestyles, Harrison and Starr went along with the idea of Klein handling their business affairs. McCartney wasn't so sure and preferred Linda's father Lee Eastman (and his son John) to handle their money. Nonetheless, the other three signed a three-year contract with Klein on May 8, 1969.

To his credit, Klein renegotiated Brian Epstein's contract with EMI, hoisting the Beatles' royalty rate from 17.5 percent to 25. As always, Klein would make out exceptionally well himself: ABKCO, his company, would net 20 percent of their royalties and 25 percent of merchandise sales—both higher percentages than usual—and according to the deal, Capitol would send all payments to Apple by way of ABKCO from September 1969 through April 1972. He also began trimming Apple's fat, doing the dirty work the Beatles themselves had no stomach for. (McCartney's interest in chairing meetings and overseeing business details had gone the way of his clean-shaven face, and his desire to remain popular meant he didn't want to fire anyone.) Numerous employees, including label head Ron Kass, were canned; Asher, having heard plenty about Klein, resigned. For DiLello, among others, the message was abundantly clear. "This was no longer an idealistic hippie dream, saving the world and giving people the chance to do whatever they want to do under the auspices of the Beatles," he said. "This was now, 'Okay, it's all about money and turning this into a real business.' They all had very lavish lifestyles. Jetting around the world for peace—someone had to pay for all that."

From the start, Peter Brown—who cultivated the air of a refined British gentleman from his neatly trimmed beard to his tasteful suits—had a visceral dislike for the far less suave Klein. Brown was also offended by Klein's assertions that Apple was in poor financial shape and saw them as Klein's calculated way of winning over the band. Within months, he and Klein were barely on speaking terms. Brown's job description remained the same, but Klein's accountant began badgering him with questions. "I wasn't happy at all, but I didn't want it to appear that Klein had pushed me out," Brown recalled. He stayed on, but when Brown and Neil Aspinall weren't reelected to the board of shareholders that year, probably thanks to Klein, Brown knew his Apple days were numbered.

As another one of his early projects, Klein also lit a fire under *Get Back*, the movie of their recording sessions they'd filmed over a year before. After *A Hard Day's Night, Help!*, and *Yellow Submarine*, the Beatles owed United Artists one more feature, so Klein made a revamped deal for a release and a soundtrack album, both now called *Let It Be*. Although engineer Glyn John had taken a first crack at making sense of the tapes and even sequenced a finished album, Klein ultimately went with Phil Spector.

Spector seemed an odd choice to oversee this particular project. His Wall of Sound was now out of vogue (as proven by the chart flop of what he saw as his masterpiece, Ike and Tina Turner's "River Deep—Mountain High" in 1966), and it also seemed the antithesis of the very idea of the consciously under-produced *Get Back* sessions. Still, he and Klein were natural cohorts: both sons of European immigrants, both rooted in the New York area (Spector was born in the Bronx, where Klein later worked). ABKCO also had a "financial participation" in hits Spector had cowritten, like "Be My Baby" and "You've Lost That Lovin' Feelin'." When the two would meet up in recording studios, they'd unintentionally look and sound like a Noo Yawk comedy duo; Lennon and Klaus Voormann would be beside themselves with laughter.

When asked why he'd hired Spector to work with the Beatles, Klein was typically blunt. "Wouldn't you want the number-one director to direct the number-one actor?" he told the *New York Post*. Klein was so confident in the unfinished *Let It Be* album that he ordered EMI to press up three million copies.

By spring, Klein had far stickier Beatle matters to sort out. McCartney's own album was no longer a secret, especially when he made it known he wanted it out fast, on April 17. Klein knew releasing it at the same time as a new Beatles album (and Starr's now completed *Sentimental Journey* record) could potentially dilute the sales of each. In his particular way, Klein went about solving the problem. After discussions with Harrison, Lennon, and Starr, he sent a letter on March 20 to Ken East, the managing director of EMI Music, which distributed Apple, asking to delay the release of McCartney's album. The only person he didn't bother to inform about his decision was McCartney.

EMI had little choice in the matter. The power of the Beatles was such that the corporation had an arm's-length relationship with Apple, which supplied EMI with release dates, finished artwork, and tapes. Other than employees of the studio on Abbey Road, hardly anyone at the company saw or worked alongside a Beatle. The imminent release of something called *Let It Be* embodied the lack of interaction between the two companies. When EMI marketing director Paul Watts heard about it, he was confused: What *was* it, exactly? And had it been recorded before or after *Abbey Road*?

The beginning of the end started on March 23. At one studio, Spector began sorting through the pile of tapes from the Twickenham and

Apple group sessions; on the same day, he also managed to stretch out "I Me Mine," the song McCartney, Harrison, and Starr had cut in January, by thirty seconds by repeating the chorus. The same day, "Billy Martin" logged his final day at EMI Studios. And also on March 23, Klein met with East to repeat his demands to postpone McCartney's album, and East agreed. In a sign of how badly communication had broken down inside the band—and how much resentment had built up toward Mc-Cartney after he'd insisted on having the Eastmans represent them—eight days went by after Klein and East's meeting before anyone reached out to McCartney.

Finally, on March 31, Lennon and Harrison sent their own letter to East, saying "it would not be in the best interests of the company" for McCartney's album to be released April 17. The same day, they dashed off another piece of correspondence, this one to McCartney himself. "To: You, From: Us," it began, followed by: "Dear Paul: We thought a lot about yours and the Beatles LPs—and decided it's stupid for Apple to put out two big albums within seven days of each other. So we sent a letter to EMI telling them to hold your release date till June 4th (there's a big Apple-Capitol convention in Hawaii then). We thought you'd come around when you realized that the Beatles album was coming out on April 24th. We're sorry it turned out like this—it's nothing personal." It was signed "Love, John and George." Extending a particularly thorny olive branch, Harrison added his own postscript: "Hail Krishna. A mantra a day keeps 'Maya' away. I hope my friend gets joy from that."

As it turned out, McCartney did take it personally. That day, Starr drove to McCartney's home on Cavendish Avenue to hand-deliver the letter. McCartney greeted his bandmate coldly, then read the letter in his parlor as Starr stood by. As McCartney later affirmed in a court affidavit, "I got really angry when Ringo told me that Klein had told him my record was not ready." That was an understatement. Appalled by the way Klein and his fellow Beatles had conspired behind his back—even though they only wanted to hold back his record for two months, not kill it altogether—McCartney exploded in a way Starr had rarely seen. "I'll finish you now!" he yelled. "You'll pay!" Starr had barely taken his coat off when McCartney told him to put it back on and leave.

Simultaneously, John Eastman, who had taken over handling McCartney's day-to-day dealings from his father, heard about the plans to postpone the record during a meeting with executives at Capitol Records in Los Angeles. Furious himself, Eastman calmed a nerve-wracked McCartney, telling him the record would come out one way or another; in fact, Eastman was already thinking about contacting Clive Davis to see if Columbia would take it. When McCartney mentioned this possibility to Harrison, Harrison shot back, "You'll stay on the fucking label. Hare Krishna." (As a Beatle associate of the time noted, Harrison, when angry, had a distinct way of making "Hare Krishna" sound like "fuck you.") In the end, McCartney got his wish: When Starr checked in with Harrison and Lennon after his confrontation with McCartney, he argued they should grant McCartney his wish and release his album on his schedule, and they did.

Shortly after, *Rolling Stone* editor Jann Wenner flew to London to interview McCartney about the impending album. McCartney asserted Klein wasn't managing him, talked about the good time he had making a record on his own, and downplayed any rifts with Lennon. Instead of talking about specific songs, he told Wenner that those details and more would be included in a special announcement accompanying the record. "I just filled it out like an essay, like a school thing," he said. When pressed by Wenner to divulge its contents, McCartney demurred. "It's much nicer as a surprise," he said.

The week of April 6 began inauspiciously enough in the land of the

Beatles. In America, "Let It Be," the elegiac ballad McCartney had written for his mother—a song with the instantly timeless feel of a church hymn composed centuries before—easily floated up to number 1. On Tuesday, April 7, John and Lee Eastman announced that their client Paul McCartney had formed his own production company, sporting the not terribly original name of McCartney Productions. Its first two projects would be an animated film based on *Rupert the Bear*, a children's cartoon celebrating its fiftieth anniversary, and the release of an album of his own, *McCartney*. That day, a meeting was scheduled at Apple Corps for April 10, at which the four Beatles would finally face each other—after months apart—to discuss plans for the release of *Let It Be*, which would be in theaters in a little over a month.

That Tuesday, DiLello was in the Press Office at Apple when Derek Taylor casually handed him a typed, four-page letter on Apple stationery. "What's this?" DiLello wondered.

The document in DiLello's hand was an "interview" with McCartney, albeit in description only. McCartney enjoyed being the jovial salesman for the band more than any of the other Beatles, but the thought of having to answer questions about the state of the Beatles appealed to him as much as seeing the frontal nudity on the cover of Lennon and Ono's *Two Virgins*. Taylor and Brown suggested McCartney write up his own question-and-answer session and supplied him with typically banal questions: "Why did you decide to make a solo album?" "Did you enjoy working as a solo?" "Were you pleased with *Abbey Road*?" As Brown watched, McCartney wrote out the answers in the living room of his St. John's Wood home, after which they were quietly typed up for distribution with the first one hundred British promotional copies of *McCartney*.

On the morning of Wednesday, April 8, Ray Connolly, a young music columnist and reporter at the *Evening Standard*, was at his desk when he received a call from Taylor. Taylor said he was about to messenger over a statement from McCartney, but asked that Connolly and the paper hold off publishing it until Friday, April 10. When the envelope arrived, Connolly flipped through it. The bulk of it was innocuous enough. In it, McCartney talked up his record and commented elliptically on where the Beatles stood as people and creative partners. McCartney said the band was split over "personal differences, business differences, musical differences," but added, "Temporary or permanent? I don't know."

The document hardly knocked Connolly out of his desk chair. Along with a group of other writers, he'd been granted much access to the Beatles over the previous few years, conducting interviews with them and spending considerable time at Apple headquarters. He'd witnessed his share of bickering and had been in the Press Office when Lennon had bolted from the meeting in Brown's office the previous September. Connolly had flown to Toronto to cover Lennon's appearance at the Rock & Roll Revival concert. Arriving at the house of rockabilly icon Ronnie Hawkins, who was lending his home to the Lennons, Connolly heard Lennon shout out his name and ask him to an upstairs bathroom. Still washing his long hair in a sink, Lennon had breathlessly told Connolly he was leaving the Beatles. Stunned by the news, Connolly realized he had the pop scoop of the decade, but Lennon told him not to write about it just yet; he'd tell him the appropriate time to break the story.

At his desk, Connolly flashed back to that and other tumultuous moments. Thinking McCartney's statement was simply of a piece with the band's increasingly public grousing, he filed it away until publication three days later. Besides, it was hard to imagine a world without the Beatles.

The next morning, Thursday, April 9, Connolly received a call at home from his editors: The *Daily Mirror* was announcing the Beatles were over. Where was *his* story? *Daily Mirror* writer Don Short, a long-time friend of the band, had received the same packet but, unlike Connolly, saw McCartney's statement as inflammatory. Short particularly focused on one back-and-forth: To the question "Do you foresee a time when Lennon-McCartney become an active songwriting partnership again?" McCartney tersely wrote out, "No." McCartney never came out and said the band was over or that he was leaving, but Short felt otherwise. "Paul is quitting the Beatles," he wrote. Disregarding Taylor's request, his editors ran Short's piece a day early. Taylor had no comment, while Mavis Smith, who worked in the Press Office with Taylor and DiLello, denied any breakup.

With the news out prematurely, McCartney went into damage-control mode. For the first time since the fall, he called Lennon at home, telling him he'd finished his album and was leaving the group. By then, Lennon had already heard about the article; Connolly had called him for comment. To McCartney, Lennon sounded relieved, and to another reporter, Lennon joked, "I was happy to hear from Paul. It was nice to find out that he was still alive. Anyway, Paul hasn't left. I've sacked him."

Privately, though, Lennon was peeved: *He'd* wanted to be the first to tell the world the Beatles—and the '60s, with which he was increasingly disillusioned—were over. Instead, it was McCartney, of all people, who'd done that—the same McCartney so intent on breathing life into the band all those years. To Lennon, the gesture felt like an ambush and a betrayal. The same process took place with Starr and Harrison: McCartney called them, but they too had already heard the news. Mal Evans, another member of the Beatles' inner circle, was at Friar Park with Harrison and Boyd that night. He left to drive back home—and then returned to the house soon after, ashen faced. A news report on the radio announced McCartney was breaking up the Beatles. Harrison took the news stoically, saying he wanted to write his own songs anyway and retreating upstairs to his bedroom. As if to drive it home further, a London variety show aired a clip of McCartney performing "Maybe I'm Amazed" from his album that night.

The next morning, Chris O'Dell, then living with the Harrisons at Friar Park, came downstairs to find Harrison and Boyd glumly reading the morning's papers. Lennon soon came by, and O'Dell watched as the two men talked in the backyard. It was the first time she'd ever seen Lennon without Ono.

The British music newsweekly *Melody Maker* called the announcement "the non-event of the year." After all, so many in the music business knew the Beatles were out of touch with each other. The previous November 11, Connolly had written an *Evening Standard* article headlined "The Day the Beatles Died," about the events of the previous fall. The same month, a *Life* magazine spread meant to put a halt to all the "Paul Is Dead" stories of the time quoted McCartney as saying, "The Beatle thing is over, it has been exploded."

Few in the media had picked up those comments then, but not this time. The *New York Times'* story, "McCartney Breaks Off with Beatles," made it into section one, normally the domain of the most urgent national and international stories. Fans converged on Apple, spilling out on Savile Row and casting blame on Klein or, in some cases, Linda McCartney. ("You can't let a woman do that to a man, can you?" explained one female fan to a reporter, as if Linda had been manipulating her husband far more than Ono had Lennon.) On the front steps of the building, an Apple employee handed out copies of McCartney's press release. Wearing his usual carefree smile along with a red frilly shirt and jacket, Starr dashed out into a waiting car and was gone. One of many earnest, somber television reporters standing outside Apple intoned, "The event is so momentous that historians may mark it as a landmark in the decline of the British Empire."

McCartney was spotted in the backseat of a dark green Rolls Royce tooling around London with Linda, Heather, and their sheepdog Martha, but no further comments were forthcoming from him or the other Beatles. Instead, their colleagues were left trying to explain what had happened. To a *Times* reporter, Klein asserted that McCartney's reasons for issuing such a statement were "personal problems." To another, he twisted a knife: "Unfortunately, he's obligated to Apple for a considerable number of years." Past the wrought-iron gates and inside Apple Corps, Taylor sat in his wicker chair and, looking increasingly besieged and sleep deprived, conducted one interview after another to explain the events of the day. "It is certain that at the moment they could not comfortably work together," he told one camera crew. Taylor wanted to remain optimistic, though: At one point he looked straight into the camera and said, "If the Beatles don't exist, *you* don't exist."

Away from the cameras, Taylor sat behind his typewriter, stuck a cigarette in his mouth, and banged out an Apple statement. "Spring is here and Leeds play Chelsea tomorrow and Ringo and John and George and Paul are alive and well and full of hope," he wrote. "The world is still spinning and so are we and so are you. When the spinning stops—that'll be the time to worry, not before. Until then, the Beatles are alive and well and the beat goes on, the beat goes on." Reading it, DiLello had no idea what Taylor meant, but it was so Derek; it said nothing, but with flair. No one knew what to say or how to react, anyway. "It was just another dismal day in a year full of them," Peter Brown recalled.

"You didn't need to do that, you know," Brown told McCartney the next day.

"But I wanted to," McCartney replied. Brown realized the statement was McCartney's way of explaining the situation to the other Beatles; given the communication breakdown between them, he couldn't do it any other way. It was also McCartney's savvy way of promoting his album. EMI was preparing to ship 480,000 copies of *McCartney*, far less than the last few Beatle albums. How better to publicize it than this?

Not surprisingly, the scheduled April 10 reunion of the Beatles at Apple Corps failed to materialize. The day before, Eastman cabled Apple to inform the company his client would not be able to make the meeting.

When Vivian Janov answered the phone in her Los Angeles home, the voice on the line announced it was Yoko Ono, calling from London. Unsure whether it was a prank, Janov handed the phone to her husband, Arthur. Arthur listened as Ono explained to him that someone at his publisher had mailed her and John Lennon a copy of Janov's three-month-old book, *The Primal Scream—Primal Therapy: The Cure for Neurosis.* Janov had no idea how that would have happened; he didn't have the Lennons' home address. Ono was saying her husband was in need of therapeutic work, and could Janov fly out to London as soon as possible to help him? Janov curtly told her he had seventy-five patients depending on him and hung up.

A certified psychologist, the curly-haired, movie-star-handsome Janov was riding the wave of the new self-help movement coming into vogue. (Also on the West Coast, another psychologist, Werner Erhard, was about to launch EST, for Erhard Seminars Training.) Forty-six years old, Janov had received a master's in social work at the University of California, where he met his future wife, Vivian. Starting in the early '50s, Janov had a private practice but was thinking bigger. Searching for clues to behavior through childhood memories wasn't Janov's idea, but he took it one thunderous step further, advocating patients unlock their inner pain and repression by screaming it out. In 1968, the Janovs opened the Primal Scream Institute on Sunset Boulevard. "In the beginning we had so many applications, we couldn't see all the people who wanted to come," recalled Vivian. After his book was published in January 1970, Janov was greeted at his office by what he called "all the druggies and lost kids who'd been in the protests against the Vietnam War."

Ono immediately called back and made the invitation harder to resist. She and Lennon would pay for the Janovs and their children to fly to London, all expenses covered. When the Janov children heard about the offer, they were so excited they ran up and down the stairs of their home for twenty minutes. With that, the Janovs began making their way to Tittenhurst in early April.

When their town car dropped them off at the estate, the Janovs were stunned by Tittenhurst's opulence and expansiveness. Lennon struck Vivian Janov as funny and charming, although her husband sensed he was also in deep psychic pain. Together, Ono and Lennon appeared earnest and serious, not quite the same playful couple who, on April 1, had issued a fake press release saying they were planning to have "dual sex change operations." After they all took seats in the kitchen, the Lennons and Janovs mutually decided to start the sessions—$6,000 for three weeks—in the recording studio being built next to the kitchen.

Still living in one of the estate's cottages, Dan Richter heard the screams whenever he walked into the kitchen. Richter was cynical about primal scream, but also knew Lennon and Ono needed some form of help—-and that primal scream was probably tied in with their desire to stop snorting smack. "Heroin isn't easy to kick," he recalled. "You don't just stop. It leaves you very empty. You're left with yourself. That's why they felt they had to do the Janov thing." Even with the studio builders coming in and out as he spoke, Lennon talked about his wayward father, the death of his mother, and how upset he was with McCartney and the breakup of the Beatles. "The drugs blew out his defense system," Janov recalled. "The sessions with the workers going back and forth in this sound room were amazing." To Janov's surprise, Lennon's father, Fred, who seemed like a sad, broken man, showed up one day; Lennon gave him some cash and sent him on his way.

When the construction noise became too much, the sessions shifted to the London hotel where the Janovs were installed. Janov also welcomed a change in cuisine: He didn't love what he called the "strange, uncooked fish" the Lennons would serve in their kitchen and was starving most of the time. But the Janovs couldn't stay in London forever, so it was agreed that the Lennons would visit Los Angeles for several months to continue their therapy. Although Lennon had earlier been denied a visa as a result of his drug bust in 1968, the therapy—medical reasons—allowed him to reenter the States. On April 23, he and Ono boarded a plane for California, leaving the rest of Apple and the world to decipher what had happened about two weeks earlier.

Just when McCartney thought he was done with the Beatles, he wasn't. In early April, he received an advance acetate of the *Let It Be* album from Spector. Only then did he learn that, on April 1, Spector had overdubbed a string section, choir, harp player, and additional drums (by Starr) onto "The Long and Winding Road," his once fairly naked ballad. An accompanying letter from Spector, addressed to all the Beatles, noted that if they had any concerns, they could contact him at his room at the Inn at the Park. (In an aside, Spector also said he thought the album should be titled *The Long and Winding Road*, not *Let It Be*.) "If there's anything you'd like done to the album," he wrote, "let me know, and I'll be glad to help." He added, though, that major changes could be a problem given the album's imminent release.

Spector had long been known for his gloriously over-the-top production style, the way he built dense, almost orchestral tracks by using multiple musicians. But even knowing what he did about Spector's approach, McCartney was livid. On April 14, he phoned the Apple office and dictated a letter to Klein by way of Apple employee Bill Oakes. In the letter, McCartney admitted he'd once considered orchestrating "The Long and Winding Road" but had "decided against it." Then he let loose: "In the future, no one will be allowed to add to or subtract from a recording of one of my songs without my permission," he decreed. His list of demands included reducing the volume of the strings, horns, and voices and mixing the Beatles' own playing higher; "harp to be removed completely at the end" and "original piano notes to be substituted." As his fourth and last condition, he spat over the phone, "Don't ever do it again," which Oakes also added into the letter.

Ultimately, McCartney's suggestions were ignored; it was either too late or no one wanted to bother to make him happy. (He later claimed he left a message for Spector at his hotel but received no response.) The backlash to McCartney's surprise announcement to the world was making itself known, especially to McCartney himself.

Two days later, Thursday, April 16, he tracked down Connolly at his home in Kensington. McCartney needed to talk, on the record, and told Connolly to meet him for lunch at Wheeler's, a fish restaurant in Soho. Given the time of day and the restaurant's busy lunchtime crowd, Connolly thought it an odd location. As expected, Wheeler's was crowded, and he, McCartney, and Linda settled into a table—of all places, right in the middle of the restaurant. As Linda ordered vegetarian meals for them all, McCartney talked about how shocked he was that his press release had been interpreted the way it had. "I didn't leave the Beatles," he told Connolly. "The Beatles have left the Beatles. But no one wanted to be the one to say the party's over." McCartney felt he'd been made the heavy in the situation, and being disliked clearly rattled him. In a stinging irony, Lennon, who was always giving him a hard time about the future of the band, was now seen as a *victim*.

Over the clatter of conversations at nearby, close-quarter tables, McCartney gave Connolly the first blow-by-blow of events of the previous six months. Lennon, he said, had dismissed McCartney's idea of live performances the previous fall. McCartney admitted Ono's constant presence was a factor in the breakup and that he had had to throw Starr out of his house the month before. He talked about the letter he'd sent to Klein about "The Long and Winding Road" and how he hadn't yet received a response. Even to an insider like Connolly, all of it was startling—as it was no doubt to the lunching businessmen around them, who craned their necks to hear what was being said. In that regard, the setting was McCartney's clear-cut attempt at public damage control.

At the luncheon's end, McCartney made one unexpected request: He wanted to read the article before it was published. Normally, Connolly would never allow his subjects to approve his text, but knowing the importance of the interview, he acquiesced.

After Derek Taylor sent him a copy of the lengthy piece, McCartney called Connolly yet again. The article was fine, he said, except for one comment he'd made about Starr. "He's *not* the best drummer in the world," McCartney said.

Connolly pointed out that, in the quote, McCartney had said Starr was "the best drummer in the world *for the Beatles*."

"Oh," McCartney said, "okay, right." Connolly could leave that part in the story.

As they spoke, Capitol, the Beatles' U.S. label, was preparing to release a 45 of "The Long and Winding Road," complete with the choir and orchestral overdubs McCartney hated so much. (When he read Connolly's interview, which included McCartney's digs at the female choir tacked onto his song, Lennon cracked, "Is that what this is all about—those bloody girls?") The following Sunday, April 19, McCartney finally returned to *The Ed Sullivan Show*, but this time alone, by way of the promo video for "Maybe I'm Amazed." The circle was complete.

James Taylor couldn't yet afford a band, so Russ Kunkel, who'd drummed on *Sweet Baby James*, went where he could for work. On May 1, Kunkel found himself in New York, doing a session for another one of

Peter Asher's clients. In his room at his hotel on Central Park South, he was preparing to return to Los Angeles when Asher called. Had Kunkel packed away his drums yet? No, Kunkel replied; they were in storage. Good, Asher said: George Harrison and Bob Dylan need a drummer, immediately. Kunkel reclaimed his drums, threw them into the back of a taxi, and headed to a Columbia Records studio.

No sooner had Kunkel arrived and begun setting up his kit when, sure enough, Dylan and his producer, Bob Johnston, strolled in; Harrison, dressed head to toe in denim, his hair and beard long, followed behind. The bass player was a hulking but affable Nashville session man named Charlie Daniels, who'd already worked with Dylan. Along with Boyd and Derek Taylor, Harrison had flown into Manhattan on April 28 to meet with Allen Klein. One night, the three of them visited Dylan at his new home in the Village, on MacDougal Street, and Dylan invited Harrison to the studio the following day.

Beyond its financial rewards, Harrison hadn't seemed to enjoy being a Beatle during the last few years. The day Lauren Bacall visited Apple, DiLello watched in horror as Harrison recoiled and bolted up the stairs as if being stalked. Yet around other musicians, particularly those who weren't the Beatles, Harrison's demeanor noticeably lightened. Such was the case as the musicians settled in with their instruments and began playing whatever came to mind. With Dylan cradling an acoustic guitar and Harrison an electric, they ambled through songs from their childhood (Sam Cooke's "Cupid" and a wobbly take on the Everly Brothers' "All I Have to Do Is Dream"), rockabilly standards (Carl Perkins' "Matchbox" and "Your True Love"), and a cowpoke classic ("Ghost Riders in the Sky").

Neither Kunkel nor Daniels was ever told the goal of the sessions— an album or not?—but it was clear Dylan and Harrison had the shared, unspoken rapport of those who'd seen it all, as well as a mutual respect Harrison found refreshing. The afternoon was the polar opposite of the stressful *Get Back* sessions. "George would say, 'Let's do "Rainy Day Women,"'" recalled Kunkel. "Usually when someone asks Bob to do a request, he's caustic to them. That wasn't the case there. They were very courteous to each other." Harrison even gamely played along when Dylan began crooning "Yesterday," McCartney's song. (As if he'd always wanted to, Harrison played a solo on it.)

No one asked Harrison how he felt about McCartney's press statement nearly three weeks before. The only time it remotely came up was when he turned to Daniels, who was playing bass, and cracked, "You want to be a Beatle?" It was just a joke, but everyone knew the context.

CHAPTER 7

Eighty miles north of Paul McCartney's farm in Argyllshire, Scotland, Art Garfunkel was anxious, and at least part of it had to do with McCartney. As soon as *Bridge Over Troubled Water* was out of their hands and in stores, Garfunkel, like Simon, was gone. Simon ventured into teaching, and Garfunkel acted as if he were a student on summer break. After taking a freighter to Tangier, he there met his girlfriend, Linda Grossman, after which they made their way to Gibraltar and then London. After driving north, they arrived in Scotland, renting a hundreds-year-old, unheated farmhouse on Kilninver outside Oban, a resort town in Argyllshire in the country's northwest—far from the music business, even farther from his partner. "American Star's Argyll Holiday," announced a headline in the *Oban Times*, complete with a photo of Garfunkel and Grossman posing with sheep.

As always, he walked. Whether on vacation or on tour with Simon, Garfunkel was known for taking long, meandering hikes by himself that allowed him to think up a new harmony part for a song or stop into gas stations and start up conversations with strangers. Given his curious, knowledge-hungry brain, the walks were relaxing—if not always for those who worked for him. Just before a Simon and Garfunkel concert in Boston in 1968, he decided to hitchhike rather than fly. Worried that Garfunkel might miss the show, their manager, Mort Lewis, attempted to talk him out of it. Garfunkel held firm and was eventually picked up by a couple who told the frizzy-haired guy in the backseat that he looked just like that singer Art Garfunkel—and then wouldn't believe him when he said he was (not even when he pulled out a driver's license to prove it).

Another time, Simon and Lewis, in a limo on the way to a show, passed Garfunkel on a highway, and Lewis stuck his thumb on his nose and twirled his fingers, the silly "screw you" gesture common to anyone who'd grown up with the Little Rascals; Simon could only laugh along.

Walking also afforded Garfunkel the time to mull things over, and few mulled the way Garfunkel did. In Scotland, strolling past homes encased by stone walls and surrounded by barren, heather-cover hills, he'd much to ponder. After the nonstop work of the previous year, he needed a break from show business and his partner. He'd also heard the new Beatles song, "Let It Be." With its piano-centered arrangement and reassuring-hug quality, it was reminiscent of the *other* kindly ballad dominating the charts, "Bridge Over Troubled Water." Garfunkel was concerned that the Beatles' new release would deflect attention from his own signature song. Back in the States, Simon himself noticed the similarities. "The first time I heard 'Let It Be,' I couldn't believe that he [McCartney] did that," he told *Rolling Stone* that spring. "They are very similar songs, certainly in instrumentation. . . . They're sort of both hopeful songs and resting peaceful songs." Simon heard that McCartney had first offered "Let It Be" to Aretha Franklin—a plan Simon also had in mind for "Bridge Over Troubled Water."

As many had already observed, Garfunkel's walks were merely one indication of how offbeat Simon's collaborator could be. As a child, he'd been methodical, thoughtful, and logical. Simon would always recall the time he encountered his friend at a Queens candy store, rattling different boxes of candy to determine which had the most pieces inside (the louder the rattle, the fewer the goodies). "Reading and teaching are Art's twin avocations," read an early Columbia press bio of Simon and Garfunkel, as if singing weren't his principal passion in life. In the *Songs of America* television special, he'd taken that comment one step further: "I can't see myself doing this five years from now . . . this entertaining, there's nothing new about it." In conversation, he would laugh at things others wouldn't think were funny. He loved making lists of things to do. He would stop into record stores and, posing as a customer, ask if a new Simon and Garfunkel album had arrived, even when one was still in the works.

The previous March 1969, he and Lewis were standing on the corner of Park Avenue and 55th Street when Garfunkel spotted an attractive brunette walking up the block. Grossman, the twenty-three-year-old daughter of a Nashville doctor and a recent graduate of architecture school, recognized Garfunkel. "You're Artie, aren't you?" she said. He told her she had a nice face, adding, "There's a little church around the corner. Do you want to go and get married?"

Startled, Grossman said goodbye and kept walking, crossing 55th Street, but Garfunkel followed her and apologized. He wrote down an address and invited her to join him at a recording studio that night. The address, it turned out, was Columbia Studios, where Simon and Garfunkel were working. "Hello, Linda," Simon said, greeting her warmly, and Grossman then watched the two work on a track for the upcoming *Bridge* album.

During the filming of *Catch-22*, Mike Nichols noticed how peculiar Garfunkel could be. A scene in a mess hall, featuring a visit by a clueless general played by Orson Welles, called for Garfunkel and his costars, including Alan Arkin and Bob Balaban, to leer and laugh as a female aide accidentally flashed a thigh. In take after take, each of the actors dredged up the required guffaws—except Garfunkel, who remained unresponsive. "He just couldn't get cheerful," Nichols would later recall.

In the end, Garfunkel's concerns about "Let It Be" overtaking "Bridge Over Troubled Water" were for naught. In the U.K., "Let It Be" only reached number 2, held back from reaching the top slot by the Simon and Garfunkel single. Even against the greatest culture force of the past decade, Simon and Garfunkel's place was secure.

When Garfunkel heard about Simon's new girlfriend, he was far from pleased. "Are you crazy?" he was overheard telling his partner. "Stay away from that Peggy Lewis." But by the spring, it was too late: Simon was already building a new and separate life of his own, and with a new companion.

Although Garfunkel tended to hole up in hotels when in New York, Simon was now living on the Upper East Side at 200 East End Avenue, across the street from the Gracie Mansion estate where New York's mayors, like the then-current one, John Lindsay, lived. Simon was a wealthy man—he paid $350,000 in income tax in 1968—and had the posh uptown home to prove it: a duplex apartment in a postwar building with views of the East River and his native Queens.

Four years earlier, when they were considering hiring Lewis as their manager, Simon and Garfunkel had met Lewis at his apartment for a meeting. There, Lewis introduced them to his wife, a pale, delicate-looking, blue-eyed beauty from Nashville fifteen years Lewis' junior. For Simon, it was hard to know what was more shocking: Peggy Ann Harper's relative youth or the fact that she was still in curlers and a robe. Born in Newport, a small town in Tennessee hill country, Harper was a child of divorce; her father, a housepainter, broke up with his wife when Peggy (born Margaret) was twelve. Since the family had to live on welfare, Harper was able to enroll in Berea College, a tuition-free school for poor students from the area.

Leaving school before graduation and unsure of a direction, Harper wound up waitressing in New York, then Atlantic City. There, she met Lewis, who was managing the Brothers Four, a commercial folk group that tapped into the Kingston Trio-fueled boom of the early '60s. Harper was dating one of its members, but soon, she and Lewis hooked up, marrying in 1965. Harper tended to keep to herself, which conflicted with Lewis' need to schmooze music business types; more often than not, she'd opt out of nights out with people in her husband's line of work.

Around the time she first met Simon and Garfunkel, she and Lewis had had a trial separation, then divorced soon after. When Harper moved by herself to the Upper East Side, Lewis didn't understand why she'd chosen to live in such a faraway part of the city—until he realized his ex-wife was now living close to Simon.

Lewis had no idea Simon was even interested in Peggy, but he didn't know the whole story. After her divorce, Harper spent time in London; by coincidence, Simon, who had a girlfriend there, was also in town and wound up spending intimate time with his manager's estranged wife. Soon enough, Harper, two years older than Simon, was sharing his East End Avenue home with him. In *Songs of America*, she made a rare public appearance, walking through a field with both men. But even then, her need for privacy came through: She was seen from the back, and only fleetingly.

Garfunkel's apprehension about Harper and Simon hooking up was largely for business reasons: He was rightly concerned they'd lose their manager in the process. As it turned out, Lewis wasn't terribly troubled by the relationship. The one person who truly had a right to be concerned was Garfunkel, especially when Simon and Harper announced they were planning to marry. Simon was so devoted to his art—continually obsessing over song lyrics and chord changes—that chances were he only had room in his life for one full-time partner. The remarkable coincidence that both New Yorkers were in relationships with women from Tennessee was small comfort.

In September 1969, Simon purchased another home, a Dutch farmhouse outside New Hope, Pennsylvania, for $200,000. The seven-room, three-floor house, nestled inside seventy acres of Bucks County real estate, felt several worlds removed from the claustrophobic intensity of Manhattan. He and Harper began spending weekends there, Harper starting a vegetable garden for their new health-food regime.

As Harper had already learned, Simon could be difficult to read. It was hard to know how he felt at any given time, and he could be moody. Whether in conversation or in interviews, he would quietly chew over a question for many minutes before delivering a carefully thought-out, precisely articulated response. (In a sign of how many qualities they shared, Garfunkel could be the same way.) He knew all too well he was beginning to lose his hair and was pained by it; Garfunkel told one friend that Simon was so sensitive that touching his head was out of the question.

In his new country home, Simon had the time and space to dwell on it all, with no one but Harper as company. He could listen to his soul and gospel records, his Schoenberg, Bach, and Bartók works, and try to determine what came next. Garfunkel, the Greenwich Village folk clubs, and the days of hustling around the Brill Building felt like ghosts from the past.

On Tuesdays, Simon returned to his weekly, early-evening commute down to the New York University building in the East Village. Teaching the songwriting course had been his idea from the start. "I wanted to do it for a while," he told *Rolling Stone*. "I like talking about songwriting." Besides, he added, "Nobody teaches anything about popular music. You have to learn it on the street." With that in mind, he'd reached out to School of the Arts dean David Oppenheim, a former Columbia Records classical-division head who'd worked on *Inside Pop: The Rock Revolution*, a 1967 CBS TV special among the first to take modern rock seriously.

Each week, Simon arrived by himself. With his baseball caps and jeans, fans hunting him down probably wouldn't have recognized him anyway. Yet even in such an informal setting, Simon brought to the class the same scrutinizing seriousness which he approached his music. The dozen students—who included the Roche sisters but not Ron

Maxwell or Joe Turrin, the fledgling theatrical composers from the audition period who were deemed too advanced—would sing or play a new
song, and Simon wouldn't hesitate to let them know if it was up to
muster or far below it. He told one—Melissa Manchester, an eighteen-
year-old New Yorker who'd attended the High School for Performing
Arts and was already an adept pianist—that she'd been absorbing too
many Laura Nyro and Joni Mitchell albums. During her audition, Simon
passed along one of the bits of career advice he occasionally doled out in
class: "Say what you have to say as simply as possible," he told her, "and
then leave before they have a chance to figure you out."

Simon might not have been adept at reading sheet music, and at times
he looked nervous, but his technical skill was apparent. He taught them
about the circle of fifths—a circular diagram that lays out the major and
minor keys in music and the relationships between different chords—
and explained that the students' songs would be more commercial if they
devised harmonies in thirds, rather than fourths and fifths, citing the
Everly Brothers as an example. Those in the class who had no idea that
Simon and Garfunkel were once Tom and Jerry were caught off guard.
"To me, Simon and Garfunkel were a break from something like the
Everly Brothers or something very pop," recalled Terre Roche. "So it
was a surprise that he was working in a very commercial pop vein. To
see that those were his roots was an eye-opener."

Simon also invited a few select music-industry friends to address the
class: classical violinist Isaac Stern and Al Kooper, the former Blues
Project and Blood, Sweat & Tears singer and keyboardist and noted session man (that was his organ churning away on Dylan's "Like a Rolling
Stone"). Simon and Kooper had known each other as teenagers in
Queens, sometimes sharing a stage at swanky society gigs, where they'd
strum standards like "Stardust" before Simon would stand up and sing
a modern rock and roll song. Simon told the class the occasional backstage tale, like the time he visited Bob Dylan's home, saw crumpled

pieces of paper strewn around—each containing fragments of lyrics—and stuffed as many as possible in his pockets. To the astonishment of the students, he sometimes brought stray musical ideas for new songs and played them, often asking their reaction, as if he himself were searching for his way.

Simon's singing partner was never one of the guests, and Simon rarely mentioned him. Few in the class thought anything of it. To students like Roche, who could still remember the exact moment in her New Jersey bedroom when she first heard "The Sound of Silence," Simon and Garfunkel were such a part of the cultural fabric that the idea they wouldn't exist was inconceivable. The only hint of anything unusual came one evening when Simon paused to talk about how hard it was to write a follow-up to a hit. Once you have one, he told them, everyone expected another, and the pressure was enormous. "To me, he was on top of the world," Terre Roche remembered. "The idea that anything he did was problematic was fascinating to me."

Simon never alluded to one specific incident that year: a lawsuit over the copyright of "El Condor Pasa." Before recording the song, Simon had been told it was a traditional South American melody, when in fact it wasn't: "El Condor Pasa" had been written by Peruvian songwriter Daniel Alomia Robles almost forty years before. Robles died in 1942, but his son sued over the credit. After they realized the mistake, Simon and his lawyer Michael Tannen settled, with no hard feelings on either side. Yet the suit was one more distasteful reminder to Simon of what had gone into the creation of one of the year's biggest-selling albums.

To those at Mission Control or any of the few watching the live feed from home, the words were almost inaudible. "I'm afraid this is going to be the last moon mission for a long time," Jim Lovell glumly reported to

Paul and Linda McCartney contemplate life in semi-exile on their farm outside Campbeltown, Scotland, January 1970. (*Evening Standard*/Getty Images)

Ringo and Maureen Starr at London's Heathrow Airport during the promotion for *The Magic Christian* that same month. (Popperfoto/Getty Images)

George Harrison and assorted Hare Krishna friends, early March. (Hulton-Deutsch/Corbis)

James Taylor backstage at the Troubadour in Los Angeles, where he played regularly throughout 1970 as the cult for *Sweet Baby James* grew. (Max B. Miller/Getty Images)

New York City police cart away the remains of Weathermen member Diana Oughton, March 10, four days after the group's Greenwich Village brownstone (in background) exploded. (Bettmann/Corbis)

John Lennon, Yoko Ono, and their newly shorn hair, London, February 9, two days after introducing their revamped look to the world during a television interview. (AP Images)

Beatle fans gather outside Apple headquarters in London, April 10, after McCartney's surprise announcement hits the press. (AP Images)

In Honolulu, Richard Nixon welcomes back Apollo 13 crew members Jack Swigert, Fred Haise, and Jim Lovell, April 18. Five days earlier, an exploding oxygen tank had crippled the flight's mission—and, in many ways, NASA itself. (JP Laffont/Sygma/Corbis)

Art Garfunkel and Paul Simon onstage at the KB Hall in Copenhagen, Denmark, April 28, during one of the only seven concerts they gave in 1970 to promote *Bridge Over Troubled Water*. (Jan Persson/Getty Images)

Students from New York's Convent of the Sacred Heart celebrate the first Earth Day by scrubbing grubby Union Square, April 22. (AP Images)

Fans flock to New York's Fillmore East to snatch up tickets to Crosby, Stills, Nash & Young's week-long stint, late May. (© 1970 Amalie R. Rothschild)

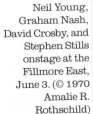

Neil Young, Graham Nash, David Crosby, and Stephen Stills onstage at the Fillmore East, June 3. (© 1970 Amalie R. Rothschild)

Chaos takes center stage at the "Bach to Rock" festival in Mountaindale, New York, July 11, one of many unsuccessful attempts throughout the year to duplicate Woodstock. (Garth Eliassen/Getty Images)

Stephen Stills and Neil Young backstage in Minneapolis, July 9, the final stop on CSNY's last tour for four years. (Henry Diltz/Morrison Hotel Gallery)

David Crosby poses with pillow flag gun and illegal substance in his hotel room prior to CSNY's July 9 Minneapolis show. (Henry Diltz/Morrison Hotel Gallery)

George Harrison and Phil Spector (with Allen Klein associate Pete Bennett, left) listening to a master of Harrison's *All Things Must Pass*, October 31. To everyone's surprise, it would become the most commercially successful of all the year's Beatle solo albums. (Bettmann/Corbis)

Poster for *Two-Lane Blacktop*, James Taylor's film debut, shot that summer with co-stars Warren Oates, Laurie Bird, and Dennis Wilson. (Everett Collection)

Keeping the dream alive at the Summer Festival for Peace at Shea Stadium, New York, August 6. The same crowd would be far less enthusiastic about Paul Simon's first post-S&G performance that day. (Marty Lederhandler/ AP Images)

Art Garfunkel, Jack Nicholson, and Candice Bergen on the Vancouver set of *Carnal Knowledge*, Garfunkel's second Mike Nichols film and the one intended to transform him into a matinee idol. (The Kobal Collection)

John, Yoko and British anti-war leader Michael X auction off the Lennons' cut hair (and a pair of Muhammad Ali's bloodied boxing shorts) at one of the Lennons' many media events throughout 1970. (Bettmann/Corbis)

Paul and Linda McCartney with baby Mary and Heather out on the town in New York, October 8. (James Garrett/New York Daily News Archive via Getty Images)

James Taylor keeps tabs on Joni Mitchell and her fans, backstage at the first Greenpeace benefit, October 16. (© Alan Katowitz 2011, all rights reserved)

one of his capsule mates. Lovell knew of what he spoke: At that moment, he and his two crew members in *Apollo 13* were adrift in space, two hundred thousand miles above earth.

The space program had emerged at the same time as Simon and Garfunkel, in the late '50s; like them, it had been pushed into orbit a few years later. In some strange way, the two entities were connected. Even John Kennedy's vision of outer space—"There is no strife, no prejudice, no hate," he told a Rice University audience the following year—seemed in sync with the emerging civil rights era (and could have been an early Simon lyric).

But what exactly was happening in the country and beyond during the first half of the year? It wasn't merely the bombs being detonated, or the fears of a looming recession, or the way a postal strike crippled the Northeast when almost a quarter of the country's postal workers left their jobs to protest low wages. Everything seemed to be taking an unexpected, unwelcome left turn compared to a few short years earlier. Unexpectedly, the most obvious example of collapse was the news that the *Odyssey* command module and its connected LEM module were stranded in darkness.

The space program hadn't been remotely glitch free, as anyone who recalled *Apollo 1* in 1967—the explosion on the launch pad, the three astronauts in the capsule dead from suffocation—knew all too well. But by decade's end, Kennedy's call to the nation to put a man on the moon had become a reality. Barely a year before, in July 1969, *Apollo 11* had actually landed there; four months later, *Apollo 12* set down near the Ocean of Storms. A month after, an adventure film called *Marooned*—about three astronauts stranded in space when their electrical power dies out—arrived, but it felt more like over-the-top science fiction than something that could actually transpire. By the time *Apollo 13* set out, on Friday, April 11, 1970, the country was so blasé about space launches that not all the networks carried it.

The launch had gone according to plan, but two days in—April 13, of all days—an oxygen tank overheated and exploded, draining the power from the main capsule. Since the mission hadn't yet reached the moon, the plot of *Marooned* was played out in real time on live television. For three days, engineers in Houston struggled to find a way to bring back the astronauts and some part of their ship, and eventually did: In what amounted to a feat of engineering genius, NASA used the moon's gravity to rocket the ship back to earth, and on April 17, the *Odyssey* nose-dived into the Pacific.

Although its mission was aborted and it never landed on the moon, *Apollo 13* was dubbed a "successful failure," a triumph of man's ingenuity over possible disaster. But the happy ending didn't extend to the program itself. NASA would continue with its remaining planned missions for two more years, but the seeds of its decline had been planted with the mishap of *Apollo 13*. By year's end, eighty-four thousand jobs in the aerospace industry would be eliminated. California alone lost out on almost one billion dollars in NASA contracts. The Kennedy dream had been blown out.

"As soon as I figure out I have nothing more to tell you, I'll stop," Simon bluntly informed his students the first night of class. As spring wound down, he accorded them one more inside peek at his business: choosing what he thought was the best student song and taking the entire class to an uptown studio, where it was recorded with some of the city's best-known studio musicians. With that, the class ended, and Simon returned to his other obligation. Four months after the release of *Bridge Over Troubled Water*, the time had finally arrived to promote it with a full-on Simon and Garfunkel tour.

The album had been doing fine without much promotion beyond the solo interview Simon had given to *Rolling Stone* while Garfunkel was abroad. On April 2, *Bridge Over Troubled Water* surpassed the two million sales mark. For ten straight weeks it was the biggest-selling album in the country, fending off challengers like *Déjà vu* and *Hey Jude*. "Cecilia," the follow-up single to the title song, began its own ascent, its rhythms a cathartic left turn from the near-religious solemnity of "Bridge Over Troubled Water."

Simon was in no major rush to head back to the road. Although he generally appeared affable and easygoing onstage, flashing a whimsical smile between songs, part of him dreaded the thought of live performance. In cabs or limos on the way to venues, he'd inevitably start to get anxious, knots forming in his stomach. He was already visiting a therapist—actor Elliott Gould's—twice a week. (He'd met Gould the year before at a Knicks game in New York, by way of their mutual friend Dustin Hoffman.) Although he was only twenty-eight, Simon told Lewis and others he was tired of touring and the dreary regimen of hotels, airports, and inadequate food. "Keep the Customer Satisfied," on *Bridge Over Troubled Water*, jovially spoke of his relief to be home—horns never blasted louder on a Simon and Garfunkel record than they did on that song—but offstage, Simon was more far disgruntled.

The thought of spending time with Garfunkel didn't particularly appeal to him either. After fifteen years of friendship, little things about his partner had begun to irk him. Simon wasn't short on eccentricities himself. To write songs, he would wait for his nails to grow a particular length so he could fingerpick the strings just right. In the studio, he could be quietly competitive: If Larry Knechtel, a skilled bass and guitar player as well as keyboardist, picked up a guitar and began playing a riff more complicated than Simon could pull off, Simon would shoot a disapproving look.

To make the situation as palatable as possible for both men, the Simon and Garfunkel spring and summer tour would barely qualify as a tour at all. Launching April 25, it would amount to a mere five European shows—one each in London, Copenhagen, Paris, and Amsterdam before one more in London—over less than two weeks. After two months off, they would then play two concerts in America, both at Forest Hills Tennis Stadium in July. This time, there would be no band, just the two of them, with Grossman and Harper along for company. (In Amsterdam, Garfunkel requested they stay at the same Amsterdam Hilton Hotel where John Lennon had had his Bed-In with Yoko Ono the year before.) Of their 1969 touring band, they only retained Knechtel, who, at their expense, would be flown with his family to every show so he could emerge from the wings and play piano on "Bridge Over Troubled Water."

In late April, Simon and Harper left Manhattan for Europe, where they met up, finally, with Garfunkel. Onstage nothing appeared remotely amiss. With only Simon's crystalline guitar for accompaniment, their voices wove around each other effortlessly and naturally. They never sang off-key, rarely missed a note. They proved they didn't need elaborate studio production to pull off "Fakin' It," the intricately arranged song from *Bookends*. After two hours and multiple encores, the Royal Albert Hall crowd was so frenetic that a British bobby had to escort both men out the back door to avoid the overeager clutches of fans.

As always, Garfunkel preferred to gaze into the crowd as if focusing on someone in the balcony, hands pushed into his jeans pockets. He frequently introduced the songs by name as if giving a lecture. ("This is an English folk song that comes out of the soundtrack of the movie that we made, called *The Graduate*," Garfunkel explained of "Scarborough Fair" in Amsterdam.) In conversation and onstage, Garfunkel exhibited a droll sense of humor and careful diction; the rare hint of his Queens upbringing came when the word "off" would emerge as "awf." Simon was looser, letting out an impish grin or rolling his shoulders and guitar as if rowing a boat.

In between the in-jokes and stagecraft, minor digs would emerge. In

Amsterdam, Garfunkel introduced "So Long, Frank Lloyd Wright" by saying, "I suggested to Paul that he write a song about" the famous architect. "I didn't know anything *about* Frank Lloyd Wright, however," Simon retorted to the crowd. "I proceeded to write the song anyway." Whenever Knechtel would begin the "Bridge" chords, Simon would walk off to cede the stage and spotlight to his partner. When Garfunkel hit the triumphant high note at the song's conclusion, the audiences would inevitably erupt as if watching an Olympic figure skater who'd just completed a perfect axel jump. Watching offstage, Simon would quietly simmer. Did the crowds realize he wrote the song? Did they know Garfunkel was merely the singer? To aggravate matters further, Garfunkel rarely cited Simon as the writer, only telling the crowd they'd be accompanied by "our piano player friend from Hollywood." Part of Simon knew his own thoughts were petty, but he couldn't help himself.

Arriving at each venue just before "Bridge Over Troubled Water" was set to start, Knechtel would walk onstage, take a seat at the piano, accompany Garfunkel, then return to his hotel room. Backstage conversation or quality time with his bosses wasn't encouraged. Knechtel didn't take it personally. By then, he'd known Simon and Garfunkel several years and was accustomed to their aloofness. Yet Knechtel still found it odd that they were so remote even from each other.

CHAPTER 8

The first stop on the Crosby, Stills, Nash & Young tour—Tuesday, May 12, at the Coliseum in Denver, Colorado—began as if nothing was awry on any fronts. Keeping with their particular tradition, the original trio walked onstage first, without Young, tuning up and eventually launching into one of their signature songs, "Suite: Judy Blue Eyes." In concert, the song was both a warm-up and a high-wire act: Would their harmonies be in tune? Would someone forget a lyric? Tonight, the singing was a little sharp and Stills rushed the tempo in the first verses, but they made it through.

Before Young joined them, Stills finally made the reference everyone knew was coming. "If the Army guys show up, just get outta the way," Stills said, using the same half-serious, half-supercilious tone he'd used to inform the Woodstock masses that the band was "scared shitless." Nash quickly interjected, "Right!" When the applause died down, Stills added, "Just move out so fast that they wouldn't even believe that you were ever *here*." Neither Stills nor his bandmates specified what they were talking about, but they didn't have to. Everyone knew what had taken place five states east and a mere eight days before, on the campus of Kent State University.

Twenty-one-year-old senior Jerry Casale was in his drawing course when he heard classes would be cut short. He wasn't surprised. All weekend, tensions had been building on Kent State's campus and in the neighborhood nearby. Now, on the late morning of Monday, May 4, rumor was that the Army or National Guard were on their way, and a noontime rally at the Commons seemed an appropriate way for students like him to vent their displeasure.

By his own admission, Casale was an "art hippie" who'd grown up in Kent and was now double-majoring in contemporary English literature and art. When he'd started as a freshman in the fall of 1966, his hair was short, his wardrobe leaning toward herringbone jackets and ties. By now, his hair fell past his earlobes, reflecting his admiration for Brian Jones, and he took his fashion tips from Dylan photographs. Like many of his fellow undergrads at Kent State, Casale was a radical in theory more than in practice. The images of Vietnam on TV every night freaked him out, but he didn't know what to do about any of it. After hearing Mark Rudd of the Students for a Democratic Society speak on campus, Casale had joined SDS in the winter of 1967. He was starting to question the war and the American culture that promoted it, but his main contribution was making fliers and posters for SDS meetings, then listening to students debate at each one.

On April 30, everyone, including the kids at Kent State, learned about a surprise American bombing campaign. "U.S. Aids Saigon Push in Cambodia with Planes, Artillery and Advisers," blared a jarring *New York Times* headline. Unexpectedly, America was invading yet another country, supposedly to help thwart the North Vietnamese troops who'd taken refuge in Cambodia. As the University of California at Santa Barbara had shown months before, campuses were already exposed nerves, but the all-new military offensive pinched those nerves doubly hard. Schools shut down, and heads of colleges warned the Nixon administration to expect a wave of protests by at least some portion of the millions enrolled in American colleges.

Kent State remained open but hardly calm. On Friday, May 1, a rally protesting the Cambodian invasion took place, and at night, the Water Street bar area became home to a handful of bonfires, hurled bottles, and police tear gas, all thanks to a motley gathering of students, bikers, and rowdy jocks. From his apartment on Water Street, Casale witnessed some of the disruptions on Friday night and heard about soldiers on campus. The next day, as news broke that the United States' bombings of North Vietnam were also increasing, an ROTC building on campus— the most obvious symbol of the Army's Kent presence—was set afire. The National Guard arrived soon after, and a second student rally was scheduled for Monday.

When Casale arrived for class on Monday, the sun-drenched conditions announced spring had finally arrived after a prolonged winter. Casale heard the ring of a bell—the rally had begun—and headed toward it. A loudspeaker or bullhorn barked out some sort of command, but the crackly words were impossible to understand. By then, almost three thousand had congregated in the Commons.

In the crowd, Casale saw a familiar face: Jeffrey Miller, a new transfer from Michigan State University. As part of his work-study scholarship, Casale had been awarded a summer campus job, helping out incoming students with paperwork and class signups. There, Casale had met Miller along with Allison Krause, a friendly, dark-haired nineteen-year-old freshman from Maryland.

For Casale and others around him, the next twenty-five minutes were a blur one moment, a slow-motion nightmare the next. First came the soldiers and the Jeeps, then the tear gas and the sight of bayonets on rifles. Then yelling, followed by tear-gas canisters being lobbed back at soldiers by a few students. Then the Guard, who, after pushing forward, appeared to head back toward the Commons. Then the seventy gas-masked soldiers in the G Troop of the 107th Calvary stopping, turning around, squatting, and pointing their bayoneted rifles.

At that point, Casale began running up the hill and to the right of

Prentice Hall, on the apex of a hill; since the Guard had sealed off the front of the campus, it seemed the only way out. Then he and everyone around him headed back down the hill toward the student parking lot. At one point, Casale looked back in the direction of the Guard, now on a ridge. From where he stood near the parking lot, the formation was a frightening sight—and doubly so when it looked to be preparing to lock and load. He couldn't imagine the guns were loaded; he assumed, if anything, they'd use their bayonets.

As Casale began running toward the parking lot, a rapid succession of what seemed like firecracker pops rang out: One after another, then multiples.

At that point, the screaming began. The bullets had flown over the heads of Casale and those in his vicinity, but they'd clearly landed somewhere. He turned to his left and, about forty feet away, saw a body slumped on the ground. At first, he didn't know who it was, but then he looked around and recognized someone—Miller, whom Casale identified from the clothing he had on at the rally. Shot in the mouth, he lay on his stomach, blood pouring out on the roadway. Soon enough, Casale realized the other body was Allison Krause.

None of it made it any sense or could be processed; mostly Casale felt as if he were going to throw up. Professors trying to mediate between students and soldiers told everyone to sit down, so Casale slumped down on the grass on the hill. Around him, people wept; others were practically shell-shocked. Eventually, the students were shepherded off campus through a corridor of soldiers. Walking home to Water Street, Casale and the other students were taunted by frat boys on the front porches of their fraternity houses. Once home, he turned on the TV and radio to find out what had happened; to his shock, initial reports claimed the students had attacked soldiers. Casale learned that two other students, William Schroeder and Sandra Scheuer, were also dead.

The school was shut down, Casale's graduation ceremony postponed.

Even when it was rescheduled, Casale wasn't allowed to attend because of his connection to SDS, and a plan to transfer to the University of Michigan at Ann Arbor fell through when his scholarship was revoked for similar reasons. With the help of a sympathetic professor, he landed a job back on the Kent State campus that fall, where he met another fellow student, Mark Mothersbaugh. Both agreed that nothing—from the hippie culture to the government—seemed to be working anymore. Society was no longer evolving; it was, they thought, devolving into chaos and numskulledness.

Since Casale didn't have the guts to join the Weathermen, the best retort he could conceive was music. He'd never been a fan of softer bands like Crosby, Stills, Nash & Young, what he called "taffy" music. But with Mothersbaugh's brother Bob, he and Mothersbaugh eventually began pounding out rudimentary blues—"devolved" music for a devolving country and era. Different times called for a different, more discordant soundtrack. Eventually, they called themselves Devo.

At their concerts, Crosby and Nash always addressed the crowds more than Stills and Young combined. Without any prompting, they'd explain what mood they were in or why they were choosing to sing a particular song; maybe they'd crack a barbed joke at the expense of the Byrds or the Hollies (neither of whom were faring as well without Crosby and Nash) or make a reference only one or the other would understand. They were determined to engage, a tradition Nash continued in Denver. "If you knew what happened to us in the last two days," he told the audience, "you wouldn't believe it."

The mishaps and bad omens actually dated back at least a month. With the CSNY tour looming, Stills had flown back into Los Angeles from London on April 14. After running his own show for nearly two months, he wasn't eager to return to California and the people who'd made him a star, but obligations were obligations. Driving back to Laurel Canyon from the airport, Stills glanced in his rearview mirror and saw a squad car. The moment was unintentionally comical, as if he was parroting the words to Crosby's "Almost Cut My Hair ("It increases my paranoia, like looking in my mirror and seeing a *po*-lice car" indeed). Whether out of paranoia or carelessness, Stills skidded into a parked car. When the patrolman approached his vehicle, Stills was holding his left hand in pain; somehow, his hand had slipped off the wheel and bashed into something inside the car. Stills wound up with a ticket and a fractured left hand, right beneath his fingers.

To everyone's aggravation, the CSNY tour was postponed for a month to allow Stills several weeks to heal. Embarrassed to tell his friends how he'd hurt himself, Stills called photographer and friend Henry Diltz two days later: "Hey, man, you wanna go to Hawaii with me?" By the next day, both were in a beach house on the North Shore, owned by a friend of Diltz's. There, they drank, played pool at the local pool hall, and gossiped about Crosby, Nash, and Young. Stills, who could only move two fingers on his hand thanks to his cast, periodically checked in with management from a pay phone at the pool hall. Girls came in and out of the house on the beach. (Coincidentally, Diltz was reading *Groupie*, a trashy cult novel called "a sex-rock odyssey.") "My fingers hurt so bad, it's got me grinnin,'" Stills wrote in a new song, "Singin' Call," whose chorus, tellingly, went, "Help me now, I got to slow down."

But there wasn't much time for slowing down, and no one was particularly interested in doing it anyway. On April 29, his injury healed, Stills returned to Los Angeles. The new starting date for the tour was May 12, in Denver, which left precious little time to rehearse thoroughly, something Stills always goaded the others into doing. If that weren't trying enough, other, more personal complications arose. Just a few weeks before, Nash had been in he and Mitchell's shared home on Lookout

Mountain Avenue when a telegram arrived from Mitchell, then vacationing in Greece: "If you hold sand too tightly, it will run through your fingers," it read. The relationship, which had been teetering on collapse for months, was over. Although it wasn't a complete surprise—Nash had felt distance between them when Mitchell had visited him and Crosby during the boat trip the month before—the delivery was still devastating. In an unnerving coincidence, *Déjà vu*, complete with Nash's ode to their life together, "Our House," had just been released.

The calamities—creative, emotional, and physical—kept coming. No sooner had he repaired his hand than Stills had a skiing accident, tearing a knee ligament. Greg Reeves' mental state also had to be dealt with. When he'd first hooked up with the band barely a year before, Reeves was shy and unassuming, as well as a fluid, sublime bass player. But something had gone awry. When he appeared at Young's home studio in Topanga for the *After the Gold Rush* sessions, he was, well, a different shade. "Greg would show up with a yellow-painted face, like pigmented or something," guitarist and keyboardist Nils Lofgren, also playing on the album, recalled. "David Briggs [Young's coproducer] would say, 'Yeah, Greg's an Indian.' As far as I could tell, he had African-American blood in him." When CSNY would arrive at airports, Reeves would act anxious around security and mutter, "Don't search my bags—I've got my medicine in there." As his bosses stood around waiting impatiently, airport officials would search Reeves' bags and find beads, bits of fur, and rabbit entrails—Reeves, it turned out, truly *did* think he was a witch doctor. When he began lobbying to sing his own songs during CSNY sets, his tenure in the band finally ended. "We said, 'We're sorry, but this is insane,'" Nash recalled. "'Just keep it all to your fucking self—just play bass.'" Reeves was promptly fired. "Things just started happening," Dallas Taylor recalled. "It was like someone was putting a jinx on us, one thing after another."

With only two days before the first show, Stills suggested a replacement. While recording at Island Studios in London, he'd met Calvin Samuels, a Caribbean-born bass player nicknamed "Fuzzy" for the way he played his instrument through a fuzz box. Homeless at the time— and often sleeping on a couch at the studio—the easygoing, gap-toothed Samuels had played in ska and reggae bands like the Equals. When he heard one of his friends was jamming with Stills, Samuels came down to watch, saw no one was playing bass, and sat in. "I heard Stephen kicked out a lot of people," Samuels recalled. "Obviously he heard something he liked. I didn't get thrown out of the room."

Ron Stone of Lookout Management, along with Stills' friend and assistant Dan Campbell, were dispatched to London to hunt down Samuels and fly him back to L.A. to replace Reeves. Given that Samuels often slept on the streets, it wasn't easy finding "a bass player named Fuzzy," as Stills described him, but somehow they did. According to Stone, a visa for Samuels was obtained at the last minute, although Samuels claimed he was turned down for a visa and had to sneak aboard a States-bound plane by confusing the attendants. Either way, he arrived in Los Angeles and was immediately driven to a rehearsal space to meet the band and audition, all in the same day. A bemused Young introduced himself, saying he wanted to meet the crazy character who'd flown all the way from London for a chance to play with them.

With his black bowler hat, black suit, and roller-skating shoes stripped of wheels, Samuels more than fit the wacky-character mold. He'd barely made the acquaintance of the others (or learned their repertoire) when, two days later, he was hustled aboard a plane for Denver with the rest of the band. It was madness, but by then, madness was becoming CSNY's normal.

"We're real loose," Young told the crowd after he came onstage in Denver and joined the trio. "This is the way it is in our living room." Nash chimed in on the same subject, with far more bluntness, but in his lilting British accent: "We decided we weren't going to rehearse too much."

At times it showed. The trio seemed shaky and under-rehearsed on the second song, "Teach Your Children," during which Stills flubbed a guitar solo and Crosby joked, "I swallowed my gum." At one point, Crosby introduced Stills' solo spot in the set while his bandmate was still in his dressing room, not emerging for a mysterious five minutes.

None of it mattered to the ten thousand who'd gathered in the arena and shouted "Right on, right *on!*" at the start and finish of every song. "Well, it sure is groovy that all you folks could come out tonight," Young aw-shucked, eliciting a loud "Outta sight!" from the audience. With Stills at the piano, they did a lovely version of "Helpless," and the Crosby and Nash harmonies snugly wrapped around Young's "Tell Me Why," another new, unreleased song. Crosby hushed the crowd with a quietly intense version of "Everybody's Been Burned," a song from the Byrds days, and Stills, alone at the piano, debuted "We Are Not Helpless," inspired by *Fail Safe*, the nuclear-war novel, and casually told the crowd he was recording his own album.

After a break, they returned for the electric set. With Stills on crutches and Samuels still stunned at the sight of more people than he'd ever beheld in an audience, the performance was bound to be peculiar. As usual, Crosby yapped the most, asking about a group of war protesters the band had passed on the way to the venue and mischievously playing the opening twelve-string riff to "Mr. Tambourine Man" to kill time while the band laboriously tuned up. Nash introduced the first performance of "Chicago," a song written a mere two weeks before, after CSNY had been invited to play at a benefit for the Chicago Seven. When Stills and Young declined, Nash wrote an impassioned plea for them to "please come to Chicago just to sing." Nash hadn't yet told Young and Stills that his lyrics were directed pointedly at them.

Matters quickly deteriorated onstage. Their lack of rehearsal time and

Samuels' unfamiliarity with the songs were apparent in slack versions of "Pre-Road Downs" from *Crosby, Stills & Nash*, "Carry On," and a new Young song cut without them for *After the Gold Rush*, "Southern Man." ("A song is a song," Samuels recalled. "I bluffed it. I fumbled my way through. You do what you have to do.") Crosby and Young complained openly about the sound system during the acoustic set, when loud popping disrupted the music, and the P.A. only grew worse with amplification.

Although the audience didn't pick up on it, the group began acting out its internal psychodrama onstage. Using his crutches, Stills pretended to conduct the band like an orchestra and in general hammed it up, much to the increasing annoyance of his bandmates. "He was milking it for all it was worth," said Nash. "He was being a jerk." Of the four of them, it was Stills who snagged the lion's share of songs during the electric set—four out of nine—due, he said, to Samuels being more familiar with Stills' tunes.

Stills' stage moves were partly an extension of his take-charge manner and military-academy year. ("He approached life in a military, organized way," recalled Diltz, who went to see the movie *Patton* with Stills during their trip to Hawaii.) But Stills, who'd seen his domination of the group diminish during the *Déjà vu* sessions, was now struggling to regain control of the band in any way he could. Young wasn't happy Reeves had been sacked and replaced with one of Stills' cohorts; it meant Young, who liked to be in charge himself, was put in a position of playing with Stills' choice of rhythm section, not his own. As the electric set carried on, Young—who only contributed one song, "Southern Man"—quietly stewed. Finally, he had had enough. As Stills sat down at the organ to begin "Long Time Gone," Young unplugged his guitar—which had been having hookup problems anyway—threw it down, and stalked off.

"Where's Neil?" Crosby asked openly. "He . . . ran?" Crosby sounded genuinely surprised, as if Young's unpredictability hadn't fully dawned on him. Nash told the crowd they were dealing with badly functioning guitars and that a fix was on the way.

But Young didn't return. The trio, with Samuels and Taylor gamely backing them, made it through the song. When it ended, Nash said a quick, "Thank you—good night," and the show abruptly ended.

Immediately after, Taylor received a call to come up to Young's hotel room. Crosby and Nash, already there, told Taylor in the bluntest terms they'd had enough of Stills. He was too crazy and domineering, and they'd decided to return to Los Angeles and scrap the tour, or maybe fire him and tour without him. Was Taylor with them or with Stills?

Taylor was stunned: He thought the show had been patchy but not terrible, and he'd been surprised when Young stormed off. Since Taylor considered Stills his friend, he told them he was staying with Stills. As they threatened, Crosby, Nash, and Young flew back to Los Angeles the next day, while Stills, unaware of their action, went onward to the next date, in Chicago, only hearing the show was canceled when he arrived at the venue for a soundcheck. "Crosby was furious at me, and Neil was disgusted," Stills recalled. "They wanted to fire me because *I* probably barely knew the songs." After fully realizing what had happened, Stills, with Taylor and Samuels, also returned to California. On the way, Taylor told him to screw the others; they'd form a group of their own. One show into their tour, CSNY had evaporated.

Three days later, on May 15, the four of them reunited, not onstage but at the Lookout Management office on La Cienega Boulevard. Roberts and Geffen laid it on the line. The tour was a big, potentially profitable one. The band was receiving an unusually high $25,000 per show. If the tour was canceled, promoters wouldn't be happy; in fact, they'd probably sue.

Atlantic had already begun preparing a press release that denied the group was disbanding. Word of the canceled Chicago show was jeopardizing ticket sales for concerts already announced; hearing the band was falling apart, fans were wary of forking over cash for shows that might not take place. The cancellations, the statement said with a degree of truth, were attributed to "knee and wrist injuries sustained by Stills and recurrence of throat problems by Graham Nash." The press release also disclosed for the first time publicly that Reeves was gone.

The meeting was a sobering experience, with grievances aired all around. "We never ran anything by our managers," Nash said. "They had to clean up the mess. But we had to face the consequences. It was a lot of money. We had to make sure the promoters weren't hurt. And the threat of lawsuits probably woke us up a little." Whether the group would actually be sued or whether the threat was a savvy management tactic to get them back together, the end result was that the four agreed to regroup and resume their tour.

Not every conflict had been resolved. That morning, Dallas Taylor had received a call from his friend and producer Paul Rothchild, who'd worked on Doors and early Crosby, Stills & Nash sessions. Rothchild asked Taylor if he was okay. Taylor didn't know what he meant. Hadn't Taylor heard or read he'd been sacked? Taylor jumped in his Ferrari and drove over to the Lookout office just as the combination group therapy session and tongue-lashing was winding down. None of them looked at him, and he knew right then it was over: Young had issued an ultimatum that Taylor, whose drumming he'd never been especially fond of, had to be replaced.

Although Taylor had never caused the band the type of consternation Reeves had, Nash felt Taylor had deluded himself into thinking he was a more integral part of the band than he was. "Because Dallas had been Stephen's hang buddy during the first record, Dallas began to think it should have been CSNY*T*," Nash recalled. "He wanted more presence and more money. It took us a little bit of explaining that he was never going to be one of us. He was a great drummer, but in CSNY there was nobody else as far as I was concerned." Taylor admitted there was disagreement over whether he should be paid as a sideman or full-time band member or whether he'd receive points on *Déjà vu*, which would represent a substantial windfall.

Onstage at Denver, Crosby had introduced Taylor, as he often did, as "our permanent drummer." But the meeting exposed the wobbliness of those words. Taylor and Stills had bonded from the earliest days of the band, but business had cleft them apart. "I never dreamed Stephen would throw me under the bus," Taylor said. "I showed my loyalty to him, but that pissed off Neil. He didn't want that camaraderie against him. I thought Stephen was my advocate. But everybody folded at that time." When Atlantic finally issued its press release, the statement now read that both Reeves and Taylor were out of the band; no replacements were mentioned. The tour would resume at the Boston Garden on May 29, roughly two weeks later.

In case anyone needed a reminder of their responsibilities, *Déjà vu* became the number 1 album in the country the day after the meeting, displacing Simon and Garfunkel's *Bridge Over Troubled Water*. The album was released to reviews both glowing ("there's no group in the country making better music than this," raved the *Chicago Tribune*, while the *Los Angeles Times'* Robert Hilburn dubbed it "easily the best rock album of the new year") and skeptical ("a lightweight collection of medium-pretty tunes, adequately performed by talented people," said the *Washington Post*, and *Rolling Stone* dubbed it "too sweet, too soothing, too perfect and too good to be true"). Nonetheless, *Déjà vu* began sailing out of stores, particularly in colleges: At the stores at the University of Boulder and the Madison branch of the University of Wisconsin, it leapfrogged over *Abbey Road* and *Bridge Over Troubled Water* to become their top seller. The fact that the names "Dallas Taylor & Greg Reeves" were embossed in gold on the cover was now a haunting memento of what had been.

● ● ● ●

Inconceivably, it was happening again, a mere ten days after Kent State.

In the immediate aftermath of the shootings, campuses either shut down or exploded. Students occupied buildings: one hundred at the University of Connecticut, protesting a no-amnesty policy toward any demonstrators, and another large group at Loyola in New Orleans. Twenty students at Eastern Michigan University were tossed in jail after pelting police. A bronze statue on the Columbia University campus in upper Manhattan wound up with a gaping hole when a makeshift bomb went off. In an unintentionally comic sidebar to events of the moment, even the music business was rattled. "Youth Unrest Cuts Disk Sales," reported *Billboard*, with one store owner grousing that students were so busy giving money to "defense funds" that they didn't have money left to buy LPs. At least, some said with relief, students weren't trashing record stores.

Like many campuses around the country, Jackson State College—a primarily African American school in the southwest section of Jackson, Mississippi—was a jumble of panic, fear, and indignation after the massacre in Ohio. On Wednesday, May 13, students took over a construction site, setting a dump truck on fire. A fire truck dispatched to the scene was hit with rocks and bottles, resulting in the inevitable aftermath—police and National Guard called in to restore order on and around the campus.

What happened next depended on who told the story. According to police, a sniper on the fourth floor of Alexander Hall, the women's dormitory, began firing at them. The students in and around the hall denied any such thing—if anything, they said, police had mistaken the sound of smashed bottles for gunfire. Whatever the cause—and no sniper was ever found—police opened fire at the building shortly after midnight on Friday, May 15.

Again, reports varied: Seven seconds of shots? Twenty-five? Nine students wounded? Eleven? Fifteen? Yet no one could argue with the number of bullet holes counted in the dorm—250—or the smell of fresh blood on the first floor, or with the grimmest results of all: two black students dead from gunshots. Philip Lafayette Gibbs, a junior studying pre-law and father of a baby about to turn eleven months, was the first casualty. James Earl Green wasn't even a student at Jackson State: A seventeen-year-old senior at the local high school, he was on his way home from a part-time job at the Rag-a-Bag grocery store, where he worked to help his widowed mother support her four children. Like those at Kent State, they were victims not of politics but of timing. Gibbs' membership in the Committee of Social Concern at a nearby Methodist Church was the closest either man came to activism.

The next day, Nixon kept a low profile, only issuing a bland statement: "In the shadow of these troubled days, this tragedy makes it urgent that every American personally undertake greater efforts toward understanding, restraint, and compassion." Not surprisingly, the comment did little to help people understand deaths that made even less sense than those at Kent State. "I think it was just a massacre," one student told a reporter. "I think it was preplanned. They came up there with the idea of killing." A token get-together at the White House with Nixon, his staff, and six Kent State students had done little to change those perceptions.

On May 26, Vice President Spiro Agnew, never known for subtlety, nuance, or love of hippies, sent a memo to John Ehrlichman, Nixon's domestic affairs advisor, about the national outbreak of antiwar protests. "We have had enough maudlin sympathy for lawbreakers emanating from other areas of government," he wrote. " . . . In my judgment, nothing makes the average American any angrier than to see the pained, self-righteous expressions of a[n Edwin] Muskie or a [Charles] Percy as they attach like leeches to the nearest Negro funeral procession . . . The polls show that the people are with [Nixon] and not with the whiners in the Senate and in the liberal community." Although he'd sounded a conciliatory note in his post-Jackson State comment, Nixon took a different stance in his office, away from prying eyes. After reading the memo, he jotted "E—I agree." It was time for law and order, and even though his popularity was waning, he pinned his hopes on his fellow Americans agreeing with him.

The sun was breaking through the clouds and drenching the redwoods when the groceries arrived. Shortly after the band meeting in Los Angeles, Crosby and Young, whose bond was becoming especially unbreakable, left town for Northern California. After stopping at Crosby's home, they piled into Young's car, toked up. and took the drive to their road manager Leo Makota's home in Pescadero, south of San Francisco. Surrounded by trees, the house on that May 19 morning couldn't have been a more ideal retreat from the craziness of the L.A. scene and CSNY turmoil. Young was also having difficulties with his wife Susan, with whom he was living at their home in Topanga. "The falling-apart stuff always involved Stills," Crosby said. "Neil and I stayed friends the whole time."

The new issue of *Life* magazine, dated May 15, spilled out onto the breakfast table along with the food. "Tragedy at Kent," announced the cover line, over a photo of students leaning over the body of another. The eleven pages that followed constituted the first, most extensive, and most unnerving look the public received of the shootings: gas-masked Guardsmen aiming to fire, a distraught girl kneeling beside Jeffrey

Miller's lifeless, jacketed body. Young looked away. He turned back and looked again. As Crosby watched, he walked over, grabbed a nearby guitar, and began writing a song. In fifteen minutes, out came an irate chant he simply called "Ohio"; Crosby worked on a harmony part while Young was writing.

Since Crosby and Young were due back in Los Angeles soon to begin rehearsals for the resuscitated tour, Crosby called Nash at home that night. Crosby rarely wavered in his role as the most excitable member the band, but this time he was noticeably charged. "You won't believe this fucking song Neil's written," he told Nash, before ordering him to book time in the studio as soon as possible. The fact that Young had written a topical song—an extremely rare occurrence, especially next to Crosby's and Stills' work—was doubly shocking. Business obligations were pulling them inexorably back together, but so were the times.

Luckily for them, a new drummer was already in hand. Another visitor to Makota's home during Crosby and Young's trip was Johnny Barbata, the lanky, shaggy-haired twenty-five-year-old former drummer for the Turtles. Makota knew Barbata socially; he was dating the sister of one of Barbata's friends. Hanging out with Crosby and Young, Barbata heard them discussing Taylor's firing, and soon enough Makota suggested Barbata step in. Since Barbata was a firm drummer who already knew most of the members of the band, the solution was easy and logical.

On May 20, the day after Young had written "Ohio," he, Crosby, and Barbata were all back in Los Angeles, with orders to meet at a massive soundstage at the Warner Brothers studio lot to begin rehearsing with the new rhythm section of Barbata and Samuels. They'd be playing on the same stage where *They Shoot Horses, Don't They?*—a drama about a Prohibition-era dance rivalry in which contestants hoofed until they dropped, in some cases dead—had been filmed the year before. The band found dark humor in the leftover sign from the production that hung over the stage: "How Long Will They Last?" Tempting fate, they posed for pictures beneath it.

Barbata knew he'd have to win over Stills, who was notoriously fussy about rhythm sections. He also well knew his and Samuels' roles—lay low and take orders—after hearing about the troubles with Taylor and Reeves. "We already knew up front what our place was," he said, "and that was fine with me." As soon as he arrived, Barbata began throwing around a football with Stills, and overall, the drummer sensed a more relaxed vibe. "They seemed excited," Barbata recalled. "They were insecure about the whole breakup and they wanted to get it right." For all his bluster, Stills could be easily wounded and sensitive. On the plane from Chicago to Los Angeles after the Denver debacle, he appeared visibly shaken that his band—the one that had finally made him a star after so many years striving for that level of recognition—could be finished.

At the soundstage over the next few days, everyone worked hard to play nice. Diltz stopped by on the afternoon of May 21; as he snapped away, the band traded grins while rehearsing, and Stills and Young huddled together in conversation. Laura Nyro, the alternately earthy and flighty New York singer, songwriter, and pianist (and Geffen client), visited, and she, Crosby, Nash, and Stills gathered around a piano, harmonizing on her song "Eli's Coming." The mood was convivial and nonconfrontational; the fact that Elliot Roberts was on the set, keeping a watchful eye on the proceedings, also helped.

That same night, Bill Halverson was at the Record Plant studio, setting up to resume work on Stills' album, when he received a call. The entire band, not just Stills, would be arriving shortly to record a new song—Young's "Ohio." ("Neil needed us *back*," Stills cracked.) Although Halverson had been an eyewitness to tension in San Francisco six months before, the four men who strode into the Record Plant and set up in a crammed corner of the studio exuded a more unified front. Stills thought the song needed another verse and had conflicting thoughts about the massacre. "I thought, there has to be more *to* this," he recalled. "I'm sure a lot of the guys in that platoon were told they didn't have live rounds. Some part of me went, 'Guys just don't *do* that—that's too much like the Germans. We're more honorable than firing into unarmed civilians.'"

But since they'd been rehearsing the song all day at the soundstage, the recording was remarkably efficient. In two takes with no overdubbing, they had a finished track; even Crosby's improvised finale, pained screams of "Four, how many more," was live. The recording, particularly the interplay between Young's twisty opening guitar figure and Stills' coiled-up leads, had a crackling energy and group dynamic rarely heard on *Déjà vu*. When it was done, they gathered around four microphones and recorded a B-side, Stills' "Find the Cost of Freedom," written but rejected for the *Easy Rider* soundtrack. In contrast to "Ohio," "Find the Cost of Freedom" was quiet, almost elegiac: a simple, dramatic showcase for their voices and Stills' acoustic lead. Young had the A-side, with Stills' song on the flip, but for once the old Springfield wars failed to materialize. "They were on a musical mission to get this done and out," Halverson recalled. "It was, 'We've got to get on the same page and make this right.'"

The tape was flown to Atlantic's offices in New York. For financial rather than political reasons, some at the company weren't thrilled: The label was in the midst of pressing up 45s of "Teach Your Children," the next single from *Déjà vu*. But "Ohio" felt like the right move at the right moment.

The afternoon following the session, Crosby, Nash, and Young went to their friend Alan Pariser's house in Hollywood. Pariser, who managed bands like Delaney and Bonnie and was a well-known scene-maker, had massive speakers in his living room, and CSNY would often light up joints and listen to their new music there. Another guest at Pariser's home that evening, Albert Grossman, wound up in a heated discussion with Crosby about politics in music. The times were so combustible that the man who had signed Dylan and Peter, Paul and Mary had mixed feelings about releasing a song about Kent State. In a remarkably fast turnaround, "Ohio" was on the radio days later, even before it was in stores.

In the meantime, the rehearsing continued on the Warner backlot. One day, a girl walked onto the soundstage, and Crosby grabbed her and planted a kiss on her. When Barbata asked who she was, Crosby said he didn't know; it was just someone hanging around. They were still a band and still rock stars, and their tour would finally resume in a little less than a week.

PART THREE

SUMMER INTO FALL
Away, I'd Rather Sail Away

CHAPTER 9

Three days into summer, Garfunkel was no longer Art. On June 24, eighteen months after its protracted and expensive shoot began in Mexico, *Catch-22* premiered at New York's Ziegfeld Theater, just north of Times Square. In the opening credits, the name "Arthur Garfunkel" appeared onscreen. He'd first used his birth name on the back cover of *Bridge Over Troubled Water*, but its appearance here now befit both his role in a prestige film and the new, distinctive role Garfunkel saw for himself, beyond pop music and his partner.

It didn't take an industry insider to see that Garfunkel's warm-glow harmonies were a huge factor in making Simon's songs palatable to radio and the masses. But whether they wanted to or not, everyone around Garfunkel made him feel like the less vital and valuable half of the duo. In early 1968, Simon and Garfunkel were booked into New York's Carnegie Hall, one of the most prestigious venues they'd yet played. The demand for tickets was so great that the promoter asked Mort Lewis to add a second show. To convince his act to perform twice in one night, Lewis knew the best strategy: Call Simon first and get his consent (after telling him there wouldn't be enough freebies to give to family members if they only did one show). If he were willing, then Garfunkel would surely go along with the decision—which was precisely what happened. Lewis always started with Simon.

Backstage at shows, fans would approach Garfunkel and ask, "Do you write the words or the music?" With noticeable discomfort, he'd always have to say neither. Garfunkel had taken a few cracks at songwriting during and soon after the Tom and Jerry days, coauthoring "Hey, Schoolgirl" with Simon. Under the culturally assimilated moniker Artie Garr, he'd cut a few singles on his own during that period, including the head-in-the-clouds ballad "Dream Alone" and the peppy whitebread doo-wop "Beat Love," the latter pushed along by a mild skiffle beat. Both were showcases for his sweet, virtuous voice and his wise-beyond-his-years views on puppy love. ("Maybe I love you and maybe I don't," he pondered to his girlfriend in the latter.)

Garfunkel had had a small hand in Simon and Garfunkel compositions—suggesting chord changes in "Bridge Over Troubled Water," for instance—but the credit, and all the publishing income, always went to Simon alone. To help smooth over any uneasy feelings, Simon began telling interviewers that Garfunkel arranged the material, although everyone knew that was merely an honorary title designed to placate Garfunkel.

Jetting down to Mexico on a plane filled with fellow *Catch-22* cast members in 1969, Garfunkel had an immediate taste of a different, more welcoming community. On the flight, Bob Balaban, then twenty-four, was so in awe of Garfunkel he didn't dare speak with him, only humming "The Sound of Silence" as a way to express his fandom. During the long, grueling hours between takes, Garfunkel and some of his costars—Alan Arkin, Tony Perkins, and Balaban—played tennis on a dilapidated court near the set, and Garfunkel and Perkins would often sing together during downtime. At Simon's rental home on Blue Jay Way in Los Angeles, visitors included another *Catch-22* actor, Charles Grodin, and Jack Nicholson. One day in the summer of 1969, Garfunkel showed Grodin an envelope with Simon's handwritten lyrics to "Bridge Over Troubled Water" scrawled on the back. "Too simple," Grodin cracked, although Garfunkel told him it would sound better with music around it. With or without Grodin's curmudgeonly jab, this alternate community was instantly intoxicating to Garfunkel; in it, he was a certified star whether or not he wrote songs.

Even if Simon was irked by Garfunkel's participation, *Catch-22* was hard to turn down. Starting with *The Green Berets* in 1968 and extending to *Patton*, which had opened in April, pro-war films hadn't vanished, even during Vietnam; part of the country wanted to see America kick some degree of butt. But by the summer of 1970, Hollywood was eager to tap into—and profit from—campus turbulence. *Getting Straight*, in theaters that May, featured Elliot Gould as a young professor navigating his way through the antiwar movement on a campus; *The Strawberry Statement*, which opened the week before *Catch-22*, found a student (played by Bruce Davison) juggling a love life and police tear-gas attacks at another fictional school. A month after *Catch-22*, Jon Voight would play a troubled student of his own in *The Revolutionary*. Each film contorted itself to appeal to ticket buyers under the age of twenty-five: "America's children lay it on the line," read the ads for *Getting Straight*, while *The Strawberry Statement* used Crosby, Stills, Nash & Young's "Ohio" and "Our House" and John Lennon's "Give Peace a Chance" on its soundtrack.

Like *M*A*S*H*, which preceded it in the spring, *Catch-22* used a different war as a metaphor for the Vietnam conflict. It was also less sensational and felt less exploitive than any of the "hip" screw-the-establishment summer movies. But Nichols' film received a far rockier reception than *M*A*S*H*. In Heller's hands, the tale of Yossarian, an American bombardier flying missions off the coast of Italy during World War II while attempting to prove his insanity to his superiors, steadily balanced sobriety and absurdity. The film version couldn't find a unifying tone between cartoonish and somber. In *Life*, critic Richard Schickel noted that Nichols and screenwriter Buck Henry had "mislaid every bit of the humor that made the novel emotionally bearable and aesthetically memorable." Less stinging but equally dismissive, *Newsweek* noted that "the cumulative effect is disjointedness instead of the coherence of craziness." *M*A*S*H* purloined much of the movie's thunder, and its karma wasn't helped when, three months before, a charred copy of *Catch-22* was found in the rubble of the West 11th Street brownstone accidentally destroyed by the Weathermen.

Nichols had been smart to cast Garfunkel as Nately; in Garfunkel's and Nichols' hands, Nately was a baby-faced nineteen-year-old and a logical extension of the vestal-virgin aspects of Garfunkel's voice and image. In his minor role, Garfunkel didn't have many opportunities to show his potential, although a scene in which Nately angrily confronted a cynical old Italian, played by veteran Marcel Dalio, showed promise. ("What are you talking about—America's not going to be *destroyed!*" he barked, condemning the old man as a "shameful opportunist.")

Not everyone agreed about Garfunkel's future in film. "He has an appealing face but sounds as if he is reading his lines from a blackboard," noted the New York *Daily News*, while the nearby *Newark Evening News* in New Jersey noted dryly that Garfunkel "has a nice face for movies but no apparent acting skills." In what amounted to a compliment, *Variety* found Garfunkel's screen presence "winsomely effeminate." Still, Nichols was impressed. Even before the première, he recruited Garfunkel for his next project, an adaptation of cartoonist and playwright Jules Feiffer's unproduced play *True Confessions*.

Simon and Lewis had no choice but to go along; at least this time, there were no album sessions scheduled for the fall, when the next film would begin shooting. "Paul felt, 'Why's he doing that?'" Lewis recalled. "'We have this successful thing we're doing.'" For those who worked with them, it wasn't hard to grasp Garfunkel's rationale. Over many years, he'd had to take a backseat to Simon in the music world, and he was still stung by Simon's early attempt to fly solo during the Tom and Jerry period. With movie roles, Garfunkel could achieve parity in their relationship. If all went well, he stood the chance of becoming an even bigger name—a movie star name. Simon may have been the primary creative force in the duo, the writer of the songs on which they harmonized so tenderly, but Garfunkel would be a man of all media. If it bothered his partner of most of the previous fifteen years, so be it.

No sooner had summer arrived than they began circling back to their early days, before the gold records and divergent interests. On July 8, the two spent a day at one of Columbia's New York studios, returning to the songs that had first drawn them together. "Barbriallen" (also known as "Barbara Allen") and "Roving Gambler" had both been covered by the Everly Brothers on *Songs Our Daddy Taught Us*, their collection of traditional and country songs from 1958. Simon took the lead on the third, the Scottish traditional song "Rose of Aberdeen."

Their love of the Everlys had manifested itself before, both on the road and in the version of "Bye Bye Love" included on *Bridge Over Troubled Water*. At their Royal Albert Hall show in London in April, they'd covered not only the Everlys' "Bye Bye Love" but two other *Songs Our Daddy Taught Us* melodies, "Lightning Express" and "Silver Haired Daddy of Mine." The new recordings, put down on tape for reasons that were never disclosed, not even to Columbia Records, had a relaxed, coffeehouse-intimate modesty, Simon even joking mid-song in "Roving Gambler" that he could sing it forever. The songs were like Switzerland—neutral ground where they could set aside their differences and revel in a sturdy melody and the sound of their joined voices.

Nine days later, they were driven out to Forest Hills Tennis Stadium for the first of two headlining shows, playing before a total of twenty-eight thousand people. Home to the tennis championship that came to be known as the U.S. Open, the open-air stadium was a mere mile and a half from Simon's childhood house in Flushing. They'd played there before, opening for the Mamas and the Papas in 1966 before graduating to headliners in 1968. With the Mamas and the Papas, they were paid only $1,000. In another sign of their achievement, they'd now be compensated $50,000 for each of the two nights. They'd also be receiving an unheard-of 90 percent of that money, with the promoter, Leonard Ruskin, only receiving the remaining 10. Before the show began, Lewis went into the office to collect his check. When Ruskin handed Lewis a check for $90,000, Lewis, for a reason he couldn't explain later, thought he should be receiving the full $100,000. "Jesus, is that *all?*" he barked. Ruskin reached over and grabbed Lewis' collar, screaming at him.

Otherwise, the first night was business, and music, as usual. With Simon wearing a Yankees cap for hometown flavor, they played a set that, more than any other, delved through their musical and shared history. While still avoiding revivals of "Hey, Schoolgirl" or other leftovers from their Tom and Jerry days, they sang a playful version of Dion's swooning doo-wop classic "A Teenager in Love" and combined "Cecilia" with "Bye Bye Love." Garfunkel shone on "For Emily, Whenever I May Find Her," Simon's song about the search for ideal love (although Garfunkel once told a friend it was about drugs). Garfunkel's voice sounded especially dreamy and willowy, Simon's guitar ripples imitating the drizzling rain evoked in his lyrics.

On cue, Larry Knechtel emerged from the wings and began playing "Bridge Over Troubled Water." Knechtel, who'd been born and raised in the sketchy, roughneck town of Bell, California, glanced around and saw a young, clearly educated crowd, the men sporting neckties. Not very rock and roll, he thought, but then, neither were his two bosses. Knechtel glanced over at Garfunkel, and the lights shining down on Garfunkel's head made it look as if a halo had encircled his head. After Knechtel left the stage, they closed, appropriately, with "Old Friends."

Other than Lewis' tussle with Ruskin, both shows at the stadium went off without incident. The concerts were so uneventful that neither the *New York Times*, *Daily News*, nor the *New York Post* bothered to publish reviews. Just before Simon and Garfunkel walked offstage the first night,

Garfunkel's girlfriend Linda Grossman took out a camera. As the moon came up over the stage—poetically recalling the "moon rose over an open field" line in "America"— she aimed and clicked. Later, she discovered the roll of film hadn't been wound correctly inside the camera, and she was left with nothing. Undocumented on all fronts, their music and image slipped away with the night.

"Welcome, brothers and sisters," read the fliers handed to those entering Downing Stadium on Randall's Island. "This concert belongs to the people." The same night as Simon and Garfunkel's first Forest Hills show, the New York Pop concerts were firing up forty miles north, on a lumpy-shaped, barely one-square-mile island on the East River between Manhattan and Queens. Tens of thousands began swarming across bridges from the boroughs—the one from Queens over a narrow strait appropriately called Hell Gate—to reach the festival grounds. While Simon and Garfunkel sang at their venue, the lineup at New York Pop promised to rattle Downing Stadium to its aging, concrete rafters. Jimi Hendrix, Mountain, and Ten Years After were on the bill, as were newer bands with younger followings, Grand Funk Railroad and Jethro Tull.

The previous summer, a young, curly-topped promoter and hustler named Michael Lang had called Lewis to gauge Simon and Garfunkel's interest in playing Woodstock, the festival Lang was co-organizing upstate. Lewis told him the two men were having "real problems" staying together and fulfilling their obligations. The day before the festival was set to begin, they were supposed to be in the studio laboring over "Bridge Over Troubled Water" and "So Long, Frank Lloyd Wright." Lewis even hinted they might not last much longer as a duo. As a result, Simon and Garfunkel missed out on the major rock and roll event of 1969.

Since then, the rock festival had become an entrenched part of the concert circuit, with promoters both reputable and otherwise casting about for a sequel to Woodstock. Even though that festival was almost a year old, its cultural—and financial—shadow was now beginning to reveal itself. The three-hour film of the event, released in theaters in March, was on its way to grossing a stunning $13 million. Its soundtrack had had three hundred thousand initial orders—huge numbers for a three-LP set with a high list price—and was the number 1 album in the country by July. Crosby, Stills, Nash & Young's version of "Woodstock" had been a radio hit in the spring. The Woodstock brand was in place to such a degree that when Long Island University announced a "Woodstock Reunion" show on campus that summer of 1970 featuring Tim Hardin and Melanie, the dean received a cease-and-desist letter from Lang's Woodstock Ventures ordering them to stop using the name.

Each week seemed to bring an announcement of a new multi-day, multi-performer festival in Hawaii, Illinois, Florida, even Japan. Sometimes the festivals announced their lineups, sometimes not. Even when they didn't, plenty of optimistic fans mailed away for tickets, assuming the event was legit and the promoters would live up to their promises.

As organizers soon learned as the 1970 concert season began, outdoor festivals that stretched out over days were rarely smooth-running machines. At Florida's Winter's End festival in the spring, rainfall was so heavy that a lake formed between the one hundred thousand ticket buyers and the facilities. The medical team on duty had to build a makeshift raft out of plywood and inner tubes in order to reach fans, including many topless girls who wound up with sunburned breasts. Keeping male concertgoers out of *that* tent itself posed a challenge to the doctors on duty.

Yet by the summer, downpours were the least of anyone's problems. The mere thought of tens or hundreds of thousands of semi-clad kids descending upon their areas sent local officials and police around the country in search of any means possible to avoid traffic jams, drug taking, and skinny-dipping. New Jersey lawyers began looking into laws to "regulate" rock festivals. Authorities in Middlefield, Connecticut, filed injunctions against a planned festival at the Powder Ridge ski resort. Although no performers were allowed to play, the fifty thousand who showed up nonetheless stayed, camping out and indulging in vast quantities of drugs on a hillside. The same scenario went down at a planned "Bach to Rock" festival in New York's Catskills. After a chaotic Soldier's Field show in July featuring the MC5, Leon Russell, and twenty thousand people, Chicago Mayor Richard Daley nixed all planned shows in his parks. A Hawaiian "World Peace Festival" was canceled before it even began after community groups fearing another Woodstock—or, worse, Altamont—shut it down. Organizers at an outdoor show in Aix-en-Provence, France, worked around a similar ban by redubbing the show a "prolonged concert" and avoiding the "festival" tag altogether.

Even when the festivals took place without incident—as they did in Indiana and Iowa—a cranky, unpleasant haze hung over them. After fans heard about the successfully crashed gates at Woodstock, a rallying cry began: Admission to such events should be free! The protest made no sense, since everyone knew the performers needed to be paid to make a living, but the cry went out nonetheless. In Amsterdam, seventy thousand barged into the Holland Pop Festival without forking over a cent, much to the annoyance of the twenty-seven thousand who had. Outside the gates of the Atlanta International Pop Festival in Byron, Georgia, over the July 4th weekend, fans chanted, screamed, and demanded to be let in without tickets. Fearing a catastrophic battle, the promoters reluctantly agreed, and ten thousand streamed in. Even as Duane Allman was leading the Allman Brothers Band through a stunning set, Lester Maddox, the state's cantankerous governor, introduced a bill in the state legislature to ban future festivals, denouncing the skinny-dippers as "immoral."

John Brower, the Canadian promoter who'd attempted to launch the

Music and Peace Conference with John Lennon, settled for a three-day Strawberry Fields Festival at a raceway in Ontario, Canada. By calling it a motorcycle race with "added entertainment," Brower and his partners were able to circumvent government interference and a planned shutdown. But even then, only 65,000 of the 150,000 who descended upon the campground to hear Sly and the Family Stone, Grand Funk Railroad, Mountain, Jethro Tull, and others actually paid. The festival ended up losing over $1 million.

At New York Pop—the name "festival" was avoided to ward off any interference—the problems began even before the gates opened. Randall's Island had once housed an orphanage and an asylum; in 1936, in time for the American Olympics trials, an outdoor stadium was built on the grounds. A month before New York Pop, Brave New World Productions, which was organizing the event, was hit with a list of demands by an ad-hoc coalition of the Young Lords—Spanish Harlem's answer to the Black Panthers—and a group of New York Yippies dubbing themselves the RYP/Off Collective. The extensive list included bail funds, defense money for Black Panthers trials, and free tickets for Spanish Harlem residents who couldn't afford them. (The festival wasn't overly pricey: $8.50 for one night, $15.00 for two, and $31.00 for all three.) If Brave New World didn't agree, the radicals would essentially ruin the festival—badmouthing it, telling everyone it was free—and the promoters reluctantly agreed to many of the demands.

With its cinderblock seats and dirt field, Downing Stadium wasn't a particularly scenic locale, and the festival, starting Friday, July 17, only seemed to grow gnarlier by the hour. As thousands set upon the gates, the promoters had no choice but to give in or risk mass injuries. The locks were removed, and tens of thousands bulldozed in without paying. Inside, an announcement on the PA warned concertgoers of bad acid making its way around the field, and a woman claiming to be a member of the renamed Weather Underground alerted the crowd that the group would attack a "symbol of American justice" shortly after the festival ended. Security was being provided by the radical collective, not police, leading to disorganization both in the crowd and backstage. "There were lots of good vibes," remembered Jimi Hazel, a teenage Bronx rock fan taken to the festival by his older brother, "and then you'd come across something."

Onstage late that first night, Hendrix was visibly unnerved by the jittery crowd and a malfunctioning sound system. "The equipment was picking up radio frequencies through the amps," Hazel recalled. "Some Spanish cab driver would come out of the amp." During "Foxey Lady," Hendrix turned to drummer Mitch Mitchell and exhaled a tired "whew." After trudging his way through a set, Hendrix told the crowd, "Fuck you, and good night," and left the stage.

When word began to spread that the promoters might not be able to pay them, many acts scheduled to play the second night—Delaney and Bonnie, Indian music composer and sitar virtuoso Ravi Shankar, and Richie Havens—either stayed in Manhattan or visited the site and left without getting anywhere near the stage. The heat and humidity soared on the second day, adding to the strain. Adhering to their increasingly erratic behavior, Sly and the Family Stone, the planned headliner for the third night, was a no-show. When New York Pop finally tumbled to a close, organizers dubbed it a financial debacle.

The next month, the third annual Isle of Wight festival off the British Isles experienced much the same turbulence. Charlie Daniels, who'd flown to Europe after the George Harrison and Bob Dylan session to play bass with Leonard Cohen, found himself onstage with Cohen, looking at fires in the distance. Security was so lax that several stoned fans wandered in front of Cohen. The throng kicked up so much dirt that everything felt covered in rust. "That was the old hippie attitude," Daniels recalled. "Everything ought to be free. Everybody will be workin' for free. *Love* ought to be free. This and that oughta be free. And the world just can't work that way." After playing "Woodstock," a rattled Joni Mitchell scolded the boisterous, not especially mellow throngs: "Will you *listen* a minute? . . . You're acting like tourists, man. Give us some respect!"

At summer's end, the head of Capitol Records suggested a fact-finding study to "save rock festivals." But it was too late. "The general consensus," *Billboard* reported after the last bonfire at the Isle of Wight cooled down, "is that it was everybody's last festival."

To the outside world—or at least to Peter Yarrow—the first suggestion of trouble in the Simon and Garfunkel camp came at another festival in midsummer. Despite Hendrix's meltdown, the Winter Concert for Peace in January had been a financial success. In April, Moratorium co-organizers including David Hawk and Sam Brown announced the Moratorium was shutting down. They cited a drop-off in public interest, Nixon's "Vietnamization" policy (withdrawing American troops to supposedly prepare the South Vietnamese for self-defense against the North), and radical elements that disrupted the generally peaceful Moratorium events. The committee was also at least $100,000 in debt.

But the November midterm elections remained in sight, and Brown, Hawk, and Yarrow, along with a ragtag group of organizers and philanthropist Stewart Mott, decided to adhere to their earlier plan of raising money for Senate and House candidates opposed to the war. Once again, Yarrow took charge of lining up the talent, this time placing one of his calls to Simon's apartment on East End Avenue.

Three years Simon's senior, Yarrow, whose goatee and earnest air lent him the look of a rabbinical student more than a folksinger, had known Simon since their Village days. He'd become a star with Peter, Paul and Mary in the years between Tom and Jerry and "The Sound of

Silence." (Yarrow would later record his own version of "Groundhog," one of the leftovers from *Bridge Over Troubled Water*.) Yarrow made his pitch, and Simon was somewhat open to performing at the concert. Then Yarrow dialed Garfunkel, who was far more hesitant. "Those were not uncomplicated discussions," Yarrow recalled of the half dozen conversations he had with Garfunkel. Simon also called his partner to recruit him. For reasons Yarrow couldn't quite ascertain, Garfunkel eventually passed. Yarrow then nudged Simon into doing the show alone, and Simon, after more conversations, agreed. At the time, Yarrow didn't think much of it; perhaps the two men merely had conflicting schedules.

By August 6, the day of the show as well as the twenty-fifth anniversary of the Hiroshima bombing, Yarrow had succeeded in assembling a respectable lineup for the Summer Festival for Peace: Creedence Clearwater Revival, Miles Davis, Poco, the Paul Butterfield Blues Band, Johnny Winter, Janis Joplin's former band Big Brother and the Holding Company, and, in his first solo performance since his London days over five years before, Paul Simon. With the help of wealthy donors, the concert committee, Peace Incorporated, had leased the fifty-seven-thousand–seat Shea Stadium for the event; a stage was erected near second base.

Yarrow was feeling less than hopeful about the times. Although he'd been involved in the October Moratorium and the following month's March on Washington, they felt like postscripts after the assassinations of King and Robert Kennedy and the assault on protesters by police at the Chicago Convention. "That was the end of a kind of momentum we could have had," he recalled. "Nineteen sixty-eight signaled the very unhappy reality that the social movement lost the possibility of being a dominant political force." Peter, Paul and Mary were themselves coming apart. A decade of nonstop touring, recording, and bickering—sometimes over the lyrics to each other's songs—had taken its toll. Noel Paul

Stookey had become a born-again Christian and, to Yarrow's discomfort, was talking about his conversion on stage. Each wanted to spend more time with their families, so they'd decided to take a hiatus once their summer concert schedule was over.

Yarrow carried on, singing at whatever rally he could find the time to attend. But he felt the political and musical shifts, especially when it came to the antiwar movement. To the frustration of many opposed to the war, Nixon's troop withdrawals—implemented at the same time he was revving up the air strikes and the Cambodian assaults—had succeeded in making the most unpopular president in decades appear a champion of peace. On June 24, changes at the Selective Service System brought both good and damaging news. Instead of drawing from the large pool of eighteen- to twenty-six-year-olds, the draft would limit its intake to nineteen-year-olds, those born in 1951. For millions of young men, the pressure was suddenly off, as the horrors of war in Southeast Asia were no longer a possibility.

As he took the stage at the Summer Festival for Peace, Yarrow and the co-organizers witnessed the change in mood for themselves. The stadium was less than half full. Even with Janis Joplin announcing on television that she would reunite onstage with Big Brother, ticket sales had been sluggish. By the time the show began in late morning, only fifteen thousand of the twenty-five thousand tickets had been sold.

Even more revealing, those who'd shown up weren't the politically charged concertgoers of the January concert, the ones with memories of the Moratorium still fresh in their brains. "The summer event was more like a music festival," recalled Hawk. "It was for people who missed out on Woodstock: 'Here's another one, at a stadium near you.'" The fans in the bleachers smoked, drank, and sailed Frisbees through the humid August air. At one point, some started leaping from the bleachers onto the Astroturf. Knowing that any destruction of the grounds would result in fines, Yarrow walked onstage and admonished the kids, saying they could feel free to jump on it, but if they did, it would be akin to jumping on a dead soldier's chest. To calm them down, he sang "Puff the Magic Dragon," which, despite its reputation as a drug song, didn't fully do the trick.

Then came the inevitable gatecrashers, the true soundtrack of the summer. Yarrow had just led the crowd in a sing-along of John Lennon's "Give Peace a Chance." ("Say it so Nixon can hear you!" he implored them.) Outside the Shea gates, a small but unruly cluster gathered, demanding to be let in for nothing. Yarrow went outside and, standing atop a fire hydrant so he could be seen and heard, pleaded with everyone to calm down. At one point, he broke down in tears. Eventually, the crowd dispersed.

By the time Simon walked out onto the Shea stage with his acoustic guitar, the crowd was no longer his. A year before, when he and Garfunkel had played Forest Hills for the second time, it had been; the response was rapturous. Two years before that, at Monterey Pop in 1967, it had been theirs too. Along with John Phillips of the Mamas and the Papas and others, Simon had helped curate the first major—and incident-free—outdoor festival of the decade. Simon's haircut was far shorter than any of those onstage—the lineup included Hendrix, the Who, and David Crosby of the Byrds sitting in for the first time with Stephen Stills and Buffalo Springfield—yet he and Garfunkel were nonetheless welcomed, the crowd clapping in time with "The 59th Street Bridge Song (Feelin' Groovy)."

By the time of the Summer Festival for Peace, the inevitable backlash had set in. It wasn't their fault that "Bridge Over Troubled Water" had become a beloved middle-of-the-road staple, covered that year by a raft of acts from Ray Conniff to Elvis Presley. But it was still ironic that the duo who'd worked so hard to beef up their antiestablishment credentials with the *Songs of America* TV special were now seen as representing all that was unthreatening, apolitical, and eye-rollingly old-fashioned. Unlike the rock acts who dominated FM radio, Simon and Garfunkel had seemingly appeared on whatever TV variety show invited them, including one hosted by banal balladeer Andy Williams. The days when *The Graduate* spoke for an entire troubled middle- and upper-middle class were suddenly over. "I consider his soft sound a cop-out," wrote *New Yorker* music critic Ellen Willis of Simon. "And I hate most of his lyrics; his alienation, like the word itself, is an old-fashioned, sentimental, West-Side-liberal bore."

At their Royal Albert Hall show in April, critic Miles Kingston defended the group—"There are very few Paul Simons around," he correctly observed—but added, "Some people hate Simon and Garfunkel because their music has no guts, because it is a middle-class look at life, because it slips too easily from idiom to idiom." With more than a touch of sexism, he dryly observed the "squads of dumpy girls half-heartedly invading" the stage during the encores. Even their groupies (whom Garfunkel later described as "the left-out kids—the loners, the bookworms, the fat girls") weren't sexy.

In a stadium the size of Shea, capturing a crowd's attention with one voice and one guitar was challenging enough. But as he began singing, Simon heard the jets overhead, on their way to JFK, and saw how far off the audience was, scattered around the bleachers rather than on the field. They wanted to party, not parse articulate rhymes, and barely noticed anyone was onstage. "He was not received all that warmly," Yarrow recalled. By the time Simon launched into his third song, "Scarborough Fair/Canticle," with its delicate, folk-club chords, apathy had turned to pockets of booing. Rather than continue, Simon stopped and left the stage. The Summer Festival for Peace continued without him.

That same summer, Simon was invited by Leonard Bernstein to collaborate on music for a Franco Zeffirelli film, *Brother Sun, Sister Moon*, about the life of St. Francis of Assisi. Over the course of two weeks, they met at Bernstein's home in Connecticut and the conductor's Manhattan apartment. Little was completed; Bernstein and Simon didn't click musically, and Bernstein withdrew from the project.

For his *Mass* the following year, though, Bernstein included a quatrain Simon had contributed, part of which read: "Half the people are stoned/And the other half are waiting for the next election." The words appeared to sum up Simon's disillusionment with both rock fans and their culture. Simon never talked much about the Summer Festival for Peace, not even with Lewis. Yet as his manager was beginning to learn, Simon didn't always tell him everything.

CHAPTER 10

Why not take a crack at "Bridge Over Troubled Water," someone at Music City Studio asked Ringo Starr. The very thought was absurd; Starr's voice, homely if likable and charming, was nothing like Art Garfunkel's. Then again, no one would have predicted that Starr would be in Nashville at the dawn of summer, surrounded by some of the city's most preeminent pickers and making, of all things, a *country* album.

For someone who'd sought to avoid as much turbulence as possible, Starr had had a taxing first half of the year. The sight of McCartney yelling at him and asking him to leave the Cavendish Avenue home had been rattling enough. In the spring, he'd learned his wife, Maureen, was pregnant with their third child, who would join four-year-old Zak and two-year-old Jason. With no further Beatle albums on the horizon, Starr needed to work as much and as quickly as possible before the baby arrived.

His first musical foray outside the Beatles had struck a misguided note. *Sentimental Journey*, the collection of non-rock standards he'd worked on throughout the winter, had been released in March. In his home country, it climbed to number 7 on the charts; out of loyalty, just enough Beatle fans in the States bought it to push it to number 22. But the album was little more than a novelty, and it was hard to tell if Starr himself was in on the joke. Everyone from faithful fans to close friends had a difficult time listening to him reinvent himself as a big-band crooner, warbling pre-rock standards like "You Always Hurt the One You Love" and Cole Porter's "Night and Day" as if he were in a local talent show. Klaus Voormann, who at Starr's request arranged a version of "I'm a Fool to Care," would cringe at the memory of the song. "I gave it a try," he recalled. "I thought if I showed it to George Martin he wouldn't like it, but he said, 'Oh, Klaus, that's very good.' But it's awful, terrible."

By way of his close friend Harrison, Starr had already moved on. In the weeks after McCartney's press statement, Harrison had decided the time had come to make an album of his own. He'd first ventured into solo waters with *Wonderwall Music*, a collection of mostly instrumental electronic tracks released in 1968 as the eponymous soundtrack for a film, but he now had a stack of songs left over from Beatle sessions as well as new ones he'd composed at Friar Park. With the encouragement of Voormann and Chris O'Dell (who helped him type out the lyrics), Harrison made plans to put his songs on tape.

The previous December, Harrison had sat in with Delaney and Bonnie (and their mutual friend Eric Clapton) on some of the American soul duo's European shows. Delaney and Bonnie Bramlett—he from a small town in Mississippi, she from St. Louis—had made their name in Los Angeles as a white-trash version of Ike and Tina Turner. Clapton had seen their fiery stage show firsthand when Delaney and Bonnie opened for his now-defunct band Blind Faith and, inspired by their R&B and soul grooves and onstage hospitality, had hooked up with them as a backup guitarist, at least temporarily.

Harrison had much the same experience. Weary of open warfare in the Beatle camp, he'd sat in with Delaney and Bonnie onstage in London in December 1969. (Lennon attended the same show, and Bonnie Bramlett was struck by how small he was in person.) At his wife's urging, Delaney Bramlett invited Harrison to join them for a few of their European shows. "I said, 'Just ask him—what's he going to do, say *no*?'" Bonnie Bramlett recalled. "He hadn't played in three years and his fucking band broke up. Ask him!" Harrison told them they should drive up to his house and simply knock on the door; his wife, Pattie Boyd, would be too polite to turn them down. The Delaney and Bonnie caravan did just that, and Harrison emerged with his guitar and hopped aboard. The experience gave him the chance to play guitar in a relaxed, nonjudgmental atmosphere, without any attendant Beatle hysteria. The Delaney and Bonnie gigs also introduced him to a group of superb American musicians—keyboardist Bobby Whitlock, bassist Carl Radle, drummer Jim Gordon—while cementing Boyd's growing infatuation with Clapton. At her and Harrison's house, Boyd told Bonnie Bramlett and Rita Coolidge, one of their backup singers, that she was in love with Clapton and was thinking of leaving Harrison. Neither Bramlett nor Coolidge knew what to say.

By way of Charlie Daniels, the bass player at his casual session with Dylan, Harrison had reached out to Pete Drake, one of Nashville's most revered pedal steel guitarists. Harrison loved the use of steel guitar on Dylan's recent albums and wanted to integrate its sweet, supple cry into his own work. At Harrison's recording sessions, Starr, who drummed on a good deal of the tracks, told Drake he was in a bind. He wanted to make another album in London, but between scheduling time and finding the right pop producer, the process could take months. Inspired by his drive into London—he was picked up in Starr's six-door Mercedes and saw piles of country cassettes strewn about—Drake flashed on an idea: Why not make a record in Nashville, a town known for its quick-turnaround schedules? With Drake producing, the whole thing most likely wouldn't take more than week.

Before he knew it, Starr, joined by Apple's Neil Aspinall, was on a plane to Nashville by way of Atlanta. Drake wasn't joking about efficiency. By the time Starr arrived in Nashville on June 22, Drake had already selected a group of songs for him. One by one, the songwriters appeared at Starr's hotel room to help him learn the material. Arriving at Music City Studio two days later, his hair and beard newly trimmed as if to prepare for more conservative surroundings, Starr found himself in a very different world than the one he'd left behind. Joining Drake in the control room was Scotty Moore, Presley's original guitar player. The studio musicians gathered around him, a formidable lineup that included guitarists Jerry Reed and Charlie Daniels, were seasoned, no-nonsense, and hardly in awe of Starr's presence. "You couldn't ignore that this was a Beatle," recalled Daniels. "But the guys were not so overwhelmed, by any stretch of the imagination. They were used to working with stars. It was, 'Hi, Ringo, we're happy to have you in town—now let's work.'"

Even when work began, no one was certain that an Englishman slipping into the role of downbeat redneck would make sense. During his first cracks at tackling the songs, Starr was visibly unnerved at the sight of Drake, an army of Nashville studio pros, and a chorus of backup singers waiting on him to complete a vocal. But gradually Starr warmed up, laughing at his own stumbles and putting everyone at ease. By the end of the third day, Nashville's assembly-line system had worked once more, resulting in fifteen finished songs.

Some of them, like "Without Her" and "Waiting," were soapy, over-baked weepers that perhaps intentionally buried Starr's voice. But Drake wisely chose blue-ribbon honky-tonk songs like "I'd Be Talking All the Time" and "Beaucoups of Blues" that cannily played into Starr's happy-loser persona. The musicianship, from Reed's speedy picking on "$15 Draw" to the airtight clip-clop beat that drove "Fastest Growing Heartache in the West," was no joke, and the album featured a genuine moment of anti-Vietnam solemnity. "Silent Homecoming" detailed the arrival of a soldier returning home in a coffin. "Proudly he had served his country/In a war he didn't seem to understand," Starr sang, making a more profound political comment in song than any of his former bandmates had yet managed.

Throughout the three days, few of the musicians knew what to make of Starr's presence in the country capitol. Most had little interaction with him, and Starr declined to speak with a *Rolling Stone* reporter covering the sessions, only answering a few questions from the young son of one of the musicians. No one dared ask him about the Beatles, and the request to cover "Bridge Over Troubled Water" was ignored. "Ringo wasn't the top country singer I've ever heard," recalled Daniels. "I have to be honest—I'm a fan of Marty Robbins. But it was an admirable thing to do."

Throughout, Starr remained his affable, unpretentious self. During a break, he and the musicians gathered in an empty lot next door for a quick photo to grace the in-progress album's artwork. "He was like one of the guys," said Ben Keith, a local picker recruited to play dobro and steel guitar, "except he had an English accent." In anticipation of a possible invasion of press or Beatle fans, three plainclothes cops guarded the studio. Their presence proved unnecessary: No one unexpected or dangerous appeared at Music City the entire time Starr was there.

○ ○ ○ ○

Arthur and Vivian Janov began working their way around the large, unfurnished room at their Primal Scream Institute on Sunset Boulevard. The patients who needed immediate help and were in palpable psychic pain were the Janovs' first priority. One by one, the Janovs approached the eighteen or so reclining on pillows or sitting on the soft rugs that had replaced the couches and office furniture once in the room. The Janovs wanted the space to be comfortable and comforting—particularly for two of the patients in the room, John Lennon and Yoko Ono.

On the other side of the country from Nashville, Lennon was having an atypical summer of his own. Several times a week, he and Ono would leave their rental house on a side street in the upscale Los Angeles neighborhood of Bel Air and drive to the Institute. To the surprise of the other patients, they readily settled into the group sessions, which lasted two to three hours each and cost a more than affordable fifty dollars a session.

Lennon and Ono's most intensive conversations, though, occurred in the Janovs' private office, a small, dimly lit room with padded-wall soundproofing for optimum privacy. "The whole thing," Arthur Janov recalled, "was to facilitate a return to the past."

With only Janov at his side (Ono would have her own separate sessions with Vivian Janov), Lennon openly spoke of his personal history. According to Janov, Lennon neither screamed nor curled up in a depressed fetal position. He would sometimes cry but mainly talked—about the Beatles, the sad life of Brian Epstein, and the songs he'd begun writing for an album he'd decided to make on his own. The conversations sometimes continued at the Bel Air home. "I went into a big discourse about religion," Janov recalled of one conversation there, "and he said, 'Well, God is a concept by which we measure our pain.' He would take all these complicated things we were talking about and put them into very simple terms, which was his genius."

Since Ono was more skeptical of primal scream, her individual sessions with Vivian Janov weren't as freewheeling. "She came from a very different background," Vivian Janov said. But during their personal time together, Janov came to realize Ono wanted to use the therapy to repair problems with her and Lennon's relationship. "They both were in some kind of turmoil over their marriage," she recalled. "That may have motivated her. She wanted to mend whatever was happening between them."

The Lennons had planned on staying four months, through the end of August, but the trip was ultimately curtailed. The reasons were never clear. Janov felt Lennon thought the FBI, at Nixon's request, was monitoring him and attempting to drive him out of the country. Vivian Janov felt he and Ono simply missed home. The fact that the Janovs filmed most of their group primal sessions may have been a factor. Arthur Janov maintained the sessions with Lennon and Ono were never filmed, but that Lennon may have heard they were, and the mere thought of leaked footage was enough to send the couple scurrying back to London. "He probably went to a group where we were filming," Janov admitted, "but I made damn sure that no film ever got out. And believe me, if I had film I could have been a multimillionaire."

By late July, they were gone. As a way to acknowledge Janov's role in helping him reconnect with buried feelings and emotions, Lennon left behind a gift: a songbook of all his Beatle lyrics, each annotated with notes and cartoons. He was leaving another part of himself behind.

Before they returned to England, Lennon and Ono swung up to San Francisco. There, with Jann Wenner of *Rolling Stone*, they finally saw *Let It Be*. The movie had premiered in the middle of May in New York, then a week later in London and Liverpool. None of the Beatles attended any of the openings, leaving reporters to resort to gawking at actress Joan Collins, writer and comic Spike Milligan (co-creator of *The Goon Show*, the revered Monty Python precursor), Apple singer Mary Hopkin, and McCartney's former girlfriend Jane Asher—hardly an A-list of British celebrities. A special train hired to escort the Beatles to the Liverpool event arrived empty.

Lennon's private premiere amounted to a daytime showing at a local theater in San Francisco. What he and the general public saw was a fairly unblemished chronicle of four men struggling to connect and work together after the thrill had gone. Even in that regard, though, *Let It Be* was a letdown. The movie's dramatic highlight was a mildly testy exchange between McCartney and Harrison, as the former attempted to show the latter how to play a new song. "I'll play, you know, whatever you want me to play," Harrison said, his voice dipped in barely controlled irritation. "Or I won't play at all if you don't want me to play. Whatever it is that'll please you, I'll do it." Otherwise, *Let It Be* was largely tedious: footage of the band rehearsing, attempting to rehearse, or killing time between rehearsals. Bashing out their new material in best Cavern Club style reduced sublime songs like "Across the Universe" to clunky thuds. In the course of six short years, the ebullient Beatles of *A Hard Day's Night* had been replaced by four grumpier, scruffier men who seemed to be existing in four different worlds. In a strange way, the film's very dullness was the point: Other than McCartney, who was happy to ham it up for the camera, the others looked disinterested in being Beatles.

Lennon later told Wenner he felt "sad" watching the film. The incessant focus on McCartney and his band-leading ways—and the much smaller amount of footage devoted to Ono—irritated Lennon as well. In another sign that something had ended, the theater was almost empty.

During the first half of the summer, McCartney was at war with the other Beatles on two different, equally frustrating fronts. First were the pop charts. On June 6, *McCartney* overtook *Déjà vu* to become the best-selling album in America; *Let It Be* was stuck at number 2. But what satisfaction McCartney took from those numbers didn't last. The following week, *Let It Be* leapt over *McCartney* to commandeer the number 1 spot, where it remained for four straight weeks.

As a movie, *Let It Be* was a muddle, and its accompanying album, especially coming after the vacuum-packed cohesion of *Abbey Road*, was a bit of a mess. It promised spontaneity but delivered it only half the time, in the relatively raw performance of "I Got a Feeling" and off-the-cuff bits of folk songs like "Maggie Mae." In contrast, the violins and horns Spector had added not only to "The Long and Winding Road" but "I Me Mine" truly did sound as if they'd been inserted at a later date. The applause at the conclusion of "Get Back," along with Lennon's instantly famous quip ("I hope we've passed the audition"), were grafted onto a studio version of the song. Starting with a cover that featured separate shots of each Beatle, the album felt stitched together with very apparent thread.

Yet for all its blemishes, *Let It Be* was still remarkable. It was impossible to dismiss an album that featured McCartney's "Let It Be" and "Get Back," Lennon's "Across the Universe," and Harrison's English-manor country blues, "For You Blue." In the movie, "Two of Us" was seen and heard in a coarse electric version dominated by one of McCartney's more camera-hogging performances. The album version, framed around acoustic guitars and a gentler give-and-take between Lennon and Mc-Cartney, was a lovely, touching eulogy. Performances like that were the album's secret weapon. Far more than anything they'd done since the pre-*Sgt. Pepper* days, *Let It Be* captured the sound of the Beatles playing and interacting together as a *band*. And in another swipe McCartney couldn't have appreciated, Spector's choir on "The Long and Winding Road" actually enhanced the emotions in the song in a way that the stripped-down version hadn't.

McCartney boasted two first-rate, fully realized songs: "Maybe I'm Amazed," an expression of love and devotion that showcased both McCartney's most earnest singing and his prowess as a lead guitarist, and "Every Night," an adult lullaby that again demonstrated McCartney's innate musicality. But arriving in tandem with his jarring news to the world, the album's whimsy and offhandedness felt off-putting, even perverse. With its goofy half-songs, instrumentals, and handmade feel, the album was so slight it made "Maxwell's Silver Hammer," the *Abbey Road* trifle so detested by Lennon, seem like heavy metal. The record's very lightheartedness felt like an affront to Beatle fans everywhere: He "left" the Beatles to bang around on drums, sing along with Linda, and try to convince fans that the trivial, cloying "Junk" should have been included on the White Album?

The second combat front opened up after both albums were battling it out in stores. Two months earlier, McCartney had done the rest of the band a favor by articulating what no one else wanted to make public: The Beatles were no longer the Beatles. Yet the way in which he'd let the world in on it left a bad taste in the mouths of Harrison, Lennon, Starr, and their friends and partners. "They never expected it to be in the paper," Chris O'Dell recalled. "Things were not good, but did Paul say, 'I did an interview in the paper tomorrow?' No. They were pissed off. It changed the complexion of things a lot."

The aftershock continued in the interactions between their now separate and warring business teams. In June, John Eastman, part of McCartney's legal team, sent a letter to Allen Klein informing Klein he'd contacted a tax advisor "for an opinion on the suggested dissolution of the partnership. It would be helpful if you too could secure an opinion." Revealing how personal things were becoming, Eastman added, with veiled sarcasm, "I suggest that you put your fertile mind to work on all the aspects."

Klein despised Eastman—a trim, officious, upper-crust type—as much as Eastman disliked him. Among other things, Klein hadn't been pleased when Eastman reportedly ordered strips of black tape placed over Klein's address on the back cover of every press review copy of *McCartney*. (Eastman would neither confirm nor deny the reports.) Klein didn't respond to Eastman's June letter, but he made his feelings known in other ways. Shortly after noon on July 29, Apple's Peter Brown phoned Klein, saying, as he recalled in a later court affidavit, that McCartney "should have some regular monthly payment from the Beatles in order to meet the expenses which he would now be paying himself rather than through Beatles and Co." (Beatles and Co. was now the official name of their business organization.) The requested amount was 1,500 pounds a month. Since EMI royalties would have to go through ABKCO before they were distributed to Apple and then the Beatles, Klein denied McCartney's request.

Even within McCartney's own company, money matters were muddy. In 1968, he'd produced one of Apple's few non-Beatle hits, Welsh singer Mary Hopkin's modern-vaudeville pop song "Those Were the Days." The single had been massive, selling millions of copies around the world.

But now Apple wanted $135,575—McCartney's fee as a producer—deducted from the funds it owed the Beatles "for individual record royalties." The other Beatles were now being financially punished for one of McCartney's outside assignments.

○ ○ ○ ○

As Charles Manson stared at him, an "X" mark freshly carved into his forehead with a razor blade (the infamous swastika came later), Vincent Bugliosi prepared to tell the world why Manson had convinced some of his followers to kill. Bugliosi knew some in the legal community would think the sad-eyed deputy district attorney of Los Angeles County was crazy. But now, in the Hall of Justice on the morning of July 24, the first day of the State of California *vs.* Charles Manson and six of his followers, Bugliosi knew the time had arrived to tell the world that the Beatles indirectly had something to do with it.

Rumors about the connection between Manson and the Beatles had first circulated in February, when an unnamed source in the District Attorney's office told the *Los Angeles Times* that prosecutors in the case were examining a possible link between the killers and the White Album. The story spread when it was picked up by the *New York Post* the following day. As laid out by the source—not Bugliosi, who denied talking to anyone in the media before the trial had begun—the idea seemed too fantastical to be true. Manson envisioned a coming war between blacks and whites in which only Manson and his followers would survive. The best way to inaugurate the war was to slaughter a bunch of white people in Los Angeles and make it appear as if African Americans had committed the crimes.

The story only grew stranger as it continued. To Manson, the entire tale was laid out in the White Album. He interpreted "Honey Pie" (which beckoned someone to "sail across the ocean") as the Beatles' message to him. "Happiness Is a Warm Gun" was a communiqué to blacks telling them to prepare to rise up and fight; "Blackbird" supposedly served the same purpose. The war itself would be called "Helter Skelter," another song on the record; the battle was laid out in the chaotic noise of "Revolution 9." In another supposed sign of his bond with the Beatles, Manson claimed he'd renamed Susan Atkins "Sadie" long before the album's "Sexy Sadie." On it went—all of it, according to Bugliosi's theory, culminating in the grisly murders the previous August of eight-months-pregnant actress Sharon Tate, coffee heiress Abigail Folger, hairdresser Jay Sebring, writer Wojiciech Frykowski, teenager Steven Parent, and supermarket executive Leno LaBianca and his wife Rosemary.

When the *Times* and *Post* stories emerged, the prevailing feeling was disbelief; *Rolling Stone* ran a skeptical commentary on the reports. But Bugliosi was convinced after two Family members, Brooks Poston and Paul Watkins, told him separately about Manson's consuming obsession with the album.

In the valleys and canyons of Los Angeles, Manson's ties with rock and roll were well known; he'd spooked plenty in the music community. Two years earlier, he and members of the Family had crashed at the home of Beach Boy Dennis Wilson; Wilson went so far as to oversee demos of Manson singing his own songs. One of them, "Cease to Exist" (retitled "Never Learn Not to Love" by Wilson), wound up on a Beach Boys album. Returning to his apartment one day, Danny Kortchmar, James Taylor's lead guitarist, found his place ransacked, guitars and equipment gone. Later, Kortchmar heard the Family may have been responsible; Manson, he heard, dispatched members of his flock to rob musicians' homes so Manson would have the gear necessary to fulfill his fantasy of being a rock star. Manson had also been angry with record producer Terry Melcher, who'd expressed interest in recording an album of Manson's songs until he saw the dark side of the diminutive cult leader. Melcher had previously lived at the Cielo Drive house where the Tate murders were committed.

Near Neil Young's home in Topanga Canyon, everyone knew about Manson. While staying in the house of David Briggs, Young's friend and producer, Nils Lofgren heard the stories about Manson's crew and saw the weapons Briggs and his friends were storing in case they came by. One day, Lofgren and Bobby Morse, one of Briggs' roommates, went to Briggs' home to pick up something for a session. "Oh, no, it's that crazy bitch," Morse said, gesturing at a girl in front of the house, standing beside a car with a flat tire. The girl asked to see another of their roommates. "He's not here," Morse said curtly. "You gotta get out of here." They quickly replaced her tire, but when the girl insisted on staying, Morse told her she couldn't. "They're bad people," Morse told Lofgren after she left, "and we don't want 'em here." Months later, when Manson and Family members were arrested on charges of murder, Lofgren recognized the girl as one of the accomplices.

The chilly repercussions extended to the U.K. Just before the murders, Dan Richter was living at the home Lennon had owned before Tittenhurst. Afraid the Lennons were next in line and that the killers might discover where he lived, the Richters moved, at Lennon and Ono's invitation, to Tittenhurst.

In his opening statement in court, Bugliosi hardly minced words when relaying his theory. "The evidence will show Manson's fanatical obsession with 'Helter Skelter,' a term he got from the English musical group the Beatles," he told the jury. "Manson was an avid follower of the Beatles and believed that they were speaking to him across the ocean through the lyrics of their songs." To bolster his case, Bugliosi entered the White Album as evidence, along with a door from Spahn Ranch (where the Family had been living) on which "Helter Skelter" had been scrawled. The lyrics to the songs were read into evidence.

To Bugliosi's surprise, no public outcry greeted his theory. Leaving the courtroom that day, no reporters besieged him to ask for further details. He didn't know whether to be shocked or not. Bugliosi himself never heard from any of the Beatles or their representatives. Even if the public, press, or his fellow lawyers thought he was insane, the jury made it clear it took his theory seriously. During the trial, they requested a stereo for the deliberation room along with their own copy of the Beatles' two-LP set.

For a moment, the Beatles themselves were almost pulled into the case when Manson's defense team sent a writ to Lennon to testify. "We feel he may want to explain the lyrics," a member of the team told the Associated Press. Reached for comment by the press, Apple spokesman Derek Taylor was pithy as always. Requesting Lennon's presence at the trial, he said, was "like summoning Shakespeare to explain *Macbeth*." Besides, he added, it was McCartney, not his former band partner, who wrote "Helter Skelter." The plan ran aground when Manson's lawyers couldn't find a way to physically administer summonses to each Beatle. Apparently, none of them knew that, during the jury-selection process that began in mid June, Lennon was in their very city, undergoing primal scream therapy.

Five months later, *Rolling Stone*'s Wenner asked Lennon about the trial and Manson's interpretations of some of his songs. "He's balmy, he's like any other Beatle kind of fan who reads mysticism into it," he said of Manson. " . . . I don't know, what's 'Helter Skelter' got to do with knifing somebody? I've never listened to the words properly, it was just noise." The trial and the association was just another death knell for his former band.

Although he'd been disturbed at the thought of being disliked by the general public, McCartney was simultaneously doing his best to extricate himself from the Beatles. To move matters along, he reached out to

Lennon first. They should "let each other out of the trap," McCartney argued in a letter sent from Scotland to his one-time bandmate. "How and why?" Lennon wrote back, scribbling his words on a photograph of himself and Ono.

Barely containing his irritation, even by mail, McCartney responded with a new letter: "*How* by signing a paper which says we hereby dissolve the partnership. *Why* because there is no partnership." Lennon's last response was a postcard in which he suggested McCartney "get the other signatures and I will think about it."

The irony couldn't have been lost on McCartney. Almost a year earlier, Lennon had declared to all who could hear that he wanted out of the band—and, on top of it, during a meeting in which McCartney pressed for ways to keep them active. Now, McCartney was the one attempting to talk Lennon into taking legal action to dissolve the partnership, something Lennon wanted more than he—or so it seemed at the time.

As the two men hashed out their Morse Code messages by mail, their once beloved Apple Corps was dying a little more each day. Press Office employee and stalwart Richard DiLello was fired after an unflattering newspaper article about the company appeared in the British press. The phones barely rang. The first week of August, the Apple Press Office was officially shut down. Even though each Beatle was at work on one project or another, there was little to publicize; Lennon by then had hired his own flak. According to the London *Evening Standard,* Apple was "little more than a center for collecting their royalties and dealing with their private affairs." The building was almost empty.

Still, gathering those royalties was someone's increasingly unpleasant job. On June 28, Eastman had informed ABKCO that McCartney needed to be paid royalties for the *McCartney* album. Finally, over two months later, on September 7, ABKCO wrote to Eastman, informing him his client was owed 391,000 British pounds from EMI for U.S. sales of *McCartney.* But, as ABKCO noted, the money wasn't forthcoming since EMI didn't know whether to send the funds to ABKCO or McCartney's own company—a matter of confusion that even EMI admitted was true. "We find ourselves in an embarrassing position," an EMI representative acknowledged in a letter to Eastman. "We have, as you will appreciate, two claimants to the same money." As a result, the funds were frozen yet again.

Even though he was hunkered down in Scotland, physically removed from the business and any of his associates, McCartney grew more exasperated. Despite the public outcry that accompanied his announcement in April, he decided to be even more explicit about the state of the band. In response to a report in *Melody Maker* that a reunion was possible, McCartney sent a handwritten letter to the newspaper printed in its August 30 issue: "My answer to the question 'Will the Beatles get together again?' is no," he wrote, a far more candid answer than the one he'd given himself months before. He added it was time "to put out of its misery the limping dog of a news story which has been dragging itself across your pages for the past year."

As summer began to fade, John Eastman and his wife flew to Edinburgh, Scotland, and drove five hours south, eventually arriving at the McCartneys' farm in Campbeltown. The trip was grueling but purposeful. During many discussions and several long hikes over four days, Eastman and McCartney talked about the next step in dissolving the Beatles. Both were worried that Klein was spending their money and not paying the required taxes. They talked about McCartney doing the inevitable: suing his bandmates and Klein, how nasty the proceedings could be, and how it would make McCartney look. Always concerned about his image, McCartney was wary but increasingly exhausted.

On another clear, brisk day, standing atop a hill that overlooked a loch, McCartney came to a decision. "Sue Klein—go ahead," he told Eastman. McCartney appeared calm and relieved. The press release accompanying his album would be far from his only surprise of the year.

CHAPTER 11

Amalie Rothschild, the twenty-three-year-old staff photographer at the Fillmore East, was in the theater's second-floor office when she heard the noisy rumble outside. "Have you seen the crowd?" one of her coworkers said, beckoning her over to the window.

Looking down upon New York's Second Avenue, Rothschild saw nothing but bodies swarming over the sidewalk, spilling onto the street, and extending around the corner onto East Sixth Street. Rothschild knew Crosby, Stills, Nash & Young were having a moment in the culture; everyone seemed to own a copy of *Déjà vu*. The critics could debate its worth relative to the work they'd done with their other bands. But something about *Déjà vu*—the sense of frailty in "4 + 20" and "Helpless," the addled paranoia of "Almost Cut My Hair," the urge to escape it all in "Our House"—summed up post-Kent State America. The dark clouds that hovered over the album, the results of the band's own personal relationships and emotional tumult, also tapped into something larger and beyond their control.

Still, no one expected quite so many people to show up to buy tickets for CSNY's six consecutive nights at the Fillmore set to begin June 2. The line grew so long, the late spring heat so stifling, that Fillmore owner Bill Graham dispatched employees with water buckets and plastic cups to cool down the masses. Grabbing her camera, Rothschild talked her way onto the roof of a building across the street to commemorate the impromptu rock-fan street carnival in front of the Fillmore.

Decades before, the Fillmore East had been a vaudeville house, then a

Loew's movie theater. In March 1968, after an earlier promoter had re-named it the Village Theater, Graham took over, transforming the build-ing into the Fillmore East, the New York sibling of his Fillmore Auditorium in San Francisco. The Fillmore's plush red seats and glass chandelier were reminders of its previous lives. But in a sign of how the culture had changed, its 2,632 seats were now given over to rock and roll: two sets a night with all the accouterments of the time, including a goopy-swirly light show and the pungent, lingering scent of dope in the air. After its opening night, which featured Big Brother and the Holding Company (with Janis Joplin) and Tim Buckley, the Fillmore East would play host to nearly every major rock act of its time. In the early months of 1970 alone, the names Jimi Hendrix, the Grateful Dead, the Kinks, and Ten Years After were all displayed on the Fillmore's marquee.

Now it would be Crosby, Stills, Nash & Young's turn. At the Warner Brothers soundstage, they'd rehearsed and nailed down a set that ac-commodated everyone. During the electric set, Stills would have three songs, Young two, and Crosby and Nash one apiece. The rhythm sec-tion was itself a compromise, since Barbata was Young's drummer of choice and Fuzzy Samuels was Stills' preferred bass player. On May 29, the tour finally resumed, at the Boston Garden. The following night, at the Baltimore Civic Center, a reviewer for the *Washington Post* wrote that the foursome "generally sounded mellow." For the moment, everything was working.

By the time they rolled into the Fillmore East on the afternoon of June 2 for their first soundcheck, Bill Graham had made the band's sta-tus clear to his staff. Gathering them outside his office, Graham ex-plained that CSNY was a major act who expected to be treated a certain way. "He talked about how everything had to be special and that they certainly thought *they* were special," recalled Allan Arkush, a New York University film student who worked part time at the theater. Graham referred to the foursome as "the American Beatles" and told the staff to give CSNY anything they wanted.

Graham's point was rammed home as soon as load-in began. As they had in Europe, CSNY were still carting around their own sound system and lighting rig. Even though the Fillmore's P.A. was considered one of the sharpest in the business, the band demanded consistency from show to show. After the CSNY trucks arrived, the Fillmore staff, working with the band's road crew, went begrudgingly to work. To accommodate CSNY's mighty spotlights, holes had to be punched into the theater's light booth. To focus as much of the audience's attention on them as possible, the band passed on the Joshua Light Show—the multi-hued liquid-light backdrop for nearly every performance at the venue—and opted for a dark black curtain. Although CSNY had headlined the Fillmore immediately after Woodstock, the theater's staff sensed how much had changed in the year since. "They had one attitude before," said Arkush, "and then they came back with a hit album and had this whole other attitude. They saw themselves as stars."

At the last minute, the band requested a Persian rug for the stage, which had to be both obtained and hastily scrubbed down. Yet even that requirement wasn't easily satisfied. "We unrolled the carpet and put equipment on it, and it wasn't clean enough," Arkush recalled. In what would become a piece of Fillmore folklore, stage hand John Ford Noonan, who detested the band and everything it stood for musically and economically, ran to a closet in the back of the theater, pulled out an industrial vacuum, rushed back to the stage, and began vacuuming ferociously, all while making sarcastically reverential comments to the band and road manager Leo Makota. Mortified, Bill Graham pretended he had a phone call and darted back to his office. Even Graham, whose hardened, street-wise demeanor reflected a childhood growing up in the Bronx, didn't want to incur the wrath of CSNY.

As Nash had grown to learn, incurring each other's ire was equally possible. "Nine o'clock and all's well, so far," he told the Fillmore audience near the beginning of one night's set. Another evening, he remarked, "Hasn't it been relaxed so far?" Following an electric version of "Help-lessly Hoping" onto which Young was now adding a tingling lead guitar, Nash looked out at the audience and said, "We like that one. Didn't you like that one? We're really enjoying this. This is *fun*."

After the debacle in Denver and the firings of Greg Reeves and Dallas Taylor, Nash sounded as if he were trying to convince both fans and him-self that his band wasn't disintegrating. Structurally, at least, the shows were stable. As ever, they opened with CSN and then Young playing an un-plugged set, followed by an electric second half with Samuels and Barbata. The acoustic performances were, as always, a blend of harmony, solipsism, and clowning around—an hour of songs, dope jokes, wisecracks about their previous bands, and references to each other. On June 4, Crosby and Nash broke into "Swanee River," and Stills cracked, "You guys are crazy," to which Nash retorted "Why do you think we play with *you* two guys?" It was the type of cutesy, self-satisfied banter that had caused one earlier critic, Tony Palmer in the *London Observer*, to grouse, "It was like being at a party where everybody knew everybody except you."

Just when the shticks became almost unbearable, they'd remind the audience why everyone was there in the first place. His voice surging one minute, dropping to a hushed whisper the next, Crosby would si-lence the adoring audience with "Triad"—his rationale for having sex with as many partners as he wanted—and Nash would join him for "The Lee Shore," Crosby's ode to his boat and the sailing life. The song's melody bobbed gently, like the *Mayan* on a tranquil evening, and he and Nash's counterpoint harmonies circled around each other in ways that expressed their deepening personal bond. Young would attempt the least hip move imaginable—a medley—and pull it off; without the sonic crush of Crazy Horse behind him, "Cowgirl in the Sand," "Down by the River," and "Cinnamon Girl" were surprisingly wistful and forlorn. Alone at the piano, Stills performed a medley of his own: a stripped-down "49 Bye Byes"—one of his many Judy Collins laments from *Crosby, Stills & Nash*—and a stomping, howling update of "For What It's Worth" with an audience-baiting section that referenced Nixon, Agnew, and "the pigs." Working himself into a lather each night, Stills always threatened to blow out his voice, but the standing ovation that invariably greeted his segment was his overdue reward.

Although CSNY were ostensibly touring to support *Déjà vu*, they rarely played songs from it. Only "Teach Your Children" was a regular part of the acoustic set, and "Carry On" in the electric portion. "You gotta keep doing new things all the time," Crosby—generally sporting the fringe jacket with tassels that was his trademark—told the Fillmore audience one evening. As if they were already moving on—or didn't want to remind themselves of what went into the making of *Déjà Vu*—they instead debuted, night after night, a slew of new or as yet unrecorded songs to reflect their tremendous creative waterfall. Nash broke out "Right Between the Eyes," about an affair he'd had on Long Island during the band's early days. Young introduced "Don't Let It Bring You Down," written in London during the first CSNY show and recently cut without them for the album he'd begun in Los Angeles. Stills played "Love the One You're With" in the acoustic set and a ballad about what he saw as his new maturity, "As I Come of Age," during the electric. Even though audiences never once heard "Wooden Ships," "Marrakesh Express," or "Helpless," they nonetheless stomped and screamed themselves nuts every night.

During the first soundcheck in the empty theater, immediately after the rug incident, another new song—"Ohio"—made its New York stage premiere. When the band finished rehearsing it that afternoon, the theater's staff gathered around Young, thanking him for writing it and extolling, "Right on!" Young accepted their praise and told them why he was moved to write the song.

Before it was performed each night, the band would introduce it as "an important song" (Nash) or "sort of a downer" (Young). On cue, the Fillmore staff would all emerge from their offices to watch CSNY blast out a song that captured the uncertainty and anger of the moment. Young would begin playing the song's doomy opening nine notes, Stills joined in, and off they went. By the end—Stills jabbing away, Barbata keeping up the incessant drumbeat, and Crosby shouting out the "How many—how many more?"—the song served as both rage and release.

All week long in New York, emotions ran high onstage and off, like thermometer mercury unexpectedly rising and plummeting. Stills dedicated "49 Bye Byes" to "Clark and his mother"—Collins, who was in the audience—while Nash sang his newly written "Simple Man," about his breakup with Mitchell, as Mitchell sat watching him in the theater. During the Fillmore nights and the remainder of the tour, Nash couldn't bring himself to play "Our House," afraid he would burst into tears while singing a song about his now-finished life with Mitchell.

On the second night, June 3, Bob Dylan—who'd moved from Woodstock to nearby MacDougal Street—decided to see what everyone was talking about. Slipping into the Fillmore, he took a seat in the sound booth to avoid recognition.[1] Wanting to impress him, Stills played four songs during his segment, including "4 + 20" and a rare solo acoustic take on Buffalo Springfield's "Bluebird." But those were two more songs than everyone had agreed upon. In the break before the electric second half, the band trudged quietly up the Fillmore's winding stairs to the small, funky dressing rooms on the upper floors. All four of them, along with Roberts, Barbata and Samuels, piled into one room and closed the door, and Nash began lacing into Stills: "Who do you think you are,

---

1. Six days later, Crosby accompanied Dylan to Princeton, where Dylan was given an honorary doctorate as he was "approaching the perilous age of thirty," the citation read. "He said it was gonna happen and I said, 'Can I come with you?' He said, 'Sure, but I don't know if I wanna go and do that.' I said, 'Let's go see.' It didn't turn out well at all because they wanted him to wear a cap and gown. He was extremely unimpressed with them all."

doing another song?" Crosby and Young stood with their heads down, silently supportive of Nash's tongue-lashing. Stills, holding a beer can, said nothing. To signify his sputtering rage, he kept squeezing the can until the foam spilled out over his right hand and onto the floor.

A terrified Barbata thought the band would dissolve then and there, before he'd played more than a handful of shows with them. After a few moments of awkward silence, the drummer finally said, "Hey, let's go play!" Roberts quickly piped in: "Yeah!" With that, everyone filed back out for the second, especially electric set. On their way to the stage, they had to step over Bill Graham and Ron Stone, tussling on the floor over the band's last-minute insistence on filming the shows for the documentary.

The volatility was never-ending. Exactly a week after Nash had castigated Stills, the band played the Spectrum in Philadelphia. One of the visitors to their individual Sheraton hotel rooms was Joel Bernstein, a newly graduated local high school student and nascent photographer who'd already shot Young and Joni Mitchell. Only eighteen, the effusive, affable Bernstein showed up at the Sheraton with a stack of prints he'd taken of the band at the Fillmore shows. In his room, Young selected one of Bernstein's shots, of him walking down the street in New York, to be the cover of his next album, *After the Gold Rush*.

Talking to Bernstein, Stills had an urgent question: "Hey, where can you play pool around here?" Bernstein mentioned his parents' house in nearby Elkins Park, just outside Philadelphia. To the teenager's shock, a limo carrying Stills and Nash appeared at the Bernsteins' three-story granite home after the show. Both hung out in Bernstein's bedroom—one of his photos of Mitchell hanging on the wall behind Nash—before all retreated to the basement to shoot pool and smoke and snort various substances. Hearing the noise, Bernstein's father rang down on the intercom: What was all the commotion? *It's just my friends from the concert*, Bernstein replied, *they came over to play pool, hope that's okay!* Still curious, Stanley Bernstein, wearing his pajamas and bathrobe, appeared, introducing himself to his son's pool friends. Luckily for his son, he either didn't notice or recognize all the white powder left over on the pool table.

As dawn arrived and their respective highs still lingered, Charles John Quarto—a bearded, gentle-mannered poet whom Nash had met in New York and who was invited along for several stops on the tour—joined Stills, Nash, and Bernstein (and a small film crew hired to document the tour) as they strolled through a nearby park. "Stephen and I sat on this huge tree trunk," remembered Quarto. "He sang and I recited for forty-five minutes. I remember Nash's face when he was looking at that. It was a beautiful thing." After their Fillmore clash, Nash and Stills had again found common ground. That week, *Billboard*'s review of one of the Fillmore sets appeared. The performance, the magazine wrote, "reversed any trend of concern and disappointment as they strummed and harmonized in a new maturity." The magazine added they had a promising future, "should CSNY stay together long enough."

Whether it was the Fillmore or any of the arenas CSNY would be hitting that summer, Ron Stone always found himself in the same place as soon as the last notes of "Find the Cost of Freedom," the traditional show closer, faded. To collect the nightly earnings, Stone would march into the venue's office and begin tallying the receipts and expenditures with the promoter. Some evenings, the work was over in minutes; other times, when the promoter would present a list of his expenses and attempt to deduct them from the band's earnings, negotiations could last until dawn. Sometimes the promoter would have a few seedy thugs standing nearby. Stone quickly caught onto the game. "Leo, did you hear *this?*" he'd call out, a signal for Makota to walk into the room. As Stone learned, the sight of the tall, burly Makota always made the tallying run a bit smoother on the band's end.

When all was done, Stone would leave with as much as $25,000 in cash—"like a drug deal every night," he recalled—and stick the envelope in the inner pocket of his jacket. If the shows piled up and he didn't have time to deposit the bills in a local bank, he'd simply pray no one knew he was walking around with about $100,000 in cash. Backstage one night, Crosby told Stone he looked pale and nervous. Stone said nothing: He didn't want Crosby to know he'd misplaced one of those overstuffed envelopes—which, to his relief, was soon recovered by a crew member.

That such large amounts of cash were floating around was just part of the changes in the economics of rock and roll. When Bill Graham gathered his staff around at the beginning of CSNY's Fillmore East run, he laid that topic on the line as well. "He'd talk about how the business was changing and how much of the money you'd have to give away to bands," recalled Arkush. Graham saw in his own Fillmore office how the business of rock was transforming, with CSNY a telling example. At Woodstock the previous August, they'd been paid $10,000, $5,000 less than Janis Joplin and the Band. But with two top 10 albums under their belts, CSNY could command more, as their managers Elliot Roberts and David Geffen well knew. Thanks to their maneuvering, CSNY would now demand over double that amount a night—and, more importantly, an unheard-of 60 percent of the gate (the money earned after expenses were recouped) compared to less than half, as other acts received. Around the country, ticket prices for the tour ran as high as $6.50. In Minneapolis, an ad-hoc group threatened a boycott when tickets were advertised at $10 each. Yet none of those protests deterred fans from flocking to see the band.

CSNY weren't alone in demanding a larger bite of the grosses. "Artists could do the math," recalled Kip Cohen, the Fillmore East's managing director. "If the gross was over $45,000, the act would get an extra

$1,000. They caught on very quickly. *Everybody* caught on very quickly, in a matter of months." Manhattan promoter Ron Delsener complained in *Billboard* that he was having trouble signing bands for his Schaefer Music Festival in Central Park. Delsener was offering a flat $2,500 a show, good money a few years before but now considered petty change. In particular, he cited Simon and Garfunkel as one example of an act that "asked so much money that I cannot even approach them."

During the first half of the year, American and world economies had bounced up and down; in the States, fears of a recession were taking hold. But the music business was generating plenty of cash, thanks to rock and roll. Firms like the William Morris Agency began hiring special booking agents to handle rock tours. In midsummer, Columbia head Clive Davis announced his label had had the best six months in its history—thanks in large part to Simon and Garfunkel—and predicted that total sales for 1970 would top those of 1969. (In the end, he was right: the figure wound up being $15 million.) A new era of consolidations was on the horizon: The year before, the Kinney Corporation, a former parking garage and cleaning-services company, had bought Warner Brothers and, in 1970, added Elektra to its stable. When those labels were merged with Atlantic, the all-powerful Warner Music Group was created.

Bill Graham sensed the financial power was shifting from promoters and their venues to the artists and their managers. To Fillmore employees, the crowds seemed increasingly too drugged up to notice anyway. Ushers would sometimes have to direct concertgoers to different seats by telling them that, no, their ticket was not blue but another color, which meant a different section.

In such an atmosphere, the Fillmore East was doomed. Acts who'd headlined there over the previous year, like the Doors and Led Zeppelin, had moved on to arenas. Graham couldn't match the money or even the amenities. At the Fillmore, backstage catering amounted to pizzas or deli sandwiches that crew members would run out and buy; soda bottles were set up in ice-filled garbage cans.

In his office, an increasingly disillusioned Graham, with help from Cohen, began working on an open letter to his industry. In it, he would announce the two Fillmores were "fighting for their very existence. . . . Economics have taken the music from the clubs, ballrooms and concert halls to the larger coliseums and festivals." (When the Fillmore opened in 1968, tickets were $3, $4, and $5; by 1970, the prices had increased by fifty cents, but only after much in-house debate.) Graham warned there were "not enough acts" to replace the ones who'd moved on to larger venues like Madison Square Garden and the Los Angeles Forum.

The finished letter ran as a full-page ad in the June 27 issue of *Billboard*. "It was a statement that had to be made, that the corporate mentality was coming in," Cohen recalled. "People could smell something was happening and it was time to cash in. It was pretty clear that the culture was changing." Graham and Cohen sat back and awaited reaction within the industry. Surely, someone other than them had to agree.

For all the disorder onstage and off, Crosby, Stills, Nash & Young appeared untouchable as the tour carried on. By the weekend of July 4, two of their singles were on the radio: "Teach Your Children" and, despite periodic problems with airplay over its content, "Ohio." After New York came shows at arenas in Philadelphia, Detroit, Portland (Oregon), Oakland, Los Angeles, and Chicago. Flying from city to city on commercial airlines, they pushed whatever envelope was available. Crosby would walk into airports smoking a joint, but the entourage of handlers, bandmates, road crew, and women around him made it hard for officials to determine the source of the odor. Crosby would eventually ditch the stash, but only when he arrived at the gate.

Yet just as the country seemed to be blowing a fuse as the summer dragged on, so did its leading rock and roll band. Between the ongoing flow of coke and pot, Crosby and Stills frequently butted heads on everything from repertoire to preferred substances. Backstage, Stone asked Samuels if the bass player, still adjusting to rock and roll lunacy, was okay; after all, he was so subdued. "I didn't worry if rock and roll guys were squabbling," Samuels recalled. "It didn't bother me because I was so accustomed to being without." Still, he told Stone he'd been taking acid every night to calm his nerves.

Even Crosby wasn't always immune. "People do the damnedest tricks on my head, man," Crosby told *Rolling Stone*'s Ben Fong-Torres after a Hollywood waitress with false teeth offered him a blowjob if he gave her tickets to one of CSNY's shows. "Things happen to me every day and I can't handle it."

The shows became symbolic of the band's internal schism. During the acoustic sets, Crosby, Nash, and Young would often huddle together in one combination or another to play one of their songs, while Stills' solo spot was always companionless. (The exception was "Love the One You're With," making its debut before Stills' recording of it had been completed; the audiences always chuckled along appreciatively when Nash introduced the title.) "There was David, Graham, and Neil, and then me—it was *Sybil* on wheels," Stills said, referencing the movie starring Sally Field as a woman who suffers from extreme multiple-personality disorder. At the rescheduled Chicago show, the critic from the *Chicago Tribune* noted Stills appeared to be "brooding" by the side of the stage.

As Nash feared, the group-therapy session in Los Angeles in May had only been a temporary fix. "We thought Stephen might use the opportunity to pull himself together a little more," Nash recalled. "And it appeared at first that he did. So we were willing to give it another shot. But it was obvious he hadn't changed at all." Stills saw it differently. As with *Déjà vu* sessions, he felt the problem lay in the music. He found the band sloppy, the shows drifting toward what he called "Grateful Dead bedlam." Stills had no interest in the type of free-form, jazz-influenced improvisational music Crosby loved. "It never had that craftsmanship quality," Stills recalled of the stage shows that summer. "It was like the Beatles' *Let It Be*: 'Let's stop doing that creative stuff in the studio and just play as a band.' But everybody was so mad at each other that they couldn't. You could feel this angst. Dealing with David and Graham became like dealing with the Irish; they didn't remember anything but the grudges." Onstage, Stills seemed to connect most with Samuels. "Me and Stephen had a different kind of bond," Samuels recalled. "We knew about playing with each other. A lot of those [Crosby, Nash and Young] songs, they're so sleepy. They weren't good performing songs."

The shows retained their share of raggedness. Nash's "Pre-Road Downs," the opener of the electric set, chugged along harder than the studio version, but could also be woozy, and the harmonies on other songs could be spotty. Hired to fly to New York and Chicago and tape the sets for a live album, engineer Bill Halverson understood part of the reason why: They'd often look at each other while singing, their mouths wandering away from the microphones in the process. Stills himself sang "Carry On" off-mic one night. From behind his drums, Barbata would sometimes hear front-row audience members complaining the band didn't sound like their records.

The contretemps between Stills and Young spilled out during jams on "Carry On" and "Southern Man" that each stretched out to close to fifteen minutes a night. ("Another song that's bound to get us in trouble," Crosby announced one night before "Southern Man," which again caught a moment: That summer, Southern senators strongly resisted an extension of the Voting Rights Act that made it easier for blacks and those eighteen and over to vote.) Rarely seeing each other when not in the arenas, Stills and Young would finally engage in conversation onstage, staring each other down with their instruments, slinging notes back and forth like tennis players.

Both men knew the spectacle benefit of these moments. "It was *entertaining*," Stills said. "Were John Coltrane and Miles Davis dueling? No. We'd go off and come back to the original theme. We'd try to imitate what the other guy was playing. It worked out pretty well." ("It's what the fans dug," recalled *Rolling Stone* writer Ben Fong-Torres, who saw a number of CSNY shows that period. "They knew the entertainment value of that.") When the two men were getting along, their to-and-fros had a playful, fluid quality. When they weren't, the mood was different: Young would come out of nowhere with a bee-sting solo and Stills would respond with a rushed barrage of notes, as if they were having a contentious argument with their instruments. Stills felt they were goaded into the exchanges by their business associates: "'He's a better guitar player!' It was destructive. I'd say, 'Neil, are we doing that or not?' And he'd say, 'No, we're just trading off.'"

Whether the exchanges were intentionally theatrical or not, CSNY had no choice but to hold it together and knew it. At the Fillmore, one particularly fervent audience during their weeklong run wouldn't let them leave without playing an additional encore. Backstage, they decided to resurrect "Woodstock." The song was never easy to pull off live; recreating the dense, multitracked harmonies of the studio version required a pinpoint accuracy they rarely managed over the din of electric guitars and drums (and inefficient stage monitors). Preparing to play the number again, Nash introduced it as "a song we haven't done for a long, long time." By then, the relatively joyous months of 1969—when a press release trumpeted them as the group "that brought happiness and laughter back to rock & roll"—seemed to reflect another lifetime.

"Hey, Crosby, someone made this for you," Nash said, sticking his head into his bandmate's Minneapolis hotel room on the afternoon of July 9. A bare-chested Crosby was lying in bed, puffing on a joint while chatting on the phone with Dylan. Several girls swirled around. Like Stills, Crosby was reveling in the applause and stature he'd felt were too long in coming. For Stills, success compensated for barely knowing his mother while growing up; for Crosby, fame and its rewards made up for the devastation of Hinton's loss. As Stone recalled, "David drowned his sorrows in some of the most beautiful women I've ever seen."

Nash tossed Crosby his gift: a pillow in the shape of a pistol, made from an American flag. Crosby chuckled and stuck it behind his back while he continued talking on the phone. Henry Diltz, who'd arrived in Minneapolis the day before, pulled out his ever-present camera and Crosby, in a playful mood, inhaled a joint and put the pillow gun against his right temple.

Crosby was merely being mischievous, but the gesture also bespoke a prevalent feeling about the tour by the time the band flew into Minneapolis for its final show. Diltz himself had been waiting over a month to fly out from Los Angeles to shoot the band. When the tour had resumed in Boston, he was poised to leave with them to snap on-the-road shots for a collection of sheet music. But the constant unrest kept delaying his departure. "I am once again in limbo over this tour," he wrote in his journal on May 26.

Diltz finally received word to fly out to Minneapolis and, upon his arrival, sensed a mixture of weariness and unease. "They had things between them, feelings good and bad," he recalled. "There was a little apprehension, a little unfriendliness. There were various energies between people." Before the show at the fourteen-thousand-seat Met Arena that had originally been set for May 2, everyone congregated in Roberts' room for an end-of-tour banquet with special guests like Young's irascible mother, Rassy, and Charles John Quarto. Before the show at the arena, CSNY gathered in a backstage bathroom and shared a joint. Starting with "Suite: Judy Blue Eyes," they played their standard set with few hitches. By then, there was no point in scratching any open wounds onstage; they were almost done.

When the show finished, all of them, along with crew and management, took over a room at the Radisson Hotel for a late-night poker game. They were newly wealthy men and unafraid to show it; over the course of the night, hundreds of dollars were tossed onto the table. Everybody was having a relaxed time until someone began banging on the door. Stone went over, pulled it open, and was face-to-face with a persistent fan. Stone told him to go away; the band needed privacy. He closed the door and returned to the table.

Another knock. Again, the same fan; again, the same do-not-disturb request. Stone slammed the door and returned to the game. Finally, a third knock. This time, Stone didn't want a conversation. Unlatching the door, he threw a punch and slammed it shut. He didn't even look to see how much damage he may have caused.

Everyone should have been aghast. Instead, they all laughed, a collective release after a particularly bumpy year. "Tremendous relief, relief beyond nothing you could imagine," recalled Stone. They'd finished the tour and wrapped up their obligations to management, promoters, and themselves. "We'd completed something without it going off the rails," recalled Nash. Yet even Nash knew how perilously close they'd come to doing just that.

CHAPTER 12

"Steve Stills got busted," James Taylor said, squatting by the side of Highway 101 outside Tucumcari, in northeast New Mexico, as *Rolling Stone* reporter Michael Goodwin looked on.

"Oh, no," said a startled Laurie Bird, whose brown shag framed a prematurely wise face. "Was it for cocaine?"

"Well, they *found* cocaine," Taylor replied with laconic terseness.

After several postponements, *Two-Lane Blacktop*, Taylor's feature-film debut, finally began shooting in and around Los Angeles the first week of August. The delays were rooted in casting and cash. Director Monte Hellman had been intrigued by the idea of recruiting non-actors; during the same time he auditioned Taylor, he also took a meeting with another, even manlier singer-songwriter, a Rhodes scholar named Kris Kristofferson. (Kristofferson and Taylor had both performed afternoon sets at the 1969 Newport Folk Festival, and Kristofferson recognized another hunky songwriting talent when he saw one.) Hellman was still considering full-time actors as well, like James Caan, a veteran of TV dramas and roles in Francis Ford Coppola and Robert Altman movies. In the end, he wanted Sam Shepard, a young East Village playwright with a dash of acting experience on his résumé. But when it looked as if his first son would be born during shooting, Shepard backed out. Hellman settled for his second choice—Taylor—but further delays ensued when the original backers bailed out. Hellman and his producer, Michael Laughlin, scrambled to find a new home for their project—eventually winding up with Universal—but as a result, the filming schedule was delayed once more.

The caravan of cast and crew had just arrived in the Albuquerque area when the Stills news broke. On August 14, local paramedics had raced to a hotel in La Jolla, California, after someone reported the sight of what looked like a sick guest crawling around a hallway. When the fire and police departments showed up, they found the man lying on his bed, seemingly having a seizure and talking incoherently. In the room next door was a naked woman; strewn about the suite were cocaine and barbiturates. Stills was promptly arrested. In the middle of the night, he called management assistant Ron Stone at home. Deciding he didn't want to drive three hours down to La Jolla—and thinking that perhaps his client would learn a thing or two after a night in jail—Stone decided not to post bail. Stills spent the night in a cell and was bailed out by Stone the next morning on a $2,500 bond. "I took some pills, got blown away, and blew my cool, and it ended up like I was ODing on pills," Stills recounted later to *Circus* magazine writer Michael Watts. " . . . I thought one of the people didn't have their key to the room and the couple across the hall were standing there and went, 'Aaargh!' I don't remember anything else until the lights went on in the room and it was full of policemen."

Few were surprised by the news. Drugs were rampant in the music business and within the CSNY camp in particular. From their managers to now former drummer Dallas Taylor, everyone knew it was best to steer clear of David Crosby's omnipresent pot stash—so potent they would feel debilitated after only a few puffs. The cocaine use that ran rampant during the *Déjà vu* sessions had become a nearly everyday indulgence, a quick stimulant with seemingly no bad consequences. "Wanna pack your nose?" someone in the band or crew would invariably ask drummer Johnny Barbata just before they walked onstage. Even during those times when he didn't indulge, Barbata would notice the changes onstage, the tempos speeding up as the high kicked in.

By summer, cocaine use beyond rock and roll had risen dramatically.

In January, the government's two-year-old Bureau of Narcotics and Dangerous Drugs first reported that the drug was making major headway into the United States: "The kids are beginning to learn that it's pretty much like speed," one agent announced. The bureau identified Chile as the largest supplier (the coca leaves themselves originated in Peru and Bolivia) and Miami as the most frequent portal of entry. In one major raid in that city, also in January 1970, agents seized twenty-three pounds of pure cocaine—more than the total amount seized in the entire country only ten years before.

Although confiscations quadrupled by the end of the '60s, the coke industry's profit margins soared—the highest-quality grade cost $50 a gram—and the smugglers became more devious. They began sneaking it into the United States by way of bras, belts, specially designed compartments in luggage—or, in one massive shipment from Paraguay in June, wrapping the drug packets like Christmas gifts. Combined with a rise in heroin trafficking (a major bust in June involved a shipment of almost two-thousand pounds from France), the shift was ominous and ugly, the stoner-world equivalent of the difference between Woodstock and Altamont.

Taylor himself wasn't immune to such indulgences. Playing before almost three thousand people at the Shady Grove Music Fair Theater in Maryland, dressed in a T-shirt and shoeless, he impressed Carl Bernstein, then the *Washington Post*'s music critic before his stint as a political reporter. In his review, Bernstein praised Taylor's "remarkable voice, full of grace and tenderness yet retaining just the slightest suggestion of a hard edge." But like many, Bernstein didn't know how hard or edgy Taylor was. After his breakdown in 1969, culminating with his stay at Austin Riggs, Taylor appeared to have fought his own recurring struggle with hard drugs to a draw. But by the summer, a combination of professional limbo, dope for the taking, and a family separation had caught up with him. The previous year, his mother, Trudy, had filed for divorce from Isaac. *Sweet Baby James* was making minor headway on the charts yet remained stuck in neutral. Albums like *Let It Be*, *Bridge Over Troubled Water*, and *Déjà vu* loomed above it. In flux and living in an atmosphere that invited experimentation—"People looked at you strangely if you *weren't* getting high," he said—Taylor began using once again.

Looking to move his client into larger venues, Taylor's manager Peter Asher had taken a gamble by booking Taylor into Carnegie Hall for two shows on June 12; each paid $5,000, Taylor's highest fees to date. To their surprise, ticket sales were brisk. A few months before, a folk legend of a previous era, Phil Ochs, had played the same austere venue, but with a more audacious idea: donning a gold lamé suit and singing Elvis, Buddy Holly, and country songs along with the protest and social commentary songs he'd written so effortlessly in the '60s. To Ochs, the revolution would only succeed if the working class and the counterculture melded. For his effort, he was booed. By the end of his second show, Ochs had won over the crowd, but the damage to his audience and psyche had been done.

No such reaction greeted Taylor during the first of his two Carnegie sets. Strolling onstage, blushing at the cheers that greeted him, he sank down into a chair and ambled through his standard set: songs from his two albums interspersed with Goffin-King's "Up on the Roof," Joni Mitchell's "For Free," and his brother Livingston's "In My Reply." "Possibly because these taut times demand it, Taylor has been hailed as a bridge over troubled waters," wrote a *Billboard* critic. "He is in a place where young people can go and be soothed, clarified and cradled."

To celebrate, Margaret Corey, one of the women swirling around Taylor, smuggled hash backstage at the hallowed hall. "It was painful and it was risky," Taylor recalled of the period. "I risked my life for *years* on drugs and also threatened other people around me or put them at risk. It just felt like an amazing release, like it solved all kinds of problems for me."

When the production for *Two-Lane Blacktop* settled down for a few days in Santa Fe, director Hellman decided on another last-minute touch of realism. He cajoled screenwriter Rudy Wurlitzer into taking a small role as a hothead conned into a race by Taylor's character, the Driver. Wurlitzer and Taylor filmed one scene together, then another in which Wurlitzer's character and his wife (played by Hellman's own wife, Jaclyn Hellman) argued in a restaurant. Sitting silently at the bar, glancing over as they argued, was Taylor's Driver. Afterward, Taylor admitted to Wurlitzer he was wasted—the bartender was serving him actual drinks during the scene.

When Hellman had first broached the idea of hiring Taylor for the role, Wurlitzer was concerned. He too had attended Milton Academy, albeit ten years before Taylor, and had heard stories about Taylor's personal demons and mental state. Taylor's lack of acting chops also set off a few alarm bells. But in the context of the movie and a new wave of filmmaking, no one else was particularly concerned. *Two-Lane Blacktop* would attempt to defy convention at every step. Taylor was hardly the only new or non-actor on the set. Bird, a teenage model with no acting experience, was cast as a runaway called the Girl, and the Beach Boys' rakishly handsome Dennis Wilson was the Driver's sidekick, the Mechanic. Balancing them out were professionals like Warren Oates, as a GTO driver who competes with Taylor and Wilson, and Harry Dean Stanton, a craggy-faced character actor twice Taylor's age.

The plot barely amounted to one: Two unnamed drifters played by Wilson and Taylor make a living conning drivers into car races they inevitably lose, allowing the drifters to make quick cash before moving on to the next town (and victim). They're committed to no one but themselves. Eventually, they meet a girl, played by Bird, who joins up with them and eventually comes between them. The Driver and Mechanic decide to race GTO (who yearns to be a dashing man's man but can't pull it off) to Washington, D.C. The winner of the race will walk away with the other's car. To ensure his project would truly feel like a road movie, Hellman took the filming to the highway. After shooting in Los Angeles in early August, cast and crew would travel across country, touching down in Santa Fe, Little Rock, Memphis, and other towns before ending in Maryville, North Carolina.

Very intentionally, *Two-Lane Blacktop* wouldn't even remotely resemble any of the year's major hits. It would be miles removed from *Airport*, a soap opera set in the sky, and *Love Story*, the maudlin melodrama about a young couple who are getting along fabulously until the beautiful young girl dies of leukemia. *Two-Lane Blacktop* wouldn't turn warfare into satire and buffoonery—as *Little Big Man*, *Catch-22*, and *M*A*S*H* had done—nor would it romanticize it, as *Patton* and the Pearl Harbor epic *Tora! Tora! Tora!* did. It wasn't a brazen attempt to tap into Vietnam protests at home, like *Getting Straight* and its ilk, nor was it an over-the-top portrait of anti-hippie violence, like *Joe*.

But in the year after *Easy Rider*, Hollywood was more than willing to fork over production dollars to left-of-center filmmakers who wanted to put their visions onscreen. As long as the kids in the movie houses didn't mind, the movies needn't have traditional heroes, storylines, or endings. Flush with his success as *Easy Rider*'s director and costar, Dennis Hopper was ensconced in Peru, taking vast amounts of drugs while filming *The Last Movie*, a convoluted movie-within-a-movie.

Universal had ponied up $850,000 for *Two-Lane Blacktop*, filmed almost simultaneously as Hopper's film. In a departure from convention that was all his own, Hellman and his movie would focus on stasis: elliptical conversations, antiheroes, and cinematography that dwelled on the desert and open road as much as on dialogue. For Wurlitzer, the film was about the country's restlessness and what he called "the end of the frontier." In rewriting the script, he'd changed the itinerary of the race, making it start out West and head east; after all, everyone knew the California dream of the early decade was dead.

The race itself wouldn't even be completed. The characters would give up midway across the country, as if there was no point to the contest anyway. Instead of a traditional plot resolution, the film would simply *stop*—the last image would look like a reel of film catching fire. *Two-Lane Blacktop* would be the ultimate road movie and, with its enigmatic plot and irregular casting and character names, a new kind of film. Despite his initial doubts, Wurlitzer came to realize Taylor was ideal for the role. "James seemed to represent a lost and bewildered innocence," he recalled, "with no apparent attachments to the past or to a defined cultural imprint." Whether he wanted to or not, Taylor would embody a newly aimless time.

Despite his alternately deadpan and irritable screen test a few months before, Taylor was thrilled when he'd been offered the role of the Driver. Other than Asher, who had his doubts, most of Taylor's friends were encouraging. "He's the next Gary Cooper," Peter Asher's girlfriend (and soon-to-be-wife) Betsy gushed to Toni Stern, Taylor's partner that spring. To Hellman, Taylor was a natural, and the director was bemused by the way Taylor always seemed prepared in the early days of filming.

Between takes, Taylor also began writing new songs. The time had come to prepare for the follow-up to *Sweet Baby James*, and Taylor had to start from scratch. Sitting in open fields while Hellman set up shots, he'd pull out his guitar and let new melodies and words flow out of him. One of the songs, "Hey Mister, That's Me up on the Jukebox," directly addressed the pressure to produce; a reference to "squeezing water from a stone" was aimed directly at Asher. ("I was trying to make him finish the songs," Asher admitted.) "Riding on a Railroad" and "Highway Song," both inspired by his experience on the traveling set, also tumbled out. The most gorgeous and emotive song to emerge from Taylor's guitar that summer, though, was "You Can Close Your Eyes," a lullaby for a visitor to the set.

Taylor had met Joni Mitchell the year before, when he'd opened for her at the Unicorn coffeehouse in Boston in March 1969. "I'm sure Joan was *most* interested," recalled then-boyfriend Graham Nash, who accompanied Mitchell to the show and even snapped a photo of her and Taylor meeting for the first time. Taylor and Mitchell then both performed at the Newport Folk Festival the following summer.

At the time, each was romantically entangled to one degree or another, Mitchell with Nash, Taylor with Margaret Corey. But by the summer of 1970, each was available. Mitchell had broken up with Nash, and Taylor's romance with Stern, who wasn't taken with life on the road or being considered Taylor's appendage, had run aground. On July 26, only a few weeks before *Two-Lane Blacktop* began shooting, Taylor and Mitchell met again, at the Mariposa Folk Festival outside Toronto, and this time, they hooked up.

Although Mitchell had far more experience in the music business and was four and a half years older, she and Taylor looked and felt like peers, and they weren't afraid to let their mutual attraction be known to everyone. In one of the first signs their affair was serious, Mitchell flew to the Arizona set for the filming. She knit Taylor a green-and-blue sweater, played guitar, and sang in the fields; they shared a motel room, inviting cast and crew for sing-alongs and bottles of wine. Taylor appeared visibly relieved by her presence. As he told *Rolling Stone*'s Goodwin, "Now I have something to do with my nights."

"I don't wanna hear about it," Taylor, as the Driver, snapped at Oates' GTO during one scene.

"What do you mean—you don't wanna hear about it?" Oates' GTO retorted.

"It's not my problem," the Driver said, dismissively.

The irritation in Taylor's voice wasn't always scripted. Mitchell eventually had to leave, chronicling her mixed feelings in "This Flight Tonight," and the movie resumed its own style of cross-country tour. As the filming dragged on for forty-two days into the beginning of fall, Taylor found the process increasingly torturous. The lengthy lags between takes were foreign to him, and he'd grow annoyed when Wilson and Bird hadn't memorized their lines. (He would also look irked when Bird would periodically start singing.) In order to maintain a sense of spontaneity, Hellman only showed his cast one page of script at a time; as a result, Taylor often felt at sea.

Drugs and moments of craziness helped alleviate the boredom and occasional stress for everyone. Taylor and Oates did mescaline. Hellman wound up having an affair with Bird, despite the presence of his wife on set. Taylor had to endure on-set acting lessons. ("They had workshop classes at the beginning of the day, 'be a tree' and that kind of bullshit," Asher recalled.) Sometimes Taylor would ignore Hellman's request to return for another take while he continued working on a chord change or a lyric.

On camera, Taylor delivered his lines with a sullen numbness, conveying emotions by way of a haunted stare or the slightest flicker of body language. To express his dissatisfaction, he would do much the same when the cameras were off. After a reporter showed up one day, Hellman convinced Taylor to join him for an interview at a local diner. Wurlitzer did most of the chatting; Taylor mostly stared down at his shoes. At one point, Wurlitzer and the writer became aware of the smell of burning flesh—and both beheld Taylor putting out a cigarette on the back of his hand. The interview was never completed. "People were telling him what to do, and he wasn't used to that," Stern recalled. "The side of his experience is that he was the creator. Maybe the way he came across on screen was the way he felt about it."

Taylor would periodically call Asher from wherever they were filming to complain about the workshops or having to move to a new town almost every day. "James had a hard time," recalled Wurlitzer. "He was never fully at ease. He was very disoriented and bored and frustrated. But he got through it." Sometimes, though, just barely. For the film's climactic race, Taylor sat behind the wheel, not realizing the car was already in reverse. When he pulled the clutch and stepped on the gas, the car jolted backward, almost flattening some of the cast. Everyone, including Taylor, was shaken. "We were lucky," Hellman said, "that no one was run over."

"That was a nightmare," Taylor told Asher when filming wrapped up. "I don't want to do that again." Asher agreed that movie stardom was probably not in his client's future. ("Management error," Asher conceded.) But no one was too troubled. Nearly six months after the release of *Sweet Baby James*, the music side of Taylor's career appeared to be finally catching fire.

The rental car pulled onto the campus of Beaver College, outside Philadelphia. In the driver's seat was Carole King. Next to her, his head down, nodding off for one reason or another, was Taylor.

The filming for *Two-Lane Blacktop* completed, Taylor had returned to the road for another string of college gigs. Together with Walter Robinson, an African American bass player who knew him from Martha's Vineyard, Taylor and King drove to and from campuses around the Northeast and Midwest. King's first album under her own name—an overly eclectic collection of pop and quasi-psychedelia called *Writer*, which featured Taylor on guitar—had just been released. But as with *Sweet Baby James*, sales were initially modest. Whatever money they stood to make would come from the road.

On their drives, Taylor, King, and Robinson were often the only ones in the car; no record company personnel, managers, or security types were around. Sitting in the backseat this weekend was a writer from the prestigious *New York Times Magazine*—Susan Braudy, who'd known several of the Weather Underground during their college days and had visited the site of the brownstone explosion in March. At the dawn of her career in publishing, Braudy had been contacted by an editor at the magazine who'd summered in Martha's Vineyard and had heard the positive murmur about Taylor. Although the newspaper hadn't run a review of Taylor's Gaslight show six months earlier, the *Times Magazine* had decided to cover this rising star.

Braudy had firsthand evidence of Taylor's growing fan base as soon as she arrived on the Beaver campus with King, Taylor, and Robinson. As they strolled across the lawns and into the gymnasium where Taylor's show would take place, girls began pointing and screaming. (Stern had experienced these episodes herself with Taylor in the spring. Walking into a venue alongside him, she was stopped by one female fan. "Are you with James Taylor?" she asked. When Stern nodded yes, the girl swooned, "You are *so* lucky.") Braudy also observed the ways in which Taylor knew how to work his particular brand of unassuming, anti-star charisma. Escorted into a basement that would serve as a de facto dressing room, Taylor found a corner and curled up in a batting cage as everyone watched—a solitary moment that also served to effectively make everyone notice him.

Once the show began, the girls in the gym were indifferent to King, occasionally booing her. They wanted the headliner and no one else. Once Taylor ambled onstage, they relaxed immediately. He told his usual self-deprecating jokes or shaggy-dog stories as if he were a modern counterculture update of Will Rogers. Then he closed his eyes and began singing. Neither Braudy nor the girls in the crowd had heard a voice quite like that, soft and gentle yet masculine and far from effeminate. His phrasing was both casual and folksy but firm and precise. Even when he'd make a reference to the coming apocalypse—telling another college audience it was coming and he was considering buying land in Nova Scotia when it arrived—few were unnerved.

Braudy would glance around the halls and see girls crying as he sang. "We love you, James!" one screamed, prompting Taylor to reply, with equal degrees of modesty and cockiness, "How many are there of you now?" The answer to that question always arrived after the performance. Lining up in front of the dressing room, girls—never boys—would press flowers, notes, or lollipops into Taylor's hands. Taylor passed some of the gifts on to King; others, like a pair of green gloves, went to Braudy.

During interviews with Braudy in his hotel rooms or at restaurants, Taylor revealed more of himself than he had to other writers by that point. He complained about the making of *Two-Lane Blacktop*. "I don't like to fight with people," he told her. "I like to please people too much, but I didn't like someone else being in control of my work." He told her his only enemy was Allen Klein, who was threatening to sue him and Peter Asher for breach of contract. (Asher and Taylor were prepared to countersue for lack of royalty payments on the first album, but Klein never followed through on his threat.) Taylor remained a Beatles fan: In a motel room during the making of *Two-Lane Blacktop*, he was overheard singing "Mean Mr. Mustard" from *Abbey Road*.

Although Braudy never saw Taylor get high, she noticed his nose always appeared to be running and he spoke in unusual cadences—very fast before slowing down. To herself, she concluded he was essentially sedated in one way or another. When the topic came up, Taylor denied he was a junkie and even talked about the detrimental effects of hard drugs. "Heroin, it deadens your senses," he told her during one conversation. "You don't think. You take all your problems and trade them in for one problem—a whole physical and mental process of deterioration. A lot of creative energy comes out of a very painful place. A lot of artists do their thing as a kind of remedial action. Junk shuts off a lot of that."

Braudy accepted his explanation. But in one of his motel rooms, she went into the bathroom and noticed a bent spoon and other drug paraphernalia on the floor behind the toilet. Braudy decided not to include it in the subsequent story that ran in the *Times Magazine*. She wasn't sure Taylor's inordinately sensitive fans were prepared to know that much about their newfound hero.

PART FOUR

FALL INTO WINTER
Gone Your Way, I'll Go Mine

CHAPTER 13

He knew the question was coming; it was only a matter of when and how to respond. But somebody was bound to bring it up. In those early days of autumn, one person or another always did.

His hair pulled back in a ponytail, his bearded face gaunt and vigilant, George Harrison took his place behind a small bank of microphones in London in the middle of September. Joined by his friend Ravi Shankar, Harrison was making his first public appearance in months to promote a series of Indian music concerts at the Royal Festival Hall. With rock fans' interest in Indian raga declining—for Western ears, the novelty had worn off—a plug by a Beatle was guaranteed to bring out the press and, with any luck, sell a few more tickets to the shows.

At first the questions from the assembled reporters focused on Harrison's love of India's music, culture, and religion, to which he'd been introduced four years before and which he had incorporated into Beatle records and his side projects. Casually dressed in denim, Harrison neither looked nor sounded happy to be on display. He answered a question about whether he still meditated with a curt "yes," then spoke of how Eastern music was far superior to Western. "These Indian singers have more soul than Aretha Franklin will ever have and you can quote me on that," he said, a revealing moment of honesty, haughtiness, or both.

Eventually, the moment he'd been dreading arrived: A reporter asked about the future of the Beatles, especially now that McCartney had published his damning letter in *Melody Maker*. To the surprise of no one who knew him, Harrison said nothing, turned, and walked away, and the press conference disintegrated. "George could be very disagreeable," recalled Apple's Peter Brown. "He was argumentative and stubborn. More than most." Then Harrison quickly paused and, over his shoulder, said, "It looks like we need a new bass player, doesn't it?" He'd tossed off that joke at least once before, in the studio with Dylan and Charlie Daniels, but this time the edge in his voice was more apparent.

Harrison had reason to be grumpy. The past few months had found him clashing with McCartney and Phil Spector, and he was beginning to suspect something was taking place between his wife, Pattie, and his friend Eric Clapton. Yet one encouraging bit of news was in the air: At the time of the press conference, Harrison had only a few more songs to complete for his first album proper, *All Things Must Pass*, whose title alone was a less-than-veiled comment on life after the Beatles.

Harrison had considered making an album even before McCartney's announcement; Chris O'Dell, the former Apple employee and Harrison friend, recalled him talking about cutting a single during the early months of 1970. But McCartney's news inspired Harrison to finally compile all the material he'd been storing away. Fresh off the *Let It Be* experience, Harrison hired Phil Spector, who, with Harrison, assembled a veritable army of musicians, from Clapton, Procol Harum's Gary Brooker, Billy Preston, and former Traffic guitarist Dave Mason to old friends Klaus Voormann and Ringo Starr. With an impressive cadre of players and nearly two dozen songs, Harrison would finally make the case for his own career, just as the other Beatles already had with their individual albums and singles.

The bushel of material amounted to a journey through Harrison's mind, past and present. The songs dating back to the waning days of the Beatles revealed the strain on his psyche and patience at the time. Written during the filming of *Let It Be*, "Wah-Wah" equated band meetings with a massive, lingering headache. Harrison would later claim "Isn't It a Pity" was a comment on a low point in an unspecified relationship—

presumably with Boyd—but its coda, a sarcastic take on the sing-along finale to McCartney's "Hey Jude," couldn't have made the subject of his words more apparent. "Run of the Mill" chronicled, with admittedly oblique imagery, the time when the business of running Apple began to wear on the band, while "Beware of Darkness" was, he later wrote, "self-explanatory"—a take on the sinister side of the music business some felt was aimed at Harrison's otherwise ally, Allen Klein.

The post-Beatles George, or the one he hoped to become now that he was free of them, poked through optimistically. His relaxed, inspiring bonding with Dylan emerged in a version of Dylan's "If Not for You" and "I'd Have You Anytime," a country-lilt ballad they'd written together. Harrison made Dylan the subject, again abstractly, of "Behind That Locked Door," a show of love and support for his songwriter friend. The Krishna George, the one who would find peace and tranquility on his own, commandeered "My Sweet Lord" and "Awaiting on You All."

Fortunately, Spector didn't allow Harrison's tendency toward stern, sour-faced lyrics to derail him. Applying his Wall of Sound approach to a rock orchestra, Spector transformed "Wah-Wah," "What Is Life," and "Awaiting on You All" into joyful cacophonies—thundering herds of multiple guitars, percussion, and choirs that did a more than commendable job of smoothing over Harrison's sometimes strained voice and rhymes ("visas" and "Jesus" in the case of the latter song). Spector brought out the hooks and energy in Harrison's songs; he even made the chant "Krishna, Krishna" in "My Sweet Lord" palatable. The ballads, like the title song, had a stately, nineteenth-century eloquence, the musical equivalent to Harrison's Friar Park mansion. From the springy guitar lick that drove "What Is Life" to Pete Drake's sweet pedal steel in "Behind That Locked Door," the album—the two LPs of original songs, anyway, not the third disc of ho-hum jam sessions with the musicians—was unflaggingly warm and inviting, as if Spector had yanked out the best side of his collaborator's personality.

Far more than McCartney's or Starr's projects, the start of Harrison's record sealed the band's fate for those who worked regularly with them. "It was, 'This is what we're going to be doing now—four solo albums,'" recalled engineer John Kurlander, who worked on some of the sessions. To Spector's frustration, though, *All Things Must Pass* took months to complete. The sessions began in late May and stretched out, languidly, throughout the summer. In a corner of the studio, Harrison constructed a small shrine, complete with lit incense sticks and a framed picture of the beloved spiritual teacher and yoga master Paramahansa Yogananda. "George took his time," Voormann recalled. "He got comfortable. He made the studio into his little home."

As the work dragged on, far longer than he expected, Spector grew bored and irascible. Drummer Alan White, who'd played on Lennon's "Instant Karma!," noticed a gun sitting on the recording console. He'd heard stories about Spector's unpredictable, explosive side, but the sight of a weapon took White and others off guard.

One day, late in the sessions, Spector showed up drunk, and Voormann watched as the producer fell backward off a chair, hurting his arm. Visibly unhappy, Harrison told Spector he'd finish the record without him. By then, the bulk of the project had been completed, and Harrison wrapped it up himself at EMI Studios in September and October. Once and only once, he popped into an adjoining room to check on the status of another historic event, the album on which John Lennon was putting the consequences of his primal scream therapy onto record for the first time.

o o o o

To Dan Richter, the change in the Lennons was apparent as soon as they returned home to Tittenhurst from Bel Air. For starters, their hair was longer, the close-cropped look of six months before relegated to history.

Lennon made jokes about gaining weight from eating too much ice cream in Hollywood, and his sense of humor, his engagement, were again on display.

So, apparently, was his relationship with Ono. "Take a picture of us," Lennon asked him one fall day, "we've got this drawing." Lennon showed Richter a sketch of a man and woman sitting together against a tree. Once, Richter had been able to tell Lennon and Ono's handwriting apart. But no longer; the penmanship on this piece of paper was such a melding of their two styles that he couldn't tell which one had drawn it. *Wow*, Richter thought, *they're even* drawing *alike*. Whatever turbulence had been taking place between Lennon and Ono had been resolved, at least for the time being.

Richter grabbed what he called a "cheap plastic camera" and the three of them headed out to the front of the main house, right off the large front yard. It was a sunny, beautifully crisp afternoon, and Lennon and Ono ran between the trees together like children just dismissed from school. "They had a lot of energy," Richter recalled. "The whole purging that had taken place with the Janov thing put them in a very positive space." With their original sketch in mind, Lennon and Ono finally sat down and leaned against a tree, Ono in Lennon's lap. Richter snapped away before Lennon and Ono reversed positions, Ono now cradling Lennon.

From the start, the photos were intended to grace the covers of separate albums Lennon and Ono had finished making after they'd arrived back in England. In late September, Lennon reached out to Starr and Voormann, telling them he had a group of new songs he wanted to record, quickly. When Voormann heard Lennon had hired Spector again, he envisioned another crowd-of-thousands production. Instead, he found himself in the studio with only Lennon and Starr, Spector keeping an exceedingly low profile and allowing Lennon to shape his own sound. (Coming on the heels of the Harrison sessions, Spector may have been humbled; he also instinctively knew Lennon was opting for a different approach and went out of his way to respect his wishes.) "Phil was very subdued and melded in," Voormann recalled. "He did not push any Phil Spector sound on us." Starr later recalled having no memory whatsoever of Spector being around.

That sound, as Voormann and Starr discovered, was naked and minimalist; most of the songs were played only by the core trio of Lennon, Voormann, and Starr. Lennon wrote out the lyrics on large pieces of paper, the chords listed underneath them. The trio ran through each song a few times, Lennon alternating between piano and guitar, and then recorded them. Voormann flubbed a few notes here and there, but in they stayed. Lennon was taking the original concept of *Let It Be* and pushing it as far as he could.

One night, Lennon insisted on recording in spite of a voice raspy from oversinging. With special guest Billy Preston accompanying him with churchly, dramatic piano flourishes, Lennon launched into "God," which worked itself up to a relentless, unapologetic list of everything in which he no longer believed: Jesus, John Kennedy, Buddha, yoga, Elvis, the Bhagavad Gita, Dylan ("Zimmerman," as he called him), and, finally, the Beatles. Beforehand, he pulled Voormann aside. The last line was going to be "I don't believe in Beatles, I just believe in me." Should he add, "and Yoko," he asked? He didn't want to hurt her feelings. Voormann didn't know what to say; it was Lennon's choice. In the final version, he had it both ways: He believed in "me . . . Yoko and me." Clearly Lennon wanted to keep everything copacetic with Ono.

If *McCartney* didn't demand much, Lennon's *Plastic Ono Band* demanded everything—complete concentration and immersion in Lennon's state of mind, and a tolerance for a sonic approach that was akin to stripped-down wood. It was pop music, but not pop like anyone, especially Beatle fans, had envisioned. "Mother," his way of confronting the mommy and daddy issues that haunted him, was more a pained mantra than a song, Lennon's voice rising up to a scream at the end of each line. "I Found Out," which lashed out equally at Jesus and Harrison's beloved Krishna, was gut-bucket Liverpool blues. "Working Class Hero," featuring just Lennon's voice and shuddering acoustic guitar strums, was as unflinching as the starkest black-and-white photograph. The songs were open wounds, the arrangements—like Lennon's voice and guitar on "I Found Out" or his equally ravaged guitar work on "Well Well Well"—scratching at them until they bled.

Lennon and Spector were savvy enough record-makers to know a few gentler moments were called for, so out came "Hold On," Lennon's reassuring words to himself, Ono, and the world, floating along on his gentle tremolo guitar, and "Love," a gorgeous quasi-prayer whose delicate arrangement—Lennon's guitar, Spector's piano, and Voormann's bass—enhanced its natural beauty. Starting with the funeral bell that opened it, *Plastic Ono Band* was neither easy to listen to nor meant to be.

During the same month of October, the band and Spector dashed off a very different project, Ono's own *Plastic Ono Band*. Again, Spector stayed largely out of the way, allowing Lennon and Ono to call the shots. If Lennon's record of the same name was his way of exorcizing his personal demons, Ono's album was Lennon's way of exercising his musical ones. The music was feral and ferocious ("Why") or defiantly eccentric ("Why Not," which sounded like country blues from outer space, thanks to the strings sticking to the magnets on Lennon's National slide guitar). Ono's voice, a quivery siren wail one minute or a delicate coo the next, rode roughshod over it all. The music was entirely improvised, and even Starr, who kept any self-indulgent tendencies as a drummer in check, let loose from time to time.

When the packaging was finished, Lennon and Ono intentionally chose a shot of Lennon leaning on Ono for *his* cover, and Ono in Lennon's lap for her own. To Richter, the idea was "classic John and Yoko. And it was a very Yoko idea, of a man and woman as yin and yang."

The choice of photographs also spoke to what Lennon told Richter were his masculine and his feminine sides, the intertwining of men and women that Ono championed.

Lennon was justly proud of both albums and knew his record especially was far more accessible than previous projects with Ono, like the sound collages of *Life with the Lions*. When executives at EMI and Apple saw the dual covers and heard the music, though, their guards went up. Why wasn't Lennon's face on the cover? "Can't you talk to him?" a label executive said to Richter one day, pulling him aside. "This is going to ruin his career. It's another nail in the coffin." In particular, they were concerned that the albums, especially Lennon's own, didn't have "that Beatles sound." What was he thinking, they thought? And why did Ono have to put out her own album too?

At the very least, the Lennons had one attentive audience. In Los Angeles, Arthur and Vivian Janov received a copy and played it for one of their group sessions at the Primal Scream Institute. Everyone, including the Janovs, listened raptly. Few could believe they were listening to a John Lennon album whose thoughts and concepts had originated in that very room on Sunset Boulevard.

In honor of Lennon's thirtieth birthday, October 9, Harrison saluted his friend in song: "It's Johnny's Birthday," a silly, playful sing-along, sounded like a carousel speeding up and slowing down. (Harrison liked it so much he included it on *All Things Must Pass*.) Despite all that had transpired and collapsed over the past year, Harrison, Lennon, and Starr remained close. Lennon stopped by at least once during the *All Things Must Pass* sessions, and Alan White found himself in the mind-boggling position of jamming with two Beatles while a third, Starr, whacked a tambourine. White asked Starr to play drums, but Starr demurred.

The odd Beatle out remained McCartney, who'd spent much of the year in Scotland and had also taken his family on vacation to Barbados. Needing another change of scenery, he, Linda, Heather, and baby Mary relocated to New York City in early fall. In Manhattan, he and Linda melted into the city woodwork, taking long, unencumbered walks through Central Park and horseback-riding in the Hamptons with Peter Brown. Nothing if not prolific, eager to work as much as possible, McCartney already had a new group of songs he wanted to start recording. During the first week of November, he rented out the *SS France* and jammed with members of the Rascals, the New York pop-soul band who'd had a string of hits ("Good Lovin'," "People Got to Be Free," "Groovin'") almost as long as the Beatles' own. Drummer Dino Danelli's moptop bangs and babyface even resembled McCartney's.

In at least one slim regard, McCartney shared one concern with his former Beatles. The previous year, the first bootleg LP—*Great White Wonder*, a collection of unreleased Dylan recordings from several stages in his career—had started mysteriously appearing in independent record stores. No one knew how the bootleggers had obtained the rare tapes, but clearly a new illicit industry had been launched. Fearing any further leaks, Charlie Daniels became the courier for Dylan's Nashville tapes to New York City. The Beatles and their representatives were also on their guard, especially when Lennon's complete set at the Toronto Rock & Roll Revival and the Beatles' 1965 Shea Stadium show became two of the next boots to slip out. In the spring, John Eastman had personally delivered *McCartney* to Capitol Records in the States. Now, in late October, Harrison and Boyd flew to New York with the master tapes for *All Things Must Pass* in hand—the one way to ensure the record didn't end up in the hands of an unauthorized middleman.

In general, money was far from a pressing concern; all the Beatles were profiting from the unflagging business of the band. In September, the

Beatles, by way of EMI, received a check for $10,738,198, representing royalties for American sales of Beatle records between September 1, 1969, and June 3, 1970. Still, little had been resolved financially between them. McCartney wasn't yet seeing any earnings from his solo album, nor were he and his team receiving what they considered fair treatment. In November, John Eastman called William Bernstein, the general counsel of United Artists, the film company that had distributed *Let It Be*. To Eastman's frustration, Bernstein refused to give any confirmation of how much the film had made or how much McCartney was owed; even if money was forthcoming, Bernstein said McCartney's "adversary position" (in Bernstein's words) with Allen Klein stood in the way.

Confusion over the royalties from the *McCartney* album dragged on. On November 12, four months after his initial inquiry, Eastman wrote to EMI, saying he thought the issue had been resolved and his client would be paid. On December 1, EMI informed Eastman that, at long last, the funds would be sent to Apple, thereby bypassing Klein. By then, the amount had grown to 487,000 British pounds. Yet the fact that McCartney and Eastman had had to endure such frustrations and foot-dragging only made them feel they'd made the right decision about how to resolve it all. By then, Eastman had brought in two other attorneys to map out an airtight strategy. In drawing up a list of possible complaints and gripes for a lawsuit, the New York-based Eastman flew back and forth to London so frequently that Pan Am knew to save him four seats in the back so he could sleep. His morning shaves took place at Heathrow.

During his visit to New York City, Harrison reached out to McCartney by phone. What began as a friendly chat turned, once again, into a shouting match. When asked for comment by a reporter, Klein denied any such conversation had occurred. But to Brown, Klein's vehement denial only confirmed that something ugly had indeed taken place and that the gashes wouldn't heal for some time.

O O O O

Everyone, not merely the four Beatles, was scattering. Feeling he had little further role in the Beatles' affairs, Brown left Apple Corps Ltd. in the fall. Robert Stigwood, the manager and music magnate who'd worked with the Bee Gees and Eric Clapton, offered Brown a job in his New York office, and Brown, who felt Klein wanted him gone anyway, took it. Quickly and quietly, Brown, one of the Beatles' key advisors and insiders for the previous three years, was out of the picture.

In search of a new line of work, Richard DiLello, the "house hippie" fired from Apple's Press Office, decided to try his hand at photography. At a festival in a small town outside London, he shot two new bands, Black Sabbath and Emerson, Lake and Palmer, whose first albums were released that fall. The music—thundering, intentionally ugly fury from Birmingham in the former, a merger of classical music chops and arena bombast in the latter—was new to many, especially DiLello. After listening to and photographing both, DiLello sensed a cultural shift around the corner. "I suddenly realized music was changing radically," he recalled. "It was a very different vibe from what the Beatles had given off. I thought we were entering a darker period."

Like a bleak murder of crows, other signs of a generational shift were circling above and around them. Lennon and Starr were both now thirty, with Simon, Garfunkel, and Crosby soon to follow in the coming year. In September, *Melody Maker* published the results of its annual readers poll. For the eight consecutive years prior, the Beatles had taken first place. Now they were usurped by Led Zeppelin. Zeppelin was rooted in the '60s—its founder, Jimmy Page, was an ex-Yardbird, and singer Robert Plant had fronted a hippie-folkie band, Band of Joy—but its monolithic music was louder and more domineering than any rock that had come before. It sternly lorded over its audience—the next generation of rock fans, the teenagers who had only faint memories of the Beatles on *The Ed Sullivan Show*. As DiLello realized, Black Sabbath, along with Grand Funk Railroad and Led Zeppelin, were the disquieting sound of a new era. It was the rise of a generation for whom the Beatles and Simon and Garfunkel, among others, were their older siblings' quaint relics from the previous decade.

o o o o

When it arrived in record stores in late September, Starr's country album, *Beaucoups of Blues*, looked the way many Beatle fans felt by year's end. On the cover, Starr sat forlornly, chin in palm and cigarette in hand. The photograph evoked the disconsolate quality of the record's down-and-out Nashville ballads, but intentionally or not, it also bespoke something about Starr's own state of mind after six uncertain months.

To help pay his bills, Starr withdrew 69,000 British pounds (about $200,000) from his Apple savings—not as much as Lennon, who'd taken out 77,000 pounds, but more than Harrison, who used a mere 19,000, and McCartney, who opted for 20,500. Although *The Magic Christian* hadn't turned him into a movie star, other roles beckoned; already, Starr was lined up to star as a heavy in *Blindman*, a violent homage to spaghetti Westerns, to begin filming the following year. His third child, a daughter named Lee, arrived in mid November.

Along with "It Don't Come Easy," he wrote and recorded another song, "Early 1970," that took playful digs at the other Beatles. The song devoted verses to McCartney's time on his farm, the Lennons' primal scream therapy, Harrison's gardening, and Starr's own limited musical chops. "When I come to town, I want to see all three," he sang optimistically at the end, as if the events of the previous year hadn't happened.

Yet many aspects of his career felt uncertain, his future far fuzzier than that of the other Beatles. The reviews of *Beaucoups of Blues* were warmer than those for *Sentimental Journey*—Starr sounded far more at ease and natural singing lachrymose country songs than sophisticated standards—yet it sold less. In America, *Beaucoups of Blues* limped to number 65 on the charts, more than forty spots lower than *Sentimental Journey*. According to Voormann, Starr had been unnerved during the recording of Lennon's and Ono's albums. "John and Yoko were sitting on chairs together and walking together," Voormann recalled. "You couldn't part them. That was very sad for Ringo. He felt he lost a friend. It was very strange for him, and he didn't feel comfortable."

As always, Starr betrayed little of his uncertainties to others; to everyone, he remained agreeable, easy-to-be-with Ringo, the man with a ready if sometimes sad smile and few cares in the world. On certain nights he could be found at Tramp, a members-only London watering hole that had opened the previous year. Starr's friend Peter Sellers was a regular, as were musicians and actors from Keith Moon to Joan Collins. In the early-morning hours of December 3, Starr ran into a friend. Greetings and champagne were shared. For both, the world was a different place than it was when they'd met ten months before. Both Starr and the friend, Stephen Stills, were now on their own.

CHAPTER 14

Thanks to a thick, crusty snowfall, the early morning of September 22 wasn't the ideal moment for a photo shoot at the Roosevelt National Forest park in northern Colorado. Nonetheless, Stephen Stills, in work boots and jeans, headed outside a rented mountain cabin with his friend Henry Diltz to snap shots for the cover of the record Stills had started in London in the winter.

No sooner had they begun than Stills told Diltz to stop; he needed something inside. Darting back in, he returned with a stuffed animal, a spotted purple giraffe, that he set in the snowdrift next to him as he began playing guitar. He didn't tell Diltz anything other than he wanted it featured in the photo that would grace the album cover. With its long neck, the giraffe was both a message to someone and a re-minder of her. "I have a thing for long, tall slender women," he recalled. "She wasn't that tall, but she looked like she was." As summer gave way to fall, she was also one of the reasons Crosby, Stills, Nash & Young were finished.

Although Rita Coolidge had entered their lives three months ear-lier, everyone in the Los Angeles music scene already seemed to know her. Born and raised in Tennessee, the daughter of a Cherokee preacher, Coolidge had begun her career singing jingles at a company in Memphis and had had a regional hit, "Turn Around and Love You." The industry still being small, one of her friends, producer Don Nix, touted her to his friend Leon Russell, then playing with Delaney and Bonnie. Before Coolidge knew it, she was driving across the country to Los Angeles with Russell, now her boyfriend, to sing on a Delaney and Bonnie album.

With her slender figure, warm smile, and waterfall of dark hair, Coolidge had a modest, unaffected magnetism, and her voice, with its touch of sultry smokiness, was equally unfussy and soulful. "She was a very charismatic girl, in a weirdly quiet way," recalled drummer Jim Keltner, who played with Delaney and Bonnie. "She was really beautiful when she made herself out to be. At other times, she looked like a little squaw with braids and everything." After recording and touring with Delaney and Bonnie from the fall of 1969 into early 1970, she was recruited by Russell to join the backup choir on Joe Cocker's "Mad Dogs & Englishmen" tour in the spring.

Once that tour wrapped up, Coolidge was back in Los Angeles, working on a record of her own. During those sessions, produced by her brother-in-law, organist Booker T. Jones of Booker T. and the MG's, she met Stills. Their first encounter was less than auspicious. "One night, he made it clear to me that the real magic of the record had nothing to do with me," Coolidge recalled. "It was because the two great musical minds of the decade, him and Booker, had come together. I thought he was arrogant." But Coolidge had to admit to herself that Stills was, in her words, "totally adorable." (When he smiled, his recessed upper-left tooth made him look down-home and less hard-boiled.)

Stills was immediately intrigued. As soon as she left the studio that day, he stayed behind and wrote and recorded a song about her, "Cherokee." Set to Jones' churning organ, it had the feel of an after-hours confessional in a smoke-drenched bar. (To lend the song an exotic twang, Stills rented an electric sitar to play on it.) He then invited her to be part of a backup choir he'd assembled for "Love the One You're With," which he'd begun recording in London and was now finishing up in Los Angeles. The track had been transformed from a solo guitar workout to a pulsating groove with congas and steel drums. At the late June session,

Coolidge found herself gathered around a microphone with Crosby, her sister Priscilla Jones, the Lovin' Spoonful's John Sebastian, and another new acquaintance, Graham Nash.

Like Stills, Nash was struck by Coolidge's voice and looks—so much so that he asked her to accompany him to the CSNY show at the Los Angeles Forum the following night, June 25. Since he was staying at Stills' house in Laurel Canyon, Nash gave Coolidge Stills' number and told her to call him to make arrangements. "And then," Coolidge recalled, "all the nonsense began."

According to Coolidge, Stills answered when she phoned the next day and told her that Nash said he'd made a mistake and couldn't take her after all—but that he, Stills, would love to drive her to the show instead. Unaware of the band's complex dynamics and only interested in seeing them perform, Coolidge said yes, and Stills picked her up at her home on Wilshire. Backstage at the show, the once-friendly Nash barely looked at her.

Stills and Coolidge began seeing each other soon after. Stills' passion was instantaneous. In quick order, he wrote and recorded another song, "Sit Yourself Down," that captured the conflicting sides of his personality, his internal conflict between taking stock and pushing himself. The ruminative lyrics talked about aging, maturing, slowing down, and buying land. The music, particularly its fervent chorus propelled by his galloping piano, a choir (again with Coolidge), and a lead guitar line that kept tugging at the melody, was anything but calm. Stills was so optimistic about his and Coolidge's budding relationship that in the song he envisioned the two of them living "on a patch of ground" later in life.

Coolidge wasn't so sure. When she met Stills, she was still recovering from her first encounter with hard-core show business insanity. The spring 1970 Joe Cocker tour was, in her words, a dose of the new brand of "rock and roll university, really tough." Every night, she'd watch as the seemingly fragile Cocker tossed down whatever pills or drugs anyone handed him as he walked onstage. She'd witnessed Cocker's band members scoring heroin at a seedy farm. Cocaine was everywhere. Walking into the lobby of one hotel, she saw half the tour members, musicians and crew alike, lining up to get shots for venereal disease. Even scarier was Cocker's drummer, Jim Gordon, whom Coolidge had dated before the tour. Watching TV one night in a hotel room, Gordon—a boyishly handsome and kinetic drummer—said he needed to talk to her outside. As soon as they stepped into the hallway, Gordon punched her so hard she fell unconscious to the floor. Later, Keltner saw a huge black shiner on her face but didn't ask what happened.[1]

Stills was nowhere near as explosive as Gordon, who was later diagnosed with schizophrenia after murdering his mother with repeated blows of a hammer. But Stills was intense in his own way: He liked to race horses at local tracks to clear his head, he indulged more than Coolidge could tolerate, and he would spend long hours, often midnight to dawn, in studios, working on his music. (At three o'clock one morning, he called a sleeping Johnny Barbata and asked him to come down, but Nash advised the drummer to pass, given how many hours Barbata would inevitably end up spending with Stills.) Almost from the start, the CSNY universe itself was too much for Coolidge. One night at Stills' house, she cooked him, Crosby, and Nash a dinner of beans and cornbread. Feeling sleepy afterward, Crosby accused her of dosing the food with acid—when, in fact, he was merely sleepy from eating so many beans. "Graham was the most elegant human being," she recalled. "The other two were pretty wacky."

In the aftermath of the Cocker tour, Coolidge needed a more stable, even-keeled force around her. The soap-opera element kicked in when she discovered what had happened the night of the CSNY show: Nash told her Stills had purposefully made up that story in order to escort

---

1. Gordon played drums on Crosby, Stills & Nash's "Marrakesh Express."

her himself. At this point, Nash made his own growing feelings about Coolidge known to her. "I talked to Rita about it and she said, 'I feel the same way,'" Nash recalled. "And I said, 'There's nothing we can do. I'm not touching you or kissing you or fucking—I'm not doing *anything* until we go to Stephen.'" Nash wound up writing a song, "Better Days," with the situation in mind: "Though you're where you want to be, you're not where you belong," he sang. "That was Rita," he said. "She was with Stephen but didn't want to be there. She wanted to be with me."

Deciding it was best to tell Stills to his face about this realignment, Nash and Coolidge drove to Stills' house to personally deliver the news of their burgeoning relationship. Sitting poolside, a stunned and humiliated Stills spit at Nash (but missed). Nash moved out of Stills' home and into a room at the Chateau Marmont. "Girls fell quite naturally in love or in lust with Graham," said Crosby. "He had that lovely British accent and was a good lover and a gentleman." Coolidge melted whenever Nash would call her "luv" with his British accent. The Coolidge triangle was far from the principal cause of any intra-band breakdown; fractures in the band had been building for months. But after the poolside conversation, Stills refused to speak to Nash, and the increasingly delicate thread that held them together finally snapped.

His pride publicly wounded, Stills drowned his sorrows in whatever way he could, one result being his drug bust in San Diego. (The charges were eventually reduced to a misdemeanor and a fine.) By the middle of September, tiring of what he called "the incestuous California scene," he rented a Lear Jet and flew to Colorado for a few weeks. Judy Collins had introduced him to the state during their relationship, and Stills rented a cabin, joined by Diltz, bass player Fuzzy Samuels, and his personal assistant Dan Campbell. With his solo album nearly complete, he buried his sorrows in work, planning sessions for another record and writing and jamming on songs in the house. "When you're sitting there dealing with all these feelings, it's, 'Oh, poor me,'" he recalled. "All this stuff is coming out."

On September 18, two days after the giraffe-enhanced photo shoot, more troubling news arrived. A call to the cabin delivered the news that Jimi Hendrix had been found dead in a hotel room in the Notting Hill section of London after choking on his own vomit. Stills was devastated and angry. "I cried and drank," he recalled. A friend awoke the next morning to find Stills cleaning out marmalade jars so he could have additional glasses to imbibe some more.

The two men had made tentative plans to record an album together, perhaps even form a band. Now those plans, like those with Coolidge, were history. It was time to flee. The hell with all of them.

○ ○ ○ ○

He couldn't tell if he was crazy, extremely high, or some combination of both. In the aftermath of Christine Hinton's death, sometimes it was hard to tell. Whatever the reason, Crosby felt her presence all around him late one September evening. Standing before a microphone in an echo chamber at Wally Heider's studio in San Francisco, Crosby told engineer Stephen Barncard to roll tape, then began singing a cappella— no words, just a full-throated blend of melody and moan. Then he sang another part, then another, ending up with six voices, each echoed back onto itself for a woebegone, eerie mass of twelve wailing Crosbys. A Grand Canyon of pain, the performance was a belated musical eulogy to her; fittingly, he called it "I'd Swear There Was Somebody Here."

To the consternation of friends and past lovers, little about Crosby's world had ever been conventional; everyone still talked about the non-stop parade of nude swimmers in his pool at his previous home in Laurel Canyon. But Crosby's life now took on something actually resembling a routine. After Hinton's fatal accident, he'd sold his house in Novato, where the *Déjà vu* cover had been shot; the place evoked too many painful memories. (Briefly, he'd lost the Halliburton case that contained some of her clothes, but after word of its disappearance or possible theft went out, it turned up amidst the Jefferson Airplane's gear.) His home became the *Mayan*, now docked in Sausalito after he and Nash had sailed it back home from Florida. Crosby lived, ate, and slept on it, often well into the afternoon.

Around seven each night, he'd drive across the Golden Gate Bridge to Heider's. Music would be his escape and salvation. In the same room where the torturous *Déjà vu* sessions had taken place a year before, Crosby began making the first record under his own name. Much like his lifestyle, it wouldn't be traditional in any form. To indulge his every whim, he booked Studio C for himself for months and put out an open call to whichever musician friends were around. For support, Jerry Garcia, Crosby's brother in outlier music, stopped by almost every night. Other members of the Dead, including Phil Lesh and Mickey Hart, visited, along with his friends from the Airplane like Paul Kantner and Grace Slick. The jam sessions and creative pokings-about, augmented by Crosby's ever-present stash, would last for hours. "Jerry and I were both pushing-the-envelope kind of people," Crosby said. "We liked doing things that other people thought were weird. They brought out an encouragement of 'there are no rules.'"

The intermingling of musicians produced the strangest yet most gorgeous music of Crosby's career. In hazy-day soundscapes like "Tamalpais High (at About 3)" and "Song with No Words (Tree with No Leaves)," harmonies and instruments bobbed and drifted, like waves lapping onto a shore and receding. Instead of singing words, Crosby—joined by Nash on the latter—sang wordless phrases rooted in the jazz records of his youth. "Song with No Words (Tree with No Leaves)" was a particularly pastoral chorale—music basking in its own stoned-out bliss—yet it also bristled; by the end, Crosby began fervently scatting around his own one-man chorus, and Jorma Kaukonen and Garcia yanked sharp, shrieking notes out of their guitars. The song heaved and lurched until, suddenly, it ended. Even songs centered around Crosby's voice and acoustic guitar were hardly campfire-sing-along material. "Traction in the Rain," inspired by the jealous looks Crosby received one day while walking through a park with Joan Baez and her sister Mimi Fariña, had a glistening, benumbed calmness. "Where Will I Be," cut at the sessions but held for a later album, was a statement of personal confusion, spaced-out and rhythmless—Crosby's comment on how both his band and his lover were part of his past, leaving him alone and directionless.

Much as Nash turned the group's interactions into fodder for new material, Crosby put CSNY's shambolic summer to song. With Garcia, Lesh, and Hart, he began rehearsing a new song, "Cowboy Movie." Driven by the brusque strums of Crosby's electric twelve-string, the song was rough and savage, Garcia playing with a piercing, angry tone rare for him. The lyrics, an Old West tale set to music, told the saga of an "Indian girl" who comes between a gang of outlaws, sowing the seeds of their destruction. The four principal characters were a "weird" cowboy named Harold, a wild-eyed gunslinger called Eli ("young and mean, and from the South"), a "Duke" good with dynamite, and the youngest, Billy; the girl, whom Harold doesn't trust from the outset, is called Raven. After both become taken with Raven, Eli and the Duke "get down to it"; Eli pulls a gun, and in the end everyone's dead except Harold. With each verse, Crosby's voice sounded raspier and more pent-up, as if he'd been smoking all night and decided to record anyway. Anyone who knew anything about the band's recent falling-out knew the characters' real names. Coolidge, for one, was not amused. "If that's the way David saw it, he has a right to think that," she recalled. "David just thought I was the Devil."

For Crosby, the recording of his album, which stretched out into the

late fall, embodied the new rock and roll: music without parameters, concrete personnel, and in some cases anything approaching a standard rock
and roll rhythm. His art would now fully become an extension of his
personal life. "The Byrds, the Hollies, and Buffalo Springfield were very
formulaic groups," Crosby recalled. "Good bands, but in a form. Kantner and I were on a quest. We were rule-breaking guys who wanted to
see more interaction between bands, more cross-pollination." Kantner
was using the same revolving-cast approach on his first record outside
the Airplane, *Blows Against the Empire*; Crosby popped up on many songs
on that one as well.

Struggling to find his identity after the problems with CSNY and
Hinton's death, Crosby would later describe himself during this time as
"not a happy camper." But to some, he'd never seemed more content—
as one friend put it, "making the best music of his life and getting laid
every night," thanks to whatever girl happened to be on the boat with
him at night after the hours in the studio. Everyone got high, made
music, and slept with whomever they wanted. The proudly esoteric
tracks Crosby was cutting would be released by a major label, Atlantic,
without any qualms. It was easy, seductively so, to imagine it would all
last forever.

During this time, word leaked out that Crosby, Nash, and Young—no
Stills inserted between them—would be releasing a single together. The
song, "Music Is Love," had its origins in an August Hollywood jam in
which Crosby began strumming and singing what he called "silly stuff"
and Young and Nash spontaneously joined in. After Nash and Young bor-
rowed the tape and overdubbed additional instruments, "Music Is Love"
wound up on Crosby's album. Its creation affirmed the way in which he,
Nash, and Young had grown closer in the aftermath of the group's col-

lapse. Nash and Young dropped by the sessions for Crosby's album; Young and Garcia traded solos on one take of "Cowboy Movie."

Young's hesitation toward a full-time commitment to CSNY gnawed at Nash (but not Crosby), but neither Nash nor Crosby felt as threatened by Young as Stills did. They couldn't help but admire his uncompromising approach to his music and presentation. ("As of this writing, Neil's about to okay the test pressing. Again," sighed a Reprise Records ad in September for Young's nearly complete *After the Gold Rush*.)

Starting with Crosby, the CSNY breakdown also played itself out geographically. During the summer, Young had bought a 140-acre ranch south of San Francisco. (His first wife, Susan, would file for divorce from him in October.) Even earlier, Nash had purchased a four-story Victorian townhouse on West Buena Vista Street in Haight-Ashbury, on the edge of Buena Park. Like Crosby, he'd grown weary of Los Angeles and envisioned himself relocating to Northern California with Mitchell. Now, that romance over, Nash decided to make the move himself. "I thought, 'Fuck, I've got a house in San Francisco, I'd better go and live there,'" he recalled. With its front-door pillars and balcony, the structure felt regal even before Nash moved in, yet he enhanced it further, installing a skylight and a bath that led into a stream with goldfish on the fourth floor. Although the three weren't within quick driving distance of each other, they were still in the same Northern California vicinity.

Since all four had songs that hadn't made it onto *Déjà vu*, the logical response was to make records of their own, whether Ahmet Ertegun, David Geffen, or Elliot Roberts liked it or not. "It was never up to management or Atlantic," Crosby said. "It was up to us." On September 7, Young became the first to release his own music that year. Recorded on and off over the previous year, *After the Gold Rush* reflected his time with Crosby, Stills, and Nash: It was more focused on acoustic songs and relatively pared-down arrangements than either of its predecessors, *Neil Young* and *Everybody Knows This Is Nowhere*. It even included a few tracks, "Southern Man" and "Tell Me Why," he'd performed with them that summer.

After the Gold Rush presented Young as both balladeer, on "Birds" and "Only Love Can Break Your Heart," and rocker, notably the whirlwind that was "When You Dance I Can Really Love," with Jack Nitzsche wildly pounding piano keys. Even throwaways like "Till the Morning Comes" (with Stills chiming in on harmony) and "Cripple Creek Ferry" felt meaty. With its preorders of four hundred thousand copies, the album was clearly a breakout, breakthrough piece of music—definitive proof that Young didn't need the other three and their mania for anything other than a larger bank account.

Although everyone expected Young to work on his own ("All of us knew we were going to do solo records, Neil above everybody," said Crosby), Nash's decision to go that route was the most telling. It was ironic that the band member who had worked hardest to preserve the group should be the one who helped fracture it, thanks to his affair with Coolidge. But in the end, the chaos on which CSNY thrived had finally unnerved even Nash. "You can only stand so much psychodrama in your life," he recalled. "I needed a break from them."

Like Crosby, he'd accumulated a batch of songs over the year and now had the luxury of time and money to commit them to tape. Over the course of several months starting in September, he casually began cutting them with a loose-knit ensemble of players he'd worked with all year, except Stills: Barbata, bassist Fuzzy Samuels, and now Coolidge, who came up from her home in Los Angeles and stayed with Nash while he recorded at the same Heider studio where Crosby was settling in.

As he'd shown when writing "Chicago" six months earlier, Nash had a tendency to relay his feelings about his musical partners or lovers in song rather than conversation. (In that way, Nash could simultaneously play the roles of good and bad cop.) *Songs for Beginners*, the album that began taking shape, continued that bent. With Coolidge supplying a fireplace-warm vocal harmony, he recorded "Simple Man," his song to Mitchell, as well as another on the same topic, "I Used to Be a King." ("In my bed, late at night, I miss you," he sang.) He chastised his fellow superstars in "There's Only One" ("Can we say it's cool/From a heated pool") and recorded "Better Days," the song inspired by Coolidge and Stills' relationship. The sessions were easygoing, the songs charmingly melodic and gentle, and Young and Crosby joined in now and then—both played on "I Used to Be a King." "Being with Graham was as easy as breathing," recalled Coolidge. "We just went in and did it, no pressure, no drugs and alcohol. That was fairly unique in those days."

The absentee band member was never far from Nash's thoughts. In "Wounded Bird," he addressed Stills directly, advising him to "take to heel or tame the horse/The choice is still your own." The song had been inspired by Stills' breakup with Judy Collins, yet it also echoed the events of the summer, especially lines like "Humble pie is always hard to swallow with your pride." This time, though, he didn't have to worry about a reaction, since his partner was over six thousand miles away. No one was sure when they'd see him next.

Days at Brookfield House in Surrey were rarely as ordinary or surreal as they were on October 22. In the morning, geese honked by the side of the pond, and an eccentric gardener named John made the rounds. On the front lawn, Stills tossed around a football with a visitor who'd just arrived from the States, comanager Elliot Roberts. At the breakfast table inside, talking and rolling joints, were Crosby and, of all people, Stills' one-time rival, Nash.

A few weeks earlier, following his Colorado detour, Stills had moved into Starr's Tudor home, which he'd begun renting in the spring. Against the advice of the band's other manager, David Geffen, Stills opted to stop renting and instead buy the house for 90,000 British pounds. (To Stills' surprise and annoyance, Allen Klein, representing Starr, unexpectedly raised by the price by 10,000 pounds at the closing.) Now Brookfield House was all his: the wandering swans, the orange grove, the separate movie theater, the doorways built so long ago that it was easy to bump one's head walking into a room.

Although Nash remained in love with Coolidge, he and Stills had mended their broken fences once more. Nash, who always worked the hardest to keep the band on an even keel, had heard the stories about Stills' excesses and decided to fly to London to see for himself. "We were very concerned," Nash said. "Everyone knew where this Stephen Stills story was headed. It wasn't as if *we* were clean, smoking dope and snorting. But we had it more under control than Stephen did."

Over breakfast, Crosby, Nash, and Henry Diltz, who'd joined Stills as houseguest, talked more immediate concerns, namely politics back home. Two weeks earlier, the Yippies in New York had received a tape featuring the voice of Bernardine Dohrn; on it, the cofounder of the Weather Underground announced "a fall offensive of youth resistance that will spread from Santa Barbara to Boston." Two days later, the group, most on the lam following the March brownstone incineration, followed through on the threat: Explosive devices went off at an ROTC building at the University of Washington and an armory in, as promised, Santa Barbara. At a press conference, attorney general John Mitchell, hardly sympathetic to antiwar protesters to begin with, snapped, "They're psychotic and out to destroy our institutions."

In tandem with an increasing number on the left, Crosby actually agreed with Mitchell for probably the first and last time in his life. Although he'd long been a vocal critic of the government, Nixon, and the Warren Commission's report on John Kennedy's assassination, Crosby was disturbed by the Weathermen. Their actions, he explained over breakfast in Stills' house, would be little more than an excuse for Nixon to declare a police state in America. "It would be instant war on us all," he told Nash and Diltz, adding the Weathermen were "fools." "Setting off bombs in office buildings was stupid," he recalled later. "All you do by going that route is become more suppressive."

The bombs had kept going off, not always by way of Weathermen associates. On the night of August 23, a stolen white Ford Falcon pulled up in front of a research building on the University of Wisconsin's Madison campus. At 3:40 A.M., an anonymous caller told police, "Hey, pig, there's a bomb on the university campus. Clear the building." Two minutes later, the truck—loaded with fertilizer, dynamite, and fuel oil—erupted into a fireball, uprooting trees and smashing windows in nearby buildings. Although the intended target was the Army Mathematics Research Center on the upper floors of the six-story building, the victim turned out to be a thirty-three-year-old research assistant (and father of three), then working in the physics department on the first floor. A manhunt ensued for the four men believed responsible, none associated with the Weathermen or other fringe groups. Most were eventually tracked down and arrested, although it would take seven years.

In Tulsa, a district judge was injured when a bomb went off in his station wagon. Firebombs crashed into police headquarters in Burlington, Massachusetts. From those and other bombings, forty people were dead, almost four hundred injured.

For Richard Nixon, all of these jarring detonations and mayhem were, in a twisted way, good news. Even before Kent State, his approval ratings had been down, mirroring the plunge in the Dow that spring. As fall approached, inflation was still on the rise, and early polls taking the public's temperature on a potential 1972 presidential race between him and Democratic Senator Edmund Muskie of Maine placed them neck and neck.

Then came the Weathermen, college demonstrations, and a general public that disliked the war but disdained scruffy campus protesters even more. (A post-Kent State clash in downtown New York, during which hard hats attacked antiwar activists, was a particularly telling sign for the administration.) Unnerved by the bombings—and comments like Dohrn's about how her group was "everywhere"—the public was happy to let the so-called Establishment put its fist down, and the administration was more than eager to exploit the law-and-order atmosphere. That fall, Agnew talked up violence and government intervention in speeches, and FBI head J. Edgar Hoover warned of "dissident elements" who "strive violently to destroy our current way of life." In an attempt to rebrand Nixon as a sympathetic figure, handlers made sure that unruly demonstrators interrupting him at rallies received ample media attention. Even one of Nixon's gaffes—declaring Charles Manson guilty of murder before his trial had even begun—worked in his favor: Of *course* Manson did it, most people thought, especially once they saw courtroom photos of the ultimate deranged hippie. (Of course, they were right in that regard: Manson and his cohorts would be found guilty of first-degree murder.) By the fall, Nixon's ratings had risen once again, and a November poll placed him eight points ahead of Muskie.

The fall midterm elections didn't go the White House's way: Democrats gained ten seats in the Senate and nineteen in the House. In a memo to Nixon two days later, special counsel Charles Colson wrote his boss, "We did not succeed in making the public believe that Democrat, Liberal permissiveness was the cause of violence and crime. . . . We didn't sell the point that violence and disorder in our society are caused directly by the rhetoric, softness, and catering to the dissidents which the Democrats have engaged in." But the White House took some comfort anyway. A Vietnam referendum on the ballot found the majority (711,000) supported Nixon's "peace plan" to end the war, compared to 440,000 who supported immediate withdrawal. "In the urban areas of the East, where fear of crime and violence is widespread," Colson also wrote, "our stand on law and order was the key issue."

The election marked the first all-out use of a relatively new Republican tactic of luring Southern white Democrats to the opposing party by way of coded reference to Democracts' alleged affiliations with black America and "liberal" leanings. In Tennessee, Republican Senate candidate William Brock— better known for the chocolate-covered cherries made by his very profitable Brock Candy Company than for any experience in politics—kept reminding voters that his opponent, Al Gore Sr., supported school busing and desegregation and was against the war and prayer in school. The GOP passed out Gore stickers and buttons to black voters in one largely African American county to make it clear to whites exactly who was in Gore's camp, and Agnew deemed Gore the "Southern regional chairman of the Eastern liberal establishment." It worked; after thirty-two years in the House and Senate, Gore lost his job on election day.

For his media profile, Nixon turned that year, as he had in 1968, to a thirty-year-old New York television producer, Roger Ailes. In a memo to Nixon in May, Ailes gave the President and his team pointers on televised appearances, such as having Nixon carry a handkerchief to wipe away perspiration and urging him to act warmer toward his own wife. ("Women voters are particularly sensitive to how a man treats his wife in public," Ailes wrote. "The more attention she gets, the happier they are.") Making the most of the medium—and scaring the hell out of white voters—were proving to be effective forms of voter persuasion, and Nixon went along, sometimes begrudgingly and sometimes willingly, with what appeared to be a trend of the future.

The Beatles continued to haunt them. On November 8, Crosby was back in San Francisco. With members of the Dead, he recorded "Laughing," written two years before about George Harrison's devotion to Indian spirituality. The song wasn't just about Harrison. ("It was a response, but not just about George," Crosby recalled. "Anybody who tells you 'I've been talking to God' is full of shit.") But it cast a wary eye on spiritual saviors in the same way Lennon had on *Plastic Ono Band*. With his layers of twelve-string guitars and Garcia's aching pedal steel guitar, which seemed to turn into a fiddle, "Laughing" was another massive, engulfing sonic cavern from the Crosby sessions. Joni Mitchell, whose bond with Crosby extended farther back than hers with Nash, contributed a spiraling, cooing harmony as well.

Whether CSNY, like the Beatles, would converge again remained an open question, the unsteady stuff of whims and moods. The informal reunion in London hadn't taken hold; to the press, Elliot Roberts declared that a group tour in the summer of 1971 was "a guess." Did Ertegun or Lookout Management make a mistake pushing for Young to join Crosby, Stills & Nash to begin with? Did they sacrifice short-term financial gain for the long-term group cohesion? Or were they always meant to come together and fall apart? "We were doing what we always intended," Stills recalled, "which was to make a couple of records together and then go away from each other for a while before we *killed* each other."

In November, the record Stills had been slaving away on all year, *Stephen Stills*, became the next sign of disharmony in the band. The album was a road map of Stills' previous six months. Some of it had been cut during his visit to London in the spring, the cover presented Stills with his mysterious, intimate-message toy giraffe, and Coolidge sang on several songs and was the subject of two others, "Cherokee" and "Sit Yourself Down." For someone who valued his privacy, Stills exposed more about his personal life on his first album than any of the rest of CSNY.

By then, each man's songs and approach to music-making reflected his personality: Nash's orderly and tidy, Crosby's laissez-faire and permissive, Young's sturdy and focused, Stills' nervy and headstrong. If *After the Gold Rush* was an indisputably well-built house of songs, *Stephen Stills* was a messy room that wouldn't have it any other way. The album moved from a raw-voiced, ferociously picked acoustic blues, "Black Queen," to a lushly orchestrated ballad, "To a Flame," pausing along the way for a nod to gospel ("Church [Part of Someone]"), a ballad that could have been part of a Greenwich Village folk repertoire ("Do for the Others"), and scene-stealing cameos by Hendrix ("Old Times Good Times") and Clapton ("Go Back Home"). Stills' creative ambitions were on full display: None of the others in his current band would have attempted, nor pulled off, a piece of orchestrated folk rock with gospel midsection like the climactic "We Are Not Helpless," complete with Ringo Starr on drums. Stills' voice, too, ran the gamut from supple to whiskey-roughed-up. In the way it moved restlessly from one genre to another, *Stephen Stills* attested to Stills' burning-at-both-ends intensity that both drove him and, as the fall progressed, threatened to derail him at any moment. (With its songs' subtle instrumental and rhythm shifts, it also pinpointed Stills' painstaking devotion to the craft of recordmaking—a vastly different approach from Young's, who preferred as much spontaneity as possible.)

Even before the album was out, Stills was already at work on its follow-up, driving himself even harder. Kept awake by any number of substances, Stills and his engineer and coproducer, Bill Halverson, would stay up for days at Island Studios in London, recording song after song, take after take, variation after variation. They cut "Change Partners," two years old but prophetic given CSNY's situation, in different tempos; at Stills' expense, the Memphis Horns were flown over from the States for a taste of the big-band rock then in vogue. "Stephen heard what was in his head and was chasing it," Halverson says. "But I was starting to lose perspective. Some of those long three or four days together, what we ended up with, we didn't want."

In London, Stills' days and nights became a nonstop blur of activity, musical and otherwise. Bill Wyman of the Rolling Stones and Robert

Plant dropped by. Stills would start recording, take a break, and go to a club, where he could watch Princess Anne dance or meet Peter Sellers, in whose former house Stills was now living. One night, he dragged Sellers back to the studio at three in the morning to hear his tapes. When Frank Zappa and the Mothers of Invention came through town, Stills jammed with them onstage and caroused with them in their dressing room later. In his brown Jaguar, he drove to an airport and flew to Amsterdam to join the Stones onstage, then partied with them until dawn in Keith Richards' hotel room. Hearing that his Mulholland Drive drag-racing buddy Steve McQueen was filming *Le Mans* outside Paris—and hoping he could write the score for the film—Stills rented a Mercedes and drove it onto a ferry bound for France. When he arrived at the race-track where they were filming, he discovered McQueen and his crew had already left.

Back in England, he tooled around the countryside in his other car, a Ferrari, and bought two Thoroughbreds from an Irish horse dealer. Deliveries for the wine cellar would appear regularly. One day's shipment included four bottles of 1960 Château Mouton Rothschild, six of Kruger, six of Dom Perignon, and four of Châteauneuf-du-Pape. Inevitably, empty bottles were scattered on the lawn near a fence. "It was wicked dangerous because there were nasty things crawling about," Stills recalled. "And I managed to walk that razor's edge. Probably not without making an utter fool of myself."

Somehow it was fitting that Stills and Starr would find themselves face-to-face again at Tramp during the first week of December. Try as they might, Crosby, Stills, Nash & Young couldn't escape the sobriquet "American Beatles" that had been bestowed upon them. "The *Let It Be* stuff was overhanging the whole year," Stills recalled, "that they were basically ready to kill each other. And I guess we got caught up in that too. We could all feel it. It permeated the whole industry. We were all getting very full of ourselves, and it was probably time to not be restricted by running everything by your mates, because some of them may understand what you're doing and some might not." Like the Beatles, CSNY had experienced it all: early camaraderie, dizzying fame, endless hours in recording studios, ample drug experimentation, mounting interpersonal tensions, and, finally, disarray. Remarkably, though, they'd managed to do it not in a decade but in a mere eighteen months.

CHAPTER 15

When Paul Simon called Clive Davis to arrange a meeting, Columbia's convivial president didn't think twice. As far as Davis knew, Simon and Garfunkel were in healthy shape professionally and financially. In early July, they'd been presented with a gold record for sales of five hundred thousand copies of "Cecilia," the galloping follow-up to "Bridge Over Troubled Water." Although the *Bridge* album was drooping on the charts—and "El Condor Pasa," its third single, failed to commandeer the airwaves the way "Bridge Over Troubled Water" and "Cecilia" had—it continued to generate substantial income for the label. One report that crossed Davis' desk cited figures from Austria, where the company made a tidy $120,000 off twenty thousand *Bridge* LPs and $60,000 from the "El Condor Pasa" single. And that was merely one relatively small market.

Besides, Davis had other, troubling matters on his mind. On the morning of October 5, the phone had rung earlier than usual in his Central Park West apartment. One of his young sons answered and delivered the news to his still-sleeping father: Janis Joplin, one of the first acts Davis signed to Columbia, was dead, her body found facedown at the Landmark Motor Hotel in Hollywood. One of her hands was still clutching a cigarette, and one of her arms carried fresh needle marks. Davis knew Joplin loved a good time—he'd noticed her taste for Southern Comfort almost from the day he'd met her—but the news was still shocking. Joplin had just completed a new album; the day before her death, she'd sat for a photo session for its cover. Whether he was naïve or in denial, Davis said he knew nothing of her fondness for heroin—which, combined with alcohol, had led to her death.

For Davis and others in the music business, it had been that kind of paralyzing fall. It wasn't merely the succession of deaths: Canned Heat's Al Wilson of an overdose in his sleeping bag on September 3, followed by Hendrix, and now Joplin. The superstars who hadn't died weren't functioning as they once had. Sly Stone, who recorded for Columbia's sister label Epic, was increasingly consumed by a drug problem, delaying his in-progress album and leading to a succession of missed concerts. In late September, Jim Morrison was found guilty of indecent exposure and profanity in a Florida courtroom, stemming from a never-proven accusation of pulling out his penis onstage with the Doors the previous year. Morrison was sentenced to six months' hard labor for the first charge, sixty days for the second. Motown still landed dazzling singles in the top 10 all year—Edwin Starr's "War," the Jackson 5's "I'll Be There," Stevie Wonder's "Signed Sealed Delivered (I'm Yours)"—but Marvin Gaye had temporarily retired from music, the Four Tops were stalled, and Wonder was in a changeover from child star to adulthood. The company, and black music in general, was in the midst of transitioning from love songs to socially conscious ones. "The Tears of a Clown," the only major hit Smokey Robinson and the Miracles had pulled off that year, was a three-year-old recording.

The government was making other, equally rattling, noises about the business. On October 14, just over a week after Joplin's overdose, Richard Nixon summoned a group of radio, news, and advertising executives to the Oval Office to talk about drugs and rock and roll. The assembled included radio programmers from around the country, the heads of ABC News and the national association of FM broadcasters, and Nixon's old friend Gene Autry, the singing cowboy who now ran the Golden West radio network. One daunting administration figure after another—John Ehrlichman, John Mitchell, officials from the Narcotics

Bureau and the FCC—issued dire warnings about the connections between drug abuse and the music, and radio executives were asked to screen songs for drug references. To ram home the point, members of a New York drug-rehab center put on a skit. No hard-and-fast rules were laid out, but the chilling effect was felt by everyone in the room.

As if he'd already received the meeting's subliminal message, Mike Curb, the young Republican head of MGM Records, announced he was dropping eighteen acts who supposedly promoted hard drugs in their songs. "I'm tired of hearing about these drugged-up acts who don't show up for a television appearance," Curb griped to a reporter. Curb didn't name the specific artists whose contracts were being terminated, only saying he'd retained Roy Orbison, former Righteous Brother Bill Medley, and, strangely, hard-living former Animals frontman Eric Burdon (whose "Spill the Wine" just happened to be a major MGM hit that summer). Given Curb's well-known political ambitions, many wondered if the move was his first step in running for office. (In fact, he would later be elected California's lieutenant governor.) Davis was the first label head to denounce Curb, publicly chiding him for what Davis called "artistic witch hunts."

Relative to this string of disquieting news, a phone call from Paul Simon was a stroll in the park, Central or otherwise. At the start, their relationship had been a little frosty. Simon seemed wary of Davis and his background in accounting. He and Garfunkel had bonded far better with Davis' predecessor, Goddard Lieberson; over their first lunch together, all three talked about classic fiction and poetry. But after Davis made the right call with the soundtrack to *The Graduate* and allowed Simon however much time he needed to craft his music, the two gradually grew tighter. Over the occasional meal, Davis listened as Simon let down his notorious guard. Despite a string of hit singles, Simon told Davis he felt he wasn't taken as seriously as some of his peers. "If you were viewed as a pop tunesmith, a hit songwriter, someone who didn't move the social frontiers forward, you were relegated to secondary consideration," Davis recalled. "Paul felt Dylan was getting more respect than him. He was keenly aware of that." An avid reader of the rock press, Davis listened, nodded, and coddled. He told Simon he was one of the great songwriters of his era, his work equal to that of Lennon and McCartney.

Even though he was in tune with Simon's neuroses, Davis wasn't prepared for the topic of conversation when Simon arrived at his office at CBS headquarters in the Black Rock building on Sixth Avenue in midtown Manhattan. After a bit of small talk, Simon told Davis he and Garfunkel were no more and that he'd be making records on his own.

The head of Columbia Records was taken aback, both by the news and the straightforwardness of Simon's declaration of independence. "It wasn't, 'What's your advice?'" Davis recalled. "He wasn't coming to ask my advice. He was coming to tell me a fact."

Davis' first impulse was to argue. It was almost impossible to imagine the two men apart (they, not CSNY, were "the American Beatles," in Davis' words) or to imagine where Simon would go as a solo artist. Garfunkel's voice was such an integral part of the duo's sound and identity. But he knew Simon too well to take such an argumentative approach, so he merely listened to Simon's reasons. "He didn't want a partner," Davis said. "Artie was a very articulate partner, but that process had worn thin with Paul. He wanted to chart his own career without having to defer to another person."

Davis wasn't happy, especially now that some of his label's biggest acts were on rocky ground. (In June, Dylan had released *Self-Portrait*, a self-destructive double LP weighed down with soggy cover versions, including Simon's "The Boxer.") Now Simon and Garfunkel looked to be history as well. "If you have kids, and they're getting a divorce, you don't applaud and say, 'Great!'" Davis said. "Divorce isn't happy news." Davis tried, instead, to gently discourage him. Would Simon sell as many records on his own as the duo? Maybe, maybe not. Simon flinched but didn't say much. By the end of the conversation, Davis sensed he couldn't alter Simon's decision. All he could do was hope the break was temporary.

O O O O

By then, Garfunkel was gone again. In September, Mike Nichols' screen adaptation of the Jules Feiffer play *True Confessions*, now retitled *Carnal Knowledge*, began filming in Vancouver, then later in Massachusetts and Manhattan. Feiffer's biting, razor-sharp-tongued script followed the sexual adventures of two close friends from their saddle-shoed college years in the '40s through facial hair and middle age in the '70s. If *Catch-22* was a seriocomic look at war, *Carnal Knowledge* would be a bleak depiction of male-female relationships in the new, sexually open era of the '70s—which, in the film, would be depicted as a soul-depleting morass of lust, infidelity, communication breakdowns, and sexual frustration.

As with *Catch-22*, Garfunkel would be taking his place alongside established actors: Jack Nicholson, fresh off *Easy Rider* and *Five Easy Pieces*, and sex-kitten pinup Ann-Margret. But there was one crucial, defining difference from the previous film. No longer just a member of an ensemble, Garfunkel would now be a costar, playing Sandy next to Nicholson's Jonathan. Thanks to Nichols' casting, he was no longer an aspiring actor; *Carnal Knowledge* would announce to the world that Art Garfunkel was a marquee name.

In Simon and Garfunkel circles, the timing raised many an eyebrow. *Catch-22* had been a difficult experience, especially for Simon. Before filming began, screenwriter Buck Henry, feeling the script had too many characters, eliminated several parts, including a small role written for Simon. Simon wasn't happy, especially once he learned that Garfunkel's part remained. To many close to them, Simon being cut from the film—

combined with the way it ate up so much of Garfunkel's time through-out 1969—was one of the principal reasons for their rift. In casting Gar-funkel in another film so quickly after *Catch-22*, was Nichols, perhaps unintentionally, helping drive a wedge between the two? Some in their circle wondered—even, it turned out, Simon himself. "There was sort of vaguely the presence of Mike Nichols around, which was discon-certing to me," he admitted to the *New York Times*, albeit two years later.

"I never brought it up with either of them," said their mutual friend Charles Grodin. "But if it was me, and my partner went off to do a movie, I wouldn't appreciate it. 'We're a team and we're doing great.' But that's me."

The net result was clear enough: With Nichols' support, Garfunkel would finally be on Simon's level. Filming *Carnal Knowledge* in Canada (for its scenes set on a campus in the '40s), Garfunkel again found himself in heady, non-rock-and-roll company. While shooting at Vic-toria College, the cast, particularly Nicholson and Garfunkel, became pals when they shared a house. Nichols asked the cast to refrain from smoking pot, which they did—except for the night when Garfunkel, Nicholson, co-star Candice Bergen, and others got high and watched Peter O'Toole in *Lawrence of Arabia*, mocking the decade-old desert classic with stoned giggles. Feiffer took Garfunkel and Nicholson to a party on the nearby set of *McCabe and Mrs. Miller*, where Garfunkel wound up in the same room as Nicholson, Warren Beatty, and Robert Altman.

Sandy's pensive, understated personality proved a perfect match for Garfunkel's own. ("Artie was just playing himself," recalled a friend of the time.) Sandy, who winds up a doctor, was another variation of the soft-spoken, pure-of-heart Nately he'd played in *Catch-22*—and, by as-sociation, the winsome characters Garfunkel embodied in Simon's songs. To Garfunkel, the combination of Jonathan and Sandy felt familiar, as if Nichols and Feiffer had based the two characters on the idea of a longtime friendship like his and Simon's. Much like Simon and Garfunkel over the years, Jonathan and Sandy were close but competitive, chummy but hard on each other. Early in the film, Nicholson's Jonathan, a rapacious, sexually driven rogue, sleeps with Susan (Bergen), the model-beautiful girl of Sandy's dreams. As *New York Times* critic Vincent Canby would comment, "It is, in effect, a series of slightly mad dialogues between two people . . . that almost always lead to new plateaus of psychic misunderstanding and emotional hurt." Those words also summed up Simon and Garfunkel in 1970.

Among those who knew Simon and Garfunkel, the breakup shouldn't have been news; even their lifestyles pointed to separate paths. Garfunkel loved nothing more than traveling, exploring, and spending time with his new Hollywood contingent. Settling down wasn't anywhere near the agenda. Simon was friends with some of the same people; like Garfunkel, he spent more time with writers, directors, and actors than with fellow musicians or pop stars. But thanks to his new marriage, Simon was more homebound. Peggy Harper was smart, witty, and attractive but, as Lewis had discovered during their brief marriage, averse to social gatherings. As a result, Simon seemed to spend more time with her at their Upper East Side apartment—which would soon give way to a brownstone—and their house in Pennsylvania.

Another sign of an impending Simon and Garfunkel divorce should have been Simon's ever-expanding tastes, particularly his fascination with rhythms and world music—a world apart from Garfunkel's attachment to more opulent, romantic pop. "Cuba Sí, Nixon No," Simon's Chuck Berry homage, wasn't the only song dropped from *Bridge Over Troubled Water*. Garfunkel had argued for a Bach choral piece Simon rejected; they also took a pass at "Feuilles-O," a Haitian ode to the powers of marijuana. All three, along with a fourth song, "Groundhog," were relegated to tape canisters.

Despite all those forewarnings, though, Clive Davis wasn't the only one caught way off guard by news of their split. Mort Lewis, their manager, knew well how each got on the other's nerves, sometimes intentionally. But when they walked offstage at Forest Hills Tennis Stadium that summer, Lewis had no idea it would be their last show. Increasingly, it was obvious what had happened: They'd effectively dissolved during the making of *Bridge Over Troubled Water* but hadn't bothered to tell anyone who handled the business of Simon and Garfunkel.

Now everything, from their strained interactions to the paucity of live concerts during the year, made sense. When he heard the news, Robert Drew, executive producer of their *Songs of America* special, flashed back to its filming. In meetings, Simon did the majority of the talking; Garfunkel mostly sat and observed. Simon wound up editing the film himself, without his partner. Most strikingly, Drew recalled how the two made subtle jokes between themselves about disbanding. "They obviously had a plan, and the plan was to separate," he recalled. "But it wasn't announced and not spoken of in that way."

Drew thought the story of their dissolution would make a riveting follow-up film, but they expressed no interest in making it. A planned live album for Columbia, culled from their fall 1969 concerts, was shelved. No press release or public statement about their dissolution would be forthcoming. (Despite his formidable ego, fanfare never appealed to Simon: That fall, he quietly donated $25,000 to the City College of New York, for what became known as its "Mrs. Robinson Fund" for teachers.) Simon and Garfunkel would recede as gently and nonaggressively as the decade.

As early as 1957, Simon was painfully aware of show business' dark side—massive fame followed by devastating, financially strapped obscurity. "Once you're down, it can be terrible," the sixteen-year-old Simon admitted to the *New York World-Telegram* during Tom and Jerry's "Hey, Schoolgirl" moment. "There's really nothing worse than someone who has been on the top and then is down." Thirteen years later, the matter still weighed on him. In the wake of the breakup, Simon knew well that Garfunkel's voice, blond Afro, and surname were more immediately identifiable to the public than his own. Simon told Lewis he was worried people would confuse him with R&B singer Joe Simon, and Davis' qualms about Simon without Garfunkel didn't help matters.

But the times were shifting in Simon's favor. As the end of 1970 neared, solidarity began going the way of solipsism. The bands, one iconic '60s act after another, were crumbling, the scrap heap growing higher with each passing month. The Beatles, CSNY, and Simon and Garfunkel—and, everyone soon learned, Peter, Paul and Mary—were only the most prominent. The Stax duo Sam and Dave, who brought volcanic energy to hits like "Hold On, I'm Comin'" and "Soul Man," announced their dissolution. The Supremes no longer included Diana Ross, who left in January to start a career of her own. A frustrated Lou Reed split from the Velvet Underground in August. Jefferson Airplane lost their original drummer, Spencer Dryden, in January, and their smooth-voiced co-lead singer, Marty Balin, would be gone by year's end. The Dave Clark Five, holdovers from the British Invasion, were now history. The Monkees, already down to only two of the four founding members, Micky Dolenz and Davy Jones, were also dust after one last ill-fated attempt to regain past glories with a final single in the spring.

Enter a new category and genre, one that could have had its own section in a record store—the solo album. A year or two before, the concept was unimaginable. Bands were collectives, united fronts; rarely if ever did a member spin off and make his or her own record on the side. The very thought was an affront to accord. Those who worked on their own, like Dylan, had always done so and were continuing the long-standing tradition of the troubadour.

By October, the group albums from earlier in the year were fading on the charts: *Déjà vu* at 24, *Bridge Over Troubled Water* at 43, *Let It Be* at 57. In their places were the remnants: albums by Harrison and Stills and Young and McCartney and Starr and, soon, Lennon and Crosby and Nash. Some were statements of individuality, others of frivolity. Either way, the collective message they sent out couldn't be denied. Be it bands, community, the antiwar movement, none of it could be relied upon anymore. The rise of the solo album embodied the new self-reliance and self-absorption: the I Don't Need Anyone Else But Myself, Thanks, statement.

Earlier in the year, Simon and Garfunkel had each grown anxious over the similarities between "Bridge Over Troubled Water" and "Let It Be." Now, as the year ended, those songs, along with those on *Déjà vu*, had more in common than any of them could've imagined. The serenity of the music turned out to be merely a cover for the hidden turbulence that lay beneath. The songs meant to comfort fans were often as not a product of recording studio magic than true collaboration. CSNY's chummy onstage banter, the way each member flattered the other after a song ended, turned out to be as much show business as reality. Even Simon's supportive words toward Garfunkel's acting aspirations in "The Only Living Boy in New York" were a camouflage for far more conflicted feelings. Whether it was the music or the country, whatever hadn't already exploded in the two previous years let loose one last time, like a final blast of steam from a manhole cover. The cover flew into the air, crashed onto the street, and gradually rolled to a stop, and everyone seemed too exhausted to retrieve and replace it.

○ ○ ○ ○

In November, Columbia Records laid claim to San Francisco. After having signed a number of local acts, including Joplin and Santana, Davis gave the go-ahead to build the label's first recording studio in the city, to be run by Roy Halee, Simon and Garfunkel's coproducer and engineer. Given Halee's association with the two men, many assumed they'd use the rooms to begin cutting new music. Instead, only one name was penciled in for sessions in December—Paul Simon.

"There was a thing called the golden age of the Beatles and when that broke up four years ago there was a huge slip-down—the energy level, the commitment disappeared," Garfunkel said in an unpublished interview years later. "It's looser now, it's more personal, it's scattered, it's gone in lots of different directions." Garfunkel began witnessing the transformation for himself. In New York in November, he, along with Dylan, caught the Fillmore East debut of Elton John, the British singer and pianist who'd released his first two American albums that year. The first had established him with "Your Song"; the second, *Tumbleweed Connection*, was suitably ambitious, an Englishman's take on American country. John was part introspective balladeer, part Tin Pan Alley showman, and entirely of a different mindset than those who'd come before.

During the *Carnal Knowledge* shoot in Vancouver, Garfunkel, Nicholson, and Bergen took a break from filming and swung by a nearby arena for a concert to benefit a new, pro-environment organization. The billed performers were Joni Mitchell and Phil Ochs. The unannounced guest was Mitchell's boyfriend, whose album was now one of the most played records in the country. The musician whom Garfunkel's partner hadn't heard of earlier in the year had left the clubs and cult following—if not his troubles—behind.

CHAPTER 16

In Vancouver, British Columbia, the Stowe family had just gathered for dinner when the phone rang. To the amazement of his children, Irving Stowe, the family's bushy-bearded patriarch, found himself on the line with Joni Mitchell, talking about her friend James.

With a group of like-minded friends in the area, Stowe, a pacifist, teacher, and convert to Quakerism, was none too thrilled when he'd heard the United States would soon be conducting nuclear tests on Amchitka, a small island off the coast of Alaska. Although the government had detonated hydrogen bombs in the area before, in 1965 and 1969, the third, planned for 1971, promised to be the most brutalizing; the five-megaton bomb threatened to extinguish sea otters, bald eagles, and any other wildlife unfortunate enough to live in the area. To protest the tests, Stowe and his wife, Dorothy, had helped launch the Don't Make a Wave Committee, and his passion for music (and the Newport Folk Festivals he'd attended) led him to consider organizing a concert to raise money for their actions, which included sailing a boat to the island as a visible act of protest.

Although Joan Baez passed on an invite to the show due to her schedule (but sent a check for $10,000), she'd suggested Mitchell. Stowe reached out to Elliot Roberts, who phoned back to say Mitchell would do it. By the time Mitchell called Stowe at home two weeks before the concert, the committee had changed its name to Greenpeace. At a meeting, Stowe had flashed a peace sign and another member replied, "Let's make it a *green* peace." The new, more compact moniker stuck.

"Hello, Joni," Stowe said, as his family—his wife, daughter, and son—quieted down and eagerly eavesdropped. Stowe cupped his hand over the phone and turned to them. "Joni wants to know if she can bring James Taylor," he whispered. "Who's James Taylor?"

The family members shrugged; they didn't know either. His fourteen-year-old daughter Barbara thought Mitchell might mean James Brown, but that didn't seem right. Back on the line, Stowe told Mitchell she could certainly bring her friend, then hung up and told his family not to mention it to anyone. "We don't know who this is," he said, "and if he's no good, it could ruin the whole concert." Later, the family ventured out to a nearby record store and, to their relief, saw *Sweet Baby James* in the window. When they asked the clerk how the album was doing, he said, excitedly, "It's number 10 on the charts!"

Like a shy kid at a prom dance, "Fire and Rain" had stood on the side-lines all year, waiting for its moment. In the spring, Warner Brothers had hesitated to release the song to radio. With its subdued tone and el-liptical lyrics, it wasn't an odds-on favorite to be a hit. "I thought it was maybe too obscure in its message," said Taylor's friend and guitarist Danny Kortchmar. "It was too dark to be a hit." The label also hesitated when soul singer R. B. Greaves, who'd had a major hit the year before with "Take a Letter, Maria," a story-song about a black executive in a failing marriage, released a cover of "Fire and Rain." No one wanted Taylor competing against his own song.

Yet "Fire and Rain," a regular part of Taylor's set on the road, was making inroads with his audiences; its understated vulnerability, unclut-tered melody, and easy-to-follow metaphors drew them in. When L.A. pop star Johnny Rivers unveiled another cover of the song in August—this one a lavish production with horns and female backup singers—Warners had no choice but to promote Taylor's own version. "Finally," announced an ad in the music press, "the original (and, we think, best) 'Fire and Rain' is now a single." The accompanying photo—Taylor playing a piano in Asher's living room, a cat hovering nearby—conveyed the singer's, and song's, hypersensitive image.

Since "Sweet Baby James" hadn't made the charts, expectations were modest; true enough, "Fire and Rain" debuted on *Billboard*'s Hot 100 chart at number 100. It didn't stay there long. Far faster than the song's tempo, stations in New York, Chicago, and Philadelphia pounced on it, as did outlets in Atlanta, New Orleans, and Athens, Georgia. During the final days of filming *Two-Lane Blacktop*, Taylor told director Monte Hellman that people were starting to respond to the song, but his delivery was so muted Hellman didn't know how big this news was. "Fire and Rain" also found its way onto playlists of stations at Knox College in Illinois, the Rochester Institute of Technology, and the State University of New York in Oswego. In one week, it vaulted from 83 to 50 before sneaking into the top 10 the week of October 17. Two weeks after that, it was the third most popular song in the country.

By then, the country, even the world, was exhausted after ten months of Vietnam-related anguish and homegrown terrorism, pandemonium and death on campus, and the collapse or failure of so much from the past decade, be it the Beatles or moon missions. The two previous years had jarringly demonstrated that social or political change was no longer in plain sight. It had all accelerated that year, so that the worlds of January 1970 and twelve months later felt like polar opposites.

What everyone—especially rock fans verging on age thirty—wanted was quiet, and pop was there to serve. The Carpenters, a brother-sister duo from Southern California who looked like student-council candidates and made polite music to match, had scored their first major hit in the spring with "(They Long to Be) Close to You"; in the fall, their second smash, "We've Only Just Begun," proved America wanted more, please. Elsewhere on the radio that fall were Bread's "It Don't Matter to Me," Elton John's "Your Song," Gordon Lightfoot's "If You Could Read My Mind," and Cat Stevens' "Wild World"—a parade of balladeers,

American, Canadian, and British, with less interest in making a racket and more in expressing their innermost feelings to unplugged, consoling backup. These were songs—superb ones, sometimes—for men who wanted women to know they were thoughtful and caring (and could make pretty good bedmates as well). Stevens' "Where Do the Children Play?" from the *Tea for the Tillerman* album that arrived that November, was mellow and eco-driven—the best of both new worlds.

Dylan turning to country music was one thing. The rise of this new genre, with the seemingly contradictory name "soft rock," was a telling sign of the times. Some of the musicians, like Stevens and Neil Diamond, were once teen-market-scrubbed pop stars who'd given themselves shaggy-dog makeovers. Some, like Lightfoot, had been making folk records for years but had grown out their hair and now looked like members of the back-to-the-land movement.

In this context, "Fire and Rain" found a home. After a year of breakdowns and death, a song about a mental collapse and a friend's suicide—by a performer only too willing to let the world know he'd spent time in "a nuthouse," as he called it onstage—felt like a natural extension of the collective mindset. The times picked "Fire and Rain" as much as any radio programmer. Taylor's good looks didn't hurt, either. In her neighborhood in Carbondale, Illinois, fourteen-year-old Shawn Colvin was babysitting for a neighbor when a friend brought over the "Fire and Rain" 45. Playing the record on the family's stereo, Colvin and her friend were instantly besotted with singer and song. ("God knows where the kid was," Colvin recalled of the child under her care.) When they found a copy of *Sweet Baby James*, Colvin, like many that fall, was immediately taken with the handsome face on the cover. "He was dark, but he was easy on the eyes," Colvin said. "We were all in love with him. Forget it. It was a good package."

The song took *Sweet Baby James* along for the ride; by late October, the album had sold eight hundred thousand copies, nearly half of them that month alone, and peaked at number 3. "The cycle has come back to romanticism," Carole King told a reporter that fall, in an unpublished interview. "People got sick of the psychedelic cloud and wanted to get softer moods. . . . He was what people were ready for and he happened to be there at the right time. His institutionalized past is also something they can identify with. A lot of people think they're going crazy: 'What I'm thinking is totally unrelated to what anyone else is thinking. Am I crazy?' James is like a friend to them." In short order, thanks to Taylor, King would be their friend as well.

Irving Stowe and his son Robert met Taylor and Mitchell at the airport the day of the concert, October 16. A limo took them to the arena, where, backstage, the two walked in hand in hand, Taylor glancing downward and Mitchell beaming for all to see. Mitchell did a few interviews, Taylor none. For an encore, they were planning to sing Dylan's "Mr. Tambourine Man" and Mitchell's "The Circle Game" together and spent time in the dressing room working out chord changes. Once that was done, Taylor seemed more interested in working his way through a bottle of Southern Comfort.

Appearing at the concert had been Mitchell's idea; after all, she was Canadian. In interviews during the previous months, though, Taylor had made it clear that his music contained no sociocultural or political messages. "I couldn't urge anybody to think a certain way politically without feeling uneasy," he told the *Times*' Susan Braudy. ". . . Just because I sing a tune people enjoy doesn't mean anybody should follow my political ideas."

Plenty of people agreed with him, but like Stowe, Bob Hunter, and other cofounders of Greenpeace, others were starting to channel their frustration—and their fears of what was happening to the planet—

into a new movement. The list of scientists warning of pending planetary doom had been growing ever since the publication of Rachel Carson's best-selling and influential *Silent Spring* in 1962, and each year brought increasingly disturbing reports of pollution and endangered species. In January 1969, a blowout at a Union Oil offshore well near Santa Barbara dumped over three million barrels of oil into Southern California waters, mucking up beaches and killing thousands of dolphins and fish. As it had at the dawn of the new year, *Mad* magazine rammed home the point harder than the mainstream media could. Its July 1970 issue included "obituaries for traditions, pastimes and other Dying-out Landmarks of the American Way of Life." Included were obits for "Efficient Customer Service," "Reliable Postal Service," "Melody in Popular Music," and "Clean Air." "Death took place at 1:33 this afternoon when the final trace, a small breathable patch above Lincoln, Nebraska, was smogged out," the magazine joked, deadpan. ". . . There will be no funeral service, due to survivors being too choked up to speak."

Inspired by the Vietnam Moratorium, a Wisconsin Democratic senator, Gaylord Nelson, proposed a "teach-in" on the environment in the spring. Before long, his idea expanded into Earth Day. On April 22, some twenty million people across the country gathered, demonstrated, swept, and planted trees. In effect, they were protesting a different kind of war. A few months later came Yale law professor Charles Reich's book, *The Greening of America*, which advocated "choosing a new lifestyle" rooted in a new, eco-minded consciousness. In his State of the Union address in January 1970, Nixon had mentioned the environment as a priority. His commitment was flimsy, his concerns more careerist than ecological. ("The hell with them," he would snap at his National Security Advisor, Henry Kissinger, during a discussion about environmentalists the following August. ". . . You know they've bled over every goddamn atomic test that's been made. We'd be fighting Japan still if they had their way.")

Always in search of ways to capitalize on a trend that would give him a boost in the polls, he'd launched an Office of Environmental Affairs in January, followed by an Environmental Protection Agency.

Something positive had finally begun to emerge from the ruins of the previous decade: a green movement that merged both political and personal concerns. The "Greenpeace Benefit" at the PNE Coliseum brought together the new and old singer-songwriter guard in one setting. Phil Ochs, who drank heavily at the Stowe household before the show, came on first and delivered a stirring set of his older topical songs, like "I Ain't Marching Anymore" and "Joe Hill." (As Ochs himself sensed, his songs were already beginning to feel like nostalgia.) Out of nervousness, Mitchell's voice broke during "Chelsea Morning," yet she recovered with a tender and occasionally rollicking set, slipping "Bonie Maronie" into her own pro-environment song, "Big Yellow Taxi."

For someone coping with substance-abuse issues, Taylor was proving himself a more than capable showman. At this and other shows that year, he was unwaveringly steady, in tune, and endearingly funny onstage. ("He hates the success," King said about Taylor that fall. "He almost reluctantly goes out onstage. But at the same time he enjoys performing.") "I've got a single out now and I'd like to play it for you, a little ditty," he said before "Fire and Rain." When they began applauding after the first two lines, he interjected, "Thank you, folks." In a self-mocking but also self-aware tone, he referred to *Sweet Baby James* as "my smash-hit album on Warner Brothers." The audience ate it all up, and the show—with Garfunkel, Nicholson, and Bergen in the crowd—wound up raising an impressive $17,000 for Greenpeace.

Taylor and Mitchell's affair continued into the autumn, friends all the while wondering how Mitchell, who was not a heroin user, was coping with his drug use and moodiness. "I'd go over there and he'd be sitting in the dark in the corner," recalled Essra Mohawk, one of Mitchell's neighbors and a singer-songwriter in her own right. "He was on heroin at the time. We all were." (Mohawk recalled regular smack deliveries to the neighborhood by way of "a very clean-cut fella in a crisp white shirt who used to come to our back door.") In spite of Taylor's recurring addiction, his and Mitchell's mutual attraction was obvious: Both were young, beautiful, and horny. In and around Los Angeles, they acted like love-struck teenagers, giggling or necking in the backs of cars. Taylor was seen wearing the vest she'd knit for him on the set of *Two-Lane Blacktop*. They traveled together, to New York and London, for each other's concerts. When she joined him at his November 7 concert at Princeton, coincidentally her twenty-seventh birthday, Taylor had the audience join him in singing "Happy Birthday" to her. The following week's issue of *Rolling Stone* went so far as to announce they were getting married.

In London for one of Mitchell's concerts, she and Taylor spent an afternoon at the apartment of none other than her former lover, Graham Nash. As Nash's friend, drummer Johnny Barbata, watched, the three passed around guitars and a hash pipe. "One would play a song and the others would say, 'Fantastic,'" recalled Barbata. "There was a lot of mutual respect." Given that Mitchell had dumped Nash about six months earlier, the situation could've been extremely awkward. According to Nash, though, no one was unnerved: They were loving the ones they were with. "We were grownups," he recalled. "James was a very shy man, with a great sense of humor. A brilliant writer." He smiled. "That motherfucker."

0 0 0 0

As soon as he took a seat behind Taylor at the Troubadour club in Los Angeles, Leland Sklar—a twenty-three-year-old bass player with the full beard and mustache of a California mountain man—knew something had changed. It was November 24, and Taylor was back at the club he'd already played several times before. Now, though, he was settling in for six nights starting Thanksgiving evening. In another sign of his success, he could afford a band—drummer Russ Kunkel, who'd played on *Sweet Baby James*, and Sklar, a Milwaukee-born musician who'd moved to California with his family and later attended college there.

That summer, Sklar had been stunned to receive a call from Peter Asher, asking if he was willing to audition for Asher's client James Taylor. Sklar didn't recognize Taylor's name; if anything, he was far more awestruck to hear the voice of one half of Peter and Gordon on the line. Asher said Taylor had heard Sklar play and had described him as "better than Paul McCartney" on the bass. Sklar suddenly recalled the time he was rehearsing with his hard-rock band Wolfgang and a mutual acquaintance had brought by a quiet, friendly, and possibly drunk friend—who, it turned out, was Taylor. To Sklar, Taylor was "one of those messed-up hippie guys" who always seemed to be crashing at various people's houses. "He'd walk around with a shirt torn down the back and he'd wear it every day," he recalled. "A pretty funky guy." At Asher's house for rehearsals, Sklar was impressed with Taylor's intricate chording and the way he played bass parts on his acoustic guitar: Maybe he was more than a messed-up hippie guy after all.

In early fall, Sklar had played his first—and he thought only—show with Taylor, at a half-filled Troubadour. But when Asher asked if he wanted to go on tour, Sklar reluctantly said good-bye to his own band to join up with Taylor. Toward the end of Taylor's sets, like another show at the Berkeley Community Theater, Kunkel and Sklar emerged from the wings to add a modest thump to "Country Road" and the new songs, "Highway Song" and "Riding on a Railroad." One reviewer detected "a crack of emotion" in Taylor with a rhythm section behind him.

For Taylor's third 1970 stint at the Troubadour, *Sweet Baby James* now a certified hit, Sklar took his seat on a folding chair behind Taylor—and instantly sensed something was different. The last time, he could see the audience chatting among themselves during the set. Now, he glanced out and saw them staring intently at the stage, singing all the words to all the songs. "It was visually obvious," Sklar said of the difference. "It was like sitting on a beach when a tsunami hits. It was so fast that you're caught off guard."

Everything about opening night felt like a combination inauguration and celebration. For dramatic flair, Asher hired Jack Belden, who'd done the horn arrangements on "Steamroller," to march onstage with his big band at the end of the show. Taylor persuaded King, who still wasn't accustomed to playing her own songs onstage, to be his opening act. Although a seasoned songwriter, King had stage fright; despite his comparative lack of professional experience, Taylor became her mentor. During soundcheck, King played a newly written song, with her own lyrics, called "You've Got a Friend." Hearing it while standing in the Troubadour balcony, Taylor was riveted and decided to record it himself one day. King decided to put it on tape as well, on an album she would start cutting in January 1971 called *Tapestry*.

On opening night, three songs into King's set, a Troubadour employee informed the audience over the sound system that the club had received a bomb threat. "As long as it's not me," King joked. (The warm laughter she received from the crowd did much to ease her jitters.) Everyone was ordered to leave as fire marshals and police swarmed in; Taylor and the musicians stood in the back alley. After a half hour, the four hundred customers were readmitted.

The police were never able to determine whether the threat was real or not; there was no way of telling if it was a political statement or, more likely, someone's way of trying to sneak into the sold-out show. After the drill was over, it would have been easy to slip into the Troubadour without a ticket stub. Then again, Taylor's new fans were proving to be an ardent lot. After the set, Sklar watched as a parent with a sick child talked her way into Taylor's dressing room and asked if he would help heal her child.

0 0 0 0

"It was very gratifying," Taylor recalled of the way *Sweet Baby James* was embraced by the public. "No question. It was what I was hoping for, that people would listen to my music and I could make a living doing it. There's no doubt it was a great thing." It was an equally great thing to his former label. To cash in on the newfound success of its former act, Apple re-released "Carolina in My Mind" from his first album. (It reached number 67 on the charts, a respectable showing for a two-year-old song from a flop album.) By year's end, Allen Klein was bragging that Taylor's Apple album had sold 400,071 copies in the U.S., along with 71,647 eight-track tapes.

The money that began streaming in sped up the growth of the James Taylor industry. Asher's management company, Marylebone Productions, was still based out of his house, but Asher was now able to afford an assistant, former Apple employee Chris O'Dell. In search of a new camper for an upcoming tour, O'Dell drove Taylor around to car dealerships. She'd met him before, in London during the Apple days when he'd crashed at her apartment, but was struck by how much more depressed he now seemed. "He hardly talked," she recalled. "It was hell trying to talk to him all the way out to somewhere south of L.A. He didn't seem like a guy who had all this great stuff going on. Either he was still on drugs or maybe *off* drugs, which maybe was the problem."

Taylor could now afford a larger band and hired Kortchmar back into the fold. Kortchmar, who'd spent much of the year recording and touring with the Laurel Canyon funk-pop band Jo Mama, made his impact felt immediately. As soon as they began rehearsing, Kortchmar started needling Taylor: "Get your ass out of that chair!" he'd bark. "Come on—you look like an old man! You gotta rock!" Honoring his friend's request—Kortchmar was a wiry stage presence himself—Taylor began standing up, but only during the last song of the set.

Being an animated showman didn't come naturally to Taylor. He'd emerged from the folksinger tradition, where perching on a chair was as standard as learning to play Weavers songs. Taylor sat onstage so frequently that by fall he'd hired a carpenter from Martha's Vineyard to build him a custom-made wooden seat: No right arm, so Taylor's guitar wouldn't bang into it, and a stand on the left arm to hold his guitar picks and glass of water. The chair was also slightly elevated to accommodate his long legs and arms. It was, Asher recalled with a laugh, "the James Taylor Chair."

The second reason for staying put onstage was the drugs. "He was still pretty strung out on serious drugs at that point," recalled Kunkel. "So sitting down was probably a better thing." Sklar, who avoided illicit anything, would often be the one to lead Taylor or one his bandmates back to the tour bus when they could barely stand. It wasn't a chore he relished, but someone had to be straight. "James didn't really talk about how he was dealing with it much," said Asher. "Perhaps I should have said, 'Are you all right?' But I didn't. Neither of us discussed our personal and emotional lives that much. He's shy; I'm English."

Since everyone else seemed to be high—one reporter spied coke and pot backstage at the Troubadour shows—Taylor's problems didn't raise any alarm bells, for those around him or Taylor himself. "I was a very functional addict," Taylor recalled. "I'm not saying it didn't get in the way of my work and my creative stuff. But I could also say in a strange way that it contributed. It was definitely something I had to go through." The drugs were just there, and as far as anyone knew, they didn't seem to be harming Taylor or anyone else.

Sensing a cultural phenomenon in the making—the rise of the new, inward pop, the anti-hard rock—*Time* magazine decided to pursue what would have been unthinkable months before: a cover story on James Taylor. In keeping with the magazine's reporting tradition, editors dispatched writers to campuses around the country to gauge Taylor's impact. Colleges were still a reliable barometer of his connection with those under twenty-five: At the student store at one of the University of Michigan campuses, *Sweet Baby James* sold out every three days.

At that and other schools, the *Time* reporters, in files not included in the final article, described Taylor's fans as "former freaks who have become more serious and mellow," people who saw Taylor as "a pleasant relief from acid music." They were "quiet, sometimes inarticulate; they certainly will not undertake the sort of diatribes that accompany much of 'heavy' rock."

"Many of them feel he is simple and sincere," filed a stringer from the Duke University campus, quoting students who deemed Taylor, in a positive way, "not an act, but a performer" who was "really good to hear when you're down." (One student added, approvingly, "I like his songs because they're all about heroin.") To another student, Taylor was proof "the Love Generation doesn't work." The Wisconsin stringer noted that Taylor's record sales on campus had eclipsed those of the Grateful Dead and Jefferson Airplane, the previous year's top sellers. "It's nice, relaxing stuff," a female student at that school observed. "It's pleasant. You don't get too excited about it." When the story finally hit newsstands the week of March 1, 1971, its cover line read, "The New Rock: Bittersweet and Low."

Not everyone was enthralled. There were grumbles that Taylor marked the end of social protest in rock. One undergrad dubbed Taylor "post-revolutionary, post-radical decadence," while another said, "With him, we've finally returned to TV, to middle-class values—he's a WASP Tom Jones." Another dismissed Taylor as "the emasculation of rock, obviating everything rock has ever tried to do." One student wondered if "the people interested in James Taylor are those who never quite got over a fascination with Simon and Garfunkel." (In his notes, the *Time* reporter added, "Upon whom it is now fashionable to dump.")

They were all right, in their respective ways, but by and large, the comments were positive and confirmed the feeling that Taylor had, accidentally and unintentionally, tapped into something larger than himself. "Sometimes you have a desire for something loud to wash all your sins away," a Wesleyan undergrad told one *Time* reporter, "and sometimes you want something quiet and lyrical." For many, there was no better way to wind down from one year, one decade, and one moment, than with James Taylor.

EPILOGUE: DECEMBER

The Caesar bangs and straightlaced-student look that had once graced Simon and Garfunkel album covers were gone. In their place on the afternoon of December 2 was Paul Simon's counterculture makeover: longish hair pulled behind his head in a knot, beard, and red-checkered work shirt.

In an interview earlier in the year, Simon had put down "San Francisco groups" and acid rock; his fastidious, perfectionist side had no use for ramshackle songwriting or musicianship. Not only did he now resemble one of those musicians; he was on their turf at Columbia's new San Francisco studio on Folsom Street, just south of the city's seedy Union Square area. In the control booth, Simon gazed through the glass at the trio of distinguished musicians he'd assembled: drummer Jim Keltner, fresh off the Delaney and Bonnie tour and sessions with Joe Cocker and Rita Coolidge; bass player Donald "Duck" Dunn from Booker T. and the MG's; and keyboard player Michael Finnigan, who'd played on Jimi Hendrix's *Electric Ladyland* and was now the singer and organ player in a local band, the Jerry Hahn Brotherhood. Given their collective roots in soul, R&B, blues, and funk, they didn't seem the model backing band for Simon. Trying to get comfortable with them, Simon joked with Dunn and told stories about his days playing rock and roll revue shows in New York.

Before work began, *Rolling Stone* reporter Ben Fong-Torres dropped by for an interview. Simon confirmed he was working on an album of his own, without Art Garfunkel, and admitted the project was a result of his partner's film career—about which Simon was still quietly stewing. In a comment Fong-Torres didn't include in the final version of the story, Simon groused that Garfunkel was "someone who had never acted and never been interested in the theater or movies until he met Mike Nichols." For attribution, he confessed he only had a handful of songs and that some of them might be "dated" in two weeks' time; he also said this was the first time he'd sung without his partner since at least 1966. Apparently Simon had already deleted memories of the Shea Stadium debacle from his mind.

After Fong-Torres left, Simon and the musicians tackled the work at hand. With loyal engineer and coproducer Roy Halee at his side, Simon asked the band to play one of his semi-formed songs. As they worked their way through it, a hard-to-read but unhappy expression took over Simon's face. To Finnigan, it was clear Simon was casting about for a direction. "It didn't have a real strong sense of purpose to me," he recalled. "Most sessions I did were a little more clear."

At one point, Simon emerged from the booth and approached Dunn, asking if he could borrow his bass. Despite Dunn's reputation as a dependable and funky player—those were his parts on Otis Redding's "Respect," Sam and Dave's "Hold On, I'm Comin'," and countless other Stax and R&B hits—Simon began playing a bass line himself to demonstrate what he wanted.

Dunn wasn't amused. "Did you fly me all the way from Memphis just to give me a bass lesson?" he snapped, caustically.

With that, the musicians took a break. In the bathroom, Keltner, another formidable player, cracked, "Well, it looks like we got fired." Finnigan was startled: What did he mean? They'd only started. Sure enough, all three were told not to come back the next day. The sessions were so exploratory they were never logged into Columbia's tape archives, and none of their work wound up on *Paul Simon*, the wonderfully eclectic and acutely personal and witty album he would release in early 1972. As he moved into the great unknown, Simon needed more time to discover how he would sound, and fit into, a new decade.

With filming of *Carnal Knowledge* wrapping up, Garfunkel was already preparing his next role. In the coming spring, he would teach a geometry course at Litchfield Preparatory School in Litchfield, Connecticut. Like his partner, he would be a singer and instructor—and, he hoped, a revered actor as well.

The long-distance calls into Stephen Stills' Elstead manor always arrived at night. "These heavy telephone things have lately gone down," Henry Diltz noted in his journal. "Calls from agents, lawyers. People in disfavor." On the line from Los Angeles during the first week of December was art director Gary Burden, who'd designed the cover for *Déjà vu*. With an eye toward a concert album for Christmas release, Atlantic had recorded Crosby, Stills, Nash & Young shows at three stops on their summer tour, New York, Los Angeles, and a rescheduled Chicago date. If the label couldn't bring them together in one place, at least they could reunite them on record—and try to convince their audience that one of the preeminent bands of the year remained intact.

Hitting the holiday deadline shouldn't have been too difficult, especially once Crosby, over Stills' objections, insisted the group not correct any of their onstage vocal flubs. But Bill Halverson, who'd overseen the recordings, knew otherwise when it came to getting all four to agree on anything. Once he finished preparing a preliminary mix of the record, he'd bring it to one of them for approval. Even if that person okayed it, the next man would reject it: Maybe it didn't sound right or didn't have enough of his songs. Shuttling back and forth between London and the West Coast, Halverson had the distinct feeling he was the only one in touch with all four musicians. Halverson also had to ensure Stills and

Young had the same number of bars of guitar solos in the "Carry On" and "Southern Man" jams—tracks so manic and messy that Halverson was forced to edit together performances from two different cities for "Carry On." The circle went around and around for months, until an album planned for November was delayed until the spring of 1971.

They remained in four different and only occasionally overlapping worlds. Stills stayed ensconced in London studios for days at a time, making the album that would become *Stephen Stills 2*. Young had completed a solo tour that, like *After the Gold Rush*, launched him into a career of his own. Thanks to his tenure with CSNY, the public knew his name, and Young was no longer the struggling solo artist of a mere year and a half before. He was already planning the early 1971 sessions that would become *Harvest*.

In San Francisco, Crosby finished his solo album, called *If I Could Only Remember My Name*, and awaited its release in February 1971. In the meantime, he continued exploring his concept of a nonrestrictive, unconventional rock and roll band. With Jerry Garcia, Phil Lesh, and Mickey Hart of the Dead, he played three nights at the Matrix club in San Francisco in the middle of December. The creative rush of the album sessions spilled out onto the club's intimate stage, the quartet playing several of its songs as well as space-jam versions of folk standards like "Motherless Child." During a largely instrumental take on the Byrds' "Eight Miles High," Garcia's guitar sweetly danced around the melody. Garcia took the lead on "Bertha," a rollicking number he'd recently finished with longtime Dead lyricist Robert Hunter.

The shows were loose and informal, occasionally too much so: At times, the singing, chords, and rhythms felt enveloped in a marijuana haze. This wasn't acid rock but acid-comedown rock. Crosby debuted "The Wall Song," which he and the Dead had taped in the fall but wouldn't release until later. The lyric, about someone "stumbling half blinded and dry as the wind," was clearly about Crosby's struggles over the past year—and, like the foggy music, hinted at a potential darkness. ("Could've been autobiographical," he later recalled.) He also gave his first public performances of "Cowboy Movie," his epic about CSNY and Coolidge. "It's dinner time," he said, sounding noticeably high. ". . . You got your Swanson TV dinner in front you ... And you tune into this bum movie on TV." CSNY's unruly summer felt more and more like a hokey shoot-'em-up western.

With Coolidge often at his side when she came up from Los Angeles, Nash opted for domesticity and home restoration, working on his own record and renovating his house. On New Year's Eve, he found himself alone in his house overlooking the Haight. Sitting down at his keyboard, he dashed off one of his recurring lonely-guy love songs. "Girl to Be on My Mind." "Come another year, I am sitting here . . . What's happening to me?" he wrote. Even for someone as levelheaded and focused as Nash, it had been that kind of twelve months.

Allen Klein was thrilled. There he was, meeting with two of his favorite clients, John Lennon and Yoko Ono, on Klein's home turf of New York. The Lennons had flown into town the first week of December, part of a trip to promote his *Plastic Ono Band* album, and they were already talking up the myriad projects they had in mind for their stay—making movies, for instance. Excitedly, Klein told them he'd hire a name like Richard Lester, who'd directed *A Hard Day's Night* and *Help!* They'd "make millions!" as a result, he told them.

No, no, Lennon and Ono patiently explained—he didn't understand. They didn't want to make that kind of movie. They wanted to make underground art films, and they wanted to direct them on their own.

Shortly before he left England, Lennon gave an interview to Ray Connolly, his friend at the *Evening Standard.* "It seems so far away, like school or college," he said of the Beatles, "because the whole thing died in my head long before all the ruckus started." Lennon's month-long visit to Manhattan bore out that comment. Checking into the Regency Hotel on Park Avenue, he and Ono threw themselves into the Manhattan art, film, and music world with a newfound frenzied intensity. To friends like Dan Richter, who accompanied them, Lennon seemed reborn. Constantly on the phone in his hotel room, making calls and plans as he wrote new songs and immersed himself in American television, Lennon was clearly not the same detached, depressed person who'd started the year in Denmark.

To Richter, Lennon clearly craved the respect of the art world—as if his Beatles music weren't legitimate enough—and he responded to Ono's way of conveying her unconventional art projects to the masses. One of his and Ono's first meetings, in the East Village, was with envelope-pushing filmmaker and writer Jonas Mekas. Ono had been making experimental movies for several years, but now that Lennon had joined in, Mekas proposed showing some of their joint films at a film festival at the Elgin, a theater in Chelsea. For the occasion, Lennon and Ono volunteered to make two new movies to premiere at the festival. Inspired by Ono's book of conceptual art projects, *Grapefruit*, they set up a camera at a space near Columbus Circle and, by word of mouth, phone calls, and any other means necessary, convinced a steady stream of musicians, actors, photographers, artists, and members of the Andy Warhol crowd to drop by. Upon their arrival, each would be asked to walk into a stall off to the side, take off their clothes, and don a robe. When they stepped in front of the camera, Richter would ask each to turn around and hand him the robe. The resulting movie, *Up Your Legs*, amounted to nearly ninety minutes of filmed butts, culminating in Lennon and Ono's own naked rears.

The next day, Ono and Lennon took over photographer Robert Frank's loft on the Bowery, where they auditioned female actresses for their second film. Given that that woman would have to lie spread-eagled on a bed as flies crawled around her, it wasn't easy to find the right person, but they ultimately did in underground actress Virginia Lust. Since flies don't normally *walk* for long periods of time, Richter used a technique he'd learned on the set of *2001: A Space Odyssey*: He and others rounded up as many live flies as possible (easy enough to do on the decrepit strip that was the Bowery), put them in coffee cans, and sprayed them with CO^2 to temporarily stun them. The flies, over two hundred of them, crawled over Lust's nude body, resulting in an even more mesmerizing short film, *Fly*.

With statements like those, Lennon wanted the world to know he was no longer a Beatle. He was an ex-Beatle, and a multimedia ex-Beatle to boot. On December 8, he sat for the first of two long interview sessions with *Rolling Stone*'s Jann Wenner. The conversations would prove cathartic for Lennon and Beatle fans alike, with their page after page of Lennon talking openly about the infighting in the band, heroin, primal scream, and McCartney's issues with Klein. "The Beatles," he said at one point, "was nothing."

Three days later came his all-out declaration of independence, *Plastic Ono Band*, the album he'd recorded in the fall. *Billboard* called it "self-determination music," certainly less snide than the magazine's assessment of Harrison's *All Things Must Pass* as "a masterful blend of rock and piety." Although no one imagined a Harrison album would make a larger impact than one by the others, *All Things Must Pass* nevertheless defied expectations. "My Sweet Lord" became a number one single, with EMI rushing to press one hundred thousand copies a week by year's end. On December 26, *All Things Must Pass* was number 2 on the album charts (*Led Zeppelin III* still commandeered the top slot), followed by *Stephen Stills* (number 4), *Sweet Baby James* (10), and Lennon's *Plastic Ono Band* (14). *After the Gold Rush* and *McCartney* were hovering nearby as well.

As a group, the Beatles had had another profitable year. The *Let It Be* album earned $1,441,766 in American sales, and a total of 2,378,000

British pounds in royalties. (ABKCO's share amounted to 475,642 pounds.) The Beatles' annual income for the year was $10.4 million. On December 28 and again two days later, two $500,000 checks for Apple Corps were delivered to ABKCO for disbursement.

But the joint venture wouldn't last long: Unbeknownst to the others, the time had arrived for McCartney and his legal team to begin the process of legally dissolving a partnership that dated back to April 1967. On December 31, David Hirst, one of McCartney's lawyers, had writs hand-delivered to Lennon, Harrison, Starr, and Klein. Among the charges, the papers claimed, was that "the Defendants have taken it on themselves to exclude the plaintiff from his proper share in the conduct of the partnership." The writ deliveries were straight out of a movie that could have been called *Let It Be: The Sequel*. Starr was at home having dinner with his wife, Maureen, when a court officer showed up. Lennon's was delivered to the Regency and Harrison's to his Friar Park estate. "*Fuck,*" Harrison said to Klaus Voormann, who was still living in a cottage on his property. Since the writ ordered them to respond within eight days, an associate in Klein's New York office signed the delivery notice on behalf of them all.

Although some assumed McCartney's team had chosen New Year's Eve for tax-deadline purposes, the reason was far simpler and pettier. The feeling was that the other Beatles and Klein had messed with McCartney's head too much during the previous twelve months. Now came payback— McCartney's way of having the last word, on the last day of the year. New Year's Eve plans resumed, but a pall hung over them. As someone in McCartney's camp said, it was his way of saying, "Welcome to 1971."

Among those who returned to school in the fall was Vietnam Moratorium co-organizer David Hawk. Like many of his fellow activists, Hawk felt the need for a break after three or more nonstop years of demonstrations, organizing, and frustrations. The midterm elections had been heartening in some regards, but the war dragged on, and the aftershock of the Summer Festival for Peace lingered: The concert lost money, not raising a cent for peace candidates. In need of downtime, Hawk resumed studies for his master's in theology at Union Theological Seminary at Columbia. "Sitting and reading," he recalled, "was a nice change." Since there was no reason to keep his hair short in order to look presentable to bureaucrats, Hawk let his locks grow out.

As Hawk noticed, the campuses were more subdued than they'd been earlier in the year. At the University of Wisconsin in Madison, the site of the infamous lethal bombing a few months before, a *Time* reporter on the James Taylor beat noted that "the campus is relatively quiet this year compared to last season, and a feeling of pensive, enlightened apathy seems to have set in." Similar reports began emerging from other media outlets probing the first semester after the deaths in Ohio. First came a *Time* report on the "New Campus Mood," which noted "a new climate on U.S. campuses this fall—a new mood of detachment that may well signal the end of large-scale student activism." The revamped activism, it reported, "generally takes the form of community work or attempts to build various kinds of communes." Frank Rich, a twenty-one-year-old student and editorial chairman of the *Harvard Crimson* (and future *New York Times* theater critic and columnist), told the magazine, "Students are still concerned about the war, racism and poverty; some are very active with ecology groups. But most are just waiting, with their pot and their Dylan records, for the grass to grow through the concrete." (By then, many had moved on to Taylor, Cat Stevens, and Neil Young, but he was still right.)

The story's angle—college students far more docile in the wake of campus turmoil—was reiterated in one outlet after another. "Kent State frightened a lot of students—there's a feeling that if you demonstrate, you get hurt," a student at Hofstra University told the *Times* in a December 20 story. Pointing out a rise in heroin use and a wave of students "tired of radical rhetoric," "endless demonstrations," and other late '60s facets of college life, the story noted that "the calm on most of the country's campuses this fall has been so pervasive as to have been almost unsettling."

The final week of the year, *Billboard* declared "Bridge Over Troubled Water" the best-selling single of 1970, the LP of the same name the top album. Although *Sweet Baby James* was fifteenth on the album list, the magazine knowingly gave its "Trendsetter Award" to James Taylor.

Taylor and manager Peter Asher were preparing to set further trends in the new year. Asher had begun mapping out a bigger-scale tour for 1971. In the surest sign of his ascension in the culture, Taylor would be moving from theaters and clubs into arenas, with some tickets priced at an unheard-of $7.50. In New York, where he'd played the tiny Gaslight the previous March, he'd be headlining Madison Square Garden. To ensure that those in the less expensive seats would be able to take in Taylor's every facial-muscle movement, massive TV monitors would be used for one of the first times in a pop tour.

In one of his last shows at an intimate theater, Taylor headlined the Fillmore East on January 25, 1971. Bill Graham's open letter to the industry, written in his Fillmore office over the summer and published in music-trade magazines soon after, had caused its share of discussion, but had had little impact. Already, younger promoters in the New York area were salivating at the idea that the Fillmore would play its final note and their venues would take its place. They knew fans had far more attachment to musicians than to where they played. The Fillmore East would shut down in June of that year, almost a year after Graham's letter.

During his show, Taylor performed a woeful rendition of the Beatles' "With a Little Help from My Friends." It was a savvy choice: Paul McCartney, his former overseer at Apple, was in the house. Once again, as at the CSNY show at the Royal Albert Hall in January, McCartney sat watching an industry buzz act perform one of his songs. When he finished, Taylor told the crowd it was "a song written by Paul McCartney and John Lennon. Mr. McCartney's in the audience tonight—let's have a big hand for Paul."

Craning its collective neck, the crowd broke into whoops and applause. It wasn't quite the pandemonium of Beatlemania. But then, nothing would be again.

CODA: OCTOBER 2009

The wrapped sandwiches piled atop a loudspeaker bore each of their initials: GN, DC, SS, JT. But there wouldn't be much time to wolf down any of them. At a multiroom facility in Manhattan in late October 2009, rehearsals were underway for the twenty-fifth-anniversary concert for the Rock & Roll Hall of Fame. Technicians hustled past security teams, who in turn kept an eye on all the musicians scurrying from room to room to practice for the next day's shows at Madison Square Garden.

By design, the concerts would present the hookups of a music geek's dreams; already, everyone was buzzing about what possible song Metallica and the Kinks' Ray Davies would play together. From outside one of the rooms came the sound of one of those groupings: Crosby, Stills & Nash playing "Love the One You're With," a song they'd cranked out thousands and thousands of times over the previous thirty-nine years, but this time with a new lead singer, James Taylor. Down the hall, after Simon and Garfunkel had finished rehearsing their set, Simon pulled aside Crosby and Nash. In a harried five minutes, the three worked out a vocal arrangement for "Here Comes the Sun," to be dedicated to one who couldn't make it, George Harrison, dead eight years from cancer.

Forty years had passed since *Bridge Over Troubled Water*, *Let It Be*, *Sweet Baby James*, and *Déjà vu* had been completed that fall and winter of 1969 into 1970. For each of these musicians, those four decades had been an ongoing tempest of hits, flops, breakups, reunions, marriages, divorces, children, drug rehab stints—the welcome-and-not gamut of life experiences. On these few days in New York, the survivors would be together once again to celebrate their music and, in an unspoken way, their very endurance.

In the intervening decades, their paths continued to cross and collide in myriad combinations. Start with the evening of March 16, 1971, when the Beatles, Simon and Garfunkel, Taylor, and CSNY were all competing for various Grammy Awards. *Bridge Over Troubled Water*, *Déjà vu*, and *Sweet Baby James* vied against each other for Album of the Year; "Bridge Over Troubled Water," "Let It Be," and "Fire and Rain" were each up for Record and Song of the Year. In each category, Simon and Garfunkel triumphed, yet neither man acted like a winner. When they left their front-row seats and walked up to the podium, they hardly looked at each other and only gave the briefest of acceptance speeches, barely acknowledging the other. When John Wayne announced the winner for best score for a movie or TV show—*Let It Be*—Paul McCartney, Linda in hand, appeared, unannounced beforehand. Wearing tennis sneakers and a blue suit, he made his way to the stage, said a quick thanks, and was gone again. (In light of his tattered image after the Beatle breakup, McCartney knew the importance of positive public relations.) It would be the only award the Beatles were handed that night; for best Duo, Group, or Chorus performance, they lost to the Carpenters. Neither the rest of the Beatles, nor Taylor nor CSNY, bothered to attend.

As the '70s lurched on, their lives and careers continued to intermingle. Crosby and Nash added their hippie-choir-boy harmonies to Taylor's recordings, most prominently "Mexico." When both Taylor and Young appeared on Johnny Cash's TV show in Nashville in 1971, Young invited Taylor to the *Harvest* sessions in town, and Taylor wound up singing harmony on "Old Man" and "Heart of Gold" (and adding a banjo part to the former). Simon and Harrison did a lovely joint performance of "Here Comes the Sun" and "Homeward Bound" on *Saturday Night Live*; Simon, Garfunkel, and Taylor cut an easy-listening remake of Sam

Cooke's "Wonderful World." Taylor and Crosby, Stills & Nash partici-
pated in the No Nukes concerts in 1979. Simon, Lennon, and Ono were
neighbors on New York's Upper West Side, where one day Simon and
Clive Davis ran into Lennon at a coffee shop, and Lennon told Simon
how much he liked his solo work without Garfunkel.

Simon and Garfunkel would reconvene fitfully—at a George Mc-
Govern rally in 1972, in a San Francisco recording studio that same year,
in New York's Central Park in 1981, for a tour two years later—but each
time the reunion never held. The familiar magic played out onstage, but
the old agitations would eventually emerge, scotching a planned album,
Think Too Much, in 1983. On his own, Simon would make some of the
finest music of his career on albums like *There Goes Rhymin' Simon* and
Still Crazy After All These Years, and Garfunkel would continue alternating between music and film roles.

Crosby, Stills, Nash & Young were on and off with each other on a
regular basis. The years would be a nonstop, dizzying go-round of solo
or duet projects and attempted or completed reunions, always followed
by the inevitable, accusation-driven collapse. There would be highlights
(Stills' expansive, career-peak *Manassas* album, Crosby and Nash's work
together, innumerable masterful Young records, CSNY's "Pushed It
Over the End" from their 1974 tour) and low points (Crosby's impris-
onment on drugs and weapon charges, the aborted Stills-Young Band
tour of 1976, woefully overproduced and anemic music throughout the
'80s). But like Simon and Garfunkel, they remained capable of stirring
up the best parts of their lives together; the quartet's 2006 tour, in support of Young's scabrous *Living with War* album, was surprisingly com-
manding and political—and, of course, included "Ohio."

Taylor would marry Carly Simon, grow more addicted to drugs and
drink, and finally kick heroin in the early '80s, during which time he and
Simon would divorce. "Last stop: Legend," *Cashbox* had declared of him
in 1970, a prediction that had come true by 2009. The man who sang

"Oh, Susannah" was now as much a part of the fabric of American music as Stephen Foster himself. Nearly everyone in his fan base could read Taylor's life—addiction, recovery, three marriages, children of varying ages, career highs and lows, deceased siblings—into their own.

The bumpy relations between the former Beatles became lore unto themselves. In March 1971, McCartney won the case against his fellow Beatles; in a rebuke to Allen Klein, a judge appointed a receivership to oversee the group's assets. Each went on to a solo career of varying success and quality, and business squabbles repeatedly reared their heads. Every so often it looked as if they might come together again, thanks to partial reunions on record or at social gatherings. But Lennon's murder in 1980 ended that speculation, and Harrison's death took the idea off the table completely.

Sometimes the connections between all four entities were eerie or inexplicable. In the late '70s, many years after Kent State, Jerry Casale's band Devo wound up playing with Young. Garfunkel partnered with Laurie Bird, Taylor's costar on *Two-Lane Blacktop*, before she took her own life in Garfunkel's New York apartment in 1979. Terre and Maggie Roche, Simon's students at NYU, would eventually release an album, 1975's *Seductive Reasoning*, with Simon's help; later, with sister Suzzy, they would become the Roches.

Even a few months before the Hall of Fame concerts, they continued to reappear in each other's lives. In February 2009, Garfunkel was a surprise guest at Simon's show at New York's Beacon Theatre, with McCartney watching in the audience. Despite the years and the rancor, their voices cozied up to each other's on "The Sound of Silence" and "The Boxer" as if they'd never been apart. Two months later, Starr and McCartney reunited at a New York benefit concert, doing a good-natured "With a Little Help from My Friends" and joking backstage about faulty memories due to too much acid. Not long after that, Taylor inducted Crosby, Stills & Nash into the Songwriters Hall of Fame. Months after the Hall of Fame concerts were over, Simon could be found on a Brooklyn stage, sweetly singing Lennon's "Hold On" from *Plastic Ono Band* as part of a tribute concert. Mirroring the technology of a new era, their collective lives remained in random shuffle mode.

Neil Young wasn't at the rehearsals, but that surprised no one; a dozen years earlier, he'd blown off his Hall of Fame induction for Buffalo Springfield. "It's always a shame not to get together with someone who I made some of the best shit of my life with," Crosby lamented during downtime. "Hopefully we'll do it again someday." Neither McCartney nor Starr would attend, either.

Those who made it to the Chelsea-neighborhood studio those October days in 2009 had been batted around by past lifestyles and age. They were all in their sixties now, if not approaching seventy, and bore the scars to prove it. Less hair and more eyewear. Crosby had a new liver. Stills had battled prostate cancer and, like many of his age and career choice, needed a hearing aid thanks to years of loud studio and stage monitors. (If he couldn't hear a question or backstage comment, Nash, ever the mediator, would repeat it to him.) Some had hair whiter than any pile of cocaine they once devoured. The high notes were harder to hit but still reachable: Singing behind Jackson Browne on "The Pretender," Nash and Crosby sounded nearly as bright as when they'd sung it with him on record in 1976.

In some ways, they remained the same. Crosby was, in his words, "a blabbermouth," a balance of cockiness and joviality. Taylor, in denim work shirt, retained his lean, sinewy frame and still projected an image of the endearingly absentminded professor. Nash was the gracious, if tough-minded, professional, Garfunkel the fastidious harmonizer (upset when he thought a cold he'd developed had affected his singing), Simon the privacy-inclined precisionist. No longer notoriously aloof, Stills was more gregarious and welcoming than in his brash youth. Although some of the old baggage remained between them, they also knew they had to rely on each other; Crosby and Stills, who'd had a frosty relationship for decades, acted more like old barroom pals than they had in years.

For one of the set finales, Crosby, Stills, Nash, and Taylor, joined by Browne and Bonnie Raitt, would sing "Teach Your Children" for what was probably CSN's 8,319th time. When they finished, Stills shouted over to Taylor at the opposite end of the line, giving him direction on playing a chord change. "When Stephen was with Buffalo Springfield, I was in the Flying Machine," Taylor reminisced during a pause in the rehearsals. "We couldn't believe our ears. They were the most exciting thing out there. And Stephen was the genius of that generation. The Springfield set the bar for us. Stephen's guitar and vocal work, I very much aspire to it. And CSN were absolutely seminal for me and profoundly inspiring." Stills then went over to Taylor and, with a guffaw, gave him a boisterous, playful slap on the right arm. Looking genuinely startled, Taylor went back to practicing the chord changes as everyone else took a break.

Settling into folding chairs, Stills told Nash he'd been woken up earlier the previous morning to promote a new CD on Howard Stern's show. "It was quite a trip," Stills said in his gravel-road voice. "He said, 'God, you're conservative—you're like Richard Nixon!'"

Nash looked aghast. "He *said* that to you?"

They both laughed. Nixon was now just a bad memory—and a relatively harmless one compared to so many in his party who'd followed. (Wiretapping the opposing party now felt like a schoolyard prank compared to starting unprovoked wars.) Many other aspects of 1970 were vague recollections too; Crosby, for one, had no recall of the night in Denver when Young stalked offstage. Simon and Garfunkel preferred not to talk about that tumultuous year at all, especially given how they'd mended their own relationship starting in the new century. Rock and roll no longer piloted the culture the way it once had, and the album itself—a cohesive, long-form piece of music that had first flourished during the era of the Beatles, Simon and Garfunkel, Taylor, and CSNY—was now a dying art form in the age of single-song downloads and digital players.

But nearly four decades on, the lessons and lesions of 1970 lingered all around them. The generation gap that cracked rock and roll apart that year, separating the older fans from the newer, next-generation ones, was now an entrenched part of the culture. The fans who demanded to be let in for free at festivals were, in essence, precursors to those who assumed music on the Internet should cost nothing. A new generation of indie-rock balladeers offered an alternative to clatter the same way Taylor once had. In record stores, polls, CD sales, and the world of video games, the Beatles still loomed as they had in 1970. (In 2010, *Abbey Road* was the best-selling record on vinyl—a format that had been newly resuscitated—and the Beatles were among the year's top ten best-selling artists, alongside Taylor Swift, Eminem, and Lady Gaga.)

The legacy of the first Earth Day and the launch of Greenpeace endured in the ever-widening green movement. Talk of manned space missions was back in the headlines—and by way of an African American president, an idea inconceivable in the fraught months of 1970. Even rock festivals, all but left for dead in 1970, had made a comeback; they'd become better planned and carried out than ever.

As the Hall of Fame concerts demonstrated, the music endured as well. The songs from those albums had been overplayed on radio and onstage, used in commercials, and in general beaten to death. But as Simon and Garfunkel traded verses on the Garden stage, "Bridge Over Troubled Water" fulfilled its destiny: It truly had become an old, revered gospel-style hymn. (Given how the two had reconciled in recent years, the lyrics took on an added resonance.) Crosby, Stills & Nash pulled off a surprisingly boisterous "Woodstock," and Crosby, despite the decades of wear and tear on his body, could still shout out a respectable "Almost Cut My Hair." As harmonized by Simon, Nash, and Crosby, "Here Comes the Sun" felt like a centuries-old folk song.

At their own concerts, Crosby, Stills & Nash had taken to playing Taylor's "You Can Close Your Eyes," written in 1970, and McCartney's "Blackbird," the song they'd sung at Royal Albert Hall so long before. As Joni Mitchell sang in that long-ago year, the seasons, they still went 'round and 'round.

ACKNOWLEDGMENTS

Writing about the music of one's youth was a dream project. Given how much time has elapsed since 1970, it was also a challenge. Memories are hazy, conflicting stories abound. To ensure as much accuracy as possible forty years on, I relied on a combination of firsthand, primary-source interviews, seemingly accurate news accounts of the time, and as much corroboration (from multiple sources) as possible.

In the main, this book is a result of interviews conducted in person, by phone, and by e-mail between November 2008 and September 2010. For starters, I have to thank David Crosby, Graham Nash, and Stephen Stills, each gracious enough to allow me to dredge through this turbulent time for them by way of in-person and telephone interviews and e-mail follow-ups. As much as they probably didn't relish talking about their ups and downs in 1970, they did it genially and patiently. I thank them for their time.

For their insights, memories, and recall, thank you to Allan Arkush, Peter Asher, Bob Balaban, Johny (formerly Johnny) Barbata, Stephen Barncard, Joel Bernstein, Jacob Brackman, Bonnie Bramlett, John Brower, Peter Brown, Vincent Bugliosi, Gerald Casale, Kip Cohen, Rita Coolidge, Stan Cornyn, Charlie Daniels, Clive Davis, Richard DiLello, Robert Drew, John Eastman, Michael Finnigan, John Fischbach, Linda Garfunkel, Charles Grodin, Bill Halverson, David Hawk, Jimi Hazel, Monte Hellman, Arthur Janov, Vivian Janov, Alan Katowitz, Jim Keltner, Danny Kortchmar, Russell Kunkel, John Kurlander, Michael Lang, Richard Langham, Mort Lewis, Nils Lofgren, Mike Medavoy, Abbot

Mills, Essra Mohawk, Terry David Mulligan, Chris O'Dell, Tom O'Neal (né Gundelfinger), Jonny Podell, Charles John Quarto, Frank Rich, Dan Richter, Susan Martin Robbins, Maggie Roche, Terre Roche, Amalie Rothschild, Calvin Samuel (formerly Samuels), John Scher, Sidney Schnoll, Leland Sklar, Joe Smith, Mark Spector, Toni Stern, Ron Stone, Barbara Stowe, Robert Stowe, Michael Tannen, Dallas Taylor, Joseph Turrin, Klaus Voormann, Paul Watts, Alan White, Nurit Wilde, Rudy Wurlitzer, and Peter Yarrow.

The James Taylor and Livingston Taylor comments are outtakes from two long interviews I conducted with them in 2001 for a magazine article on James. Larry Knechtel and Ben Keith, musicians who combined consummate skill with splendid humility, both passed away shortly after I spoke with them, and my condolences goes out to their families.

Thank you to Susan Braudy, Ray Connolly, Ben Fong-Torres, Ellen Sander, and Ritchie Yorke for documenting the times, the music, and the people behind them—and then helping me relive the era through their memories, insights, and transcripts. Henry Diltz was generous with his time, memories, journal entries, and remarkable photo archive.

Dave Zimmer deserves special mention for his friendship, advice, and patience with all my annoying phone calls and e-mails. His detailed, year-by-year chronicle, *Crosby, Stills & Nash: The Biography*, is the required text for current or future historians of the band and the scene that created them. Our mutual friend Raymond Foye was also a supportive and helpful pal in this process, as was the legendary Debbie Gold, whose recurring refrain—"Is there any other way I can help?"—is rarely heard music to the ears of authors and historians.

For helping me reach out to the appropriate parties or assisting in various ways, thank you, Malcolm Addey, Andy Adelewitz, Jeff Albright, Tony Arancio, Lisa Arzt, Jane Ayer, Nick Bailey, Tonya Bell-Green at Carnegie Hall, Gene Bowen, Kelly Bowen, Todd Brodginski, Christoph Buerger, Bud Buschardt, Frank Carrado, Atty Castle, Kay Clary at BMI,

Liz Campanile, Tom Cording at Sony, Charles Cross, Michelle Delgado, Donna Dickman, Mika El-Baz, Jason Elzy, Denis Farley, Heidi Ellen Robinson Fitzgerald, Jim Flammia, Michael Fremer, Roger Friedman, Brian Galindo, Rick Gershon, Jill Gillett at Paradigm, Steve Gillette, Erica Hagen, Mike Heatley, Kathy Heintzelman, Meghan Helsel, Martha Hertzberg, David Hochman, Mike Holtzman, Michael Jensen, Jeff Jones at Apple, Meghan Kehoe, Harvey Kleinman at Pryor Cashman, Steve Knopper, Candace Lake, Evan Lamberg, Joe Lawrence, Diane Levinson, Susan Makarichez, Bob Merlis, Buddha and Cree Miller, Ryan Moore, Nelly Neben, Susan Novak, Mollie O'Neal, Binky Philips, Niki Roberton, Drew Rosenfeld, Richard Sandford, Gigi Semone, Adam Sharp, Bill Siegmund at the Audio Engineering Society, Susan Smith, Jim Steinblatt at ASCAP, Ken Stowar of CIUT, Gary Strobl, Anya Strzemien, Paula Szeigis, Alison Teal, Mary Tower, Traci Thomas, Yolanda Vega, Christina Voormann, Jonathan Wolfson, and Josh Young. Despite his insanely busy schedule, Bruce Feiler once again took the time to offer advice and wise counsel.

With her customary thoroughness and expediency, Anna Brenner excavated plenty of terrific archival material while attending to her burgeoning directorial career. For additional research assistance, many thanks to Lee Abrams; Pete Asch at the New York University Archives; Jennifer Burke at the Selective Service System; Gordon Carmadelle at Musicians Local 47; David Coleman at the Presidential Recordings Program at the University of Virginia; Claude Hall; Dan Levy; Chris Miller; Sean O'Heir; David Priest, who helped me navigate the National Archives in London; my old friend and Beatle and Dylan expert Steve Schwartz; Larry Shannon; and Tom Tierney at Sony.

At *Rolling Stone*, many thanks to Will Dana, Jason Fine, Jonathan Ringen, Michael Endelman, and Nathan Brackett for the work, support, and extra time they afforded me to complete this book. Also at *RS*, thanks to Brian Hiatt and Andy Greene for sharing their thoughts and notes and to Alison Weinflash for the back issues on CD-ROM, which saved me days of library time. Michele Romero's determined, exhaustive archival dig into numerous photo archives resulted in the terrific photos inside.

My agent Erin Hosier of Dunow, Carlson & Lerner (no Nash *or* Young) was supportive from the moment I e-mailed her with the idea for this book. Writers can hope for nothing more than Erin's energy and enthusiasm. Ben Schafer at Da Capo was again an encouraging and sharp editor, always up for a chat and always knowing when to ask (or not) for updates. For the third time in my career, Martha Trachtenberg brought her astute copyediting skills to one of my manuscripts, from which it emerged unquestionably improved. Thanks to Kathleen Kelly for the extra pair of eyes. Many thanks to Marco Pavia, Kate Burke, and everyone at Da Capo and the Perseus Books Group.

Music has been a part of my family life for as long as I can recall. My mother, Raymonde, and my late father, Cliff, constantly played records on the family stereo in our New Jersey living room, and my sisters Linda Virginia and Colette initiated me into the music covered in this book by way of the LPs and singles wafting out of their bedrooms. My wife, Maggie, helped me conceive this project and, with her usual wisdom, astuteness, and breadth of knowledge, kept me on message when it came to the themes and presentation. Our daughter Maeve still doesn't know what to make of those large, circular black objects called "records" floating around the house. But she knows they have something to do with music, and that's good enough for me.

NOTES AND SOURCES

In addition to my own primary-source interviews mentioned earlier, the following books and magazine articles were also sources for some of the information in this book. Archives of the following publications were consulted regularly: the *New York Times*, *Rolling Stone*, the *Los Angeles Times*, the *Washington Post*, and *Billboard*. The Time Inc. library was also a mecca of research and information.

BOOKS:

Ayers, Bill, *Fugitive Days: Memoirs of an Anti-War Activist* (Beacon, 2009)

Boyd, Pattie, *Wonderful Tonight* (Harmony, 2007)

Braudy, Susan, *Family Circle* (Knopf, 2003)

Bronson, Fred, *The Billboard Book of Number 1 Hits* (Billboard, 2003)

Brown, Peter, and Steven Gaines, *The Love You Make* (McGraw-Hill, 1983)

Bugliosi, Vincent, with Curt Gentry, *Helter Skelter: The True Story of the Manson Murders* (Norton, 2001)

Caputo, Philip, *13 Seconds: A Look Back at the Kent State Shootings* (Chamberlain Brothers, 2003)

Cross, Charles, *Room Full of Mirrors: A Biography of Jimi Hendrix* (Hyperion, 2005)

Davis, Clive, with James Willwerth, *Clive: Inside the Music Business* (Ballantine, 1975)

DiLello, Richard, *The Last Cocktail Party* (Playboy, 1972)

Ehrlichman, John, *Witness to Power: The Nixon Years* (Simon & Schuster, 1982)

Emerick, Geoff, *Here, There and Everywhere: My Life Recording the Music of the Beatles* (Gotham, 2006)

Fawcett, Anthony, *John Lennon: One Day at a Time* (Grove, 1981)

Feiffer, Jules, *Backing into Forward* (Nan A. Talese/Doubleday, 2010)

Gitlin, Todd, *The Sixties: Years of Hope, Days of Rage* (Bantam, 1993)

Giuliano, Geoffrey, *The Lost Beatles Interviews* (Cooper Square, 2002)

Goldman, Albert, *The Lives of John Lennon* (Morrow, 1988)

Goodman, Fred, *The Mansion on the Hill* (Times Books, 1997)

Graham, Bill, and Robert Greenfield, *Bill Graham Presents: My Life Inside Rock and Out* (Doubleday, 1992)

Guralnick, Peter, *Careless Love: The Unmaking of Elvis Presley* (Little, Brown, 1999)

Harrison, George, *I Me Mine* (Chronicle, 2002)

Hoffman, Abbie, *Soon to Be a Major Motion Picture* (Putnam, 1980)

Hoskyns, Barney, *Hotel California* (Wiley, 2006)

Kingston, Victoria, *Simon & Garfunkel: The Biography* (Fromm, 1998)

Lang, Michael, with Holly George-Warren, *The Road to Woodstock* (Ecco, 2009)

Lewisohn, Mark, *The Beatles Day By Day* (Harmony, 1990)

Lewisohn, Mark, *The Complete Beatles Chronicle* (Harmony, 1992)

Lovell, Jim, and Jeffrey Kluger, *Lost Moon: The Perilous Voyage of Apollo 13* (Houghton Mifflin, 1994)

Luftig, Stacy (editor), *The Paul Simon Companion* (Schirmer, 1997)

McDonough, Jimmy, *Shakey: Neil Young's Biography* (Random House, 2002)

Norman, Philip, *Shout!: The Beatles in Their Generation* (Fireside, 1981)

O'Dell, Chris, with Katherine Ketcham, *Miss O'Dell* (Touchstone, 2009)

O'Neil, Thomas, *The Grammys: The Ultimate Unofficial Guide to Music's Highest Honor* (Perigee, 1993)

Oudes, Bruce (editor), *From: The President—Richard Nixon's Secret Files* (Harper and Row, 1989)

Perlstein, Rick, *Nixonland* (Scribner, 2008)

Reeves, Richard, *President Nixon: Alone in the White House* (Simon & Schuster, 2001)

Rogan, Johnny, *Crosby, Stills, Nash & Young: The Visual Documentary* (Omnibus, 1996)

Sandercombe, W. Fraser (ed.), *The Beatles Press Reports 1961-1970* (Collector's Guide, 2007)

Santelli, Robert, *Aquarius Rising: The Rock Festival Years* (Delta, 1980)

Schulman, Bruce Jr., *The Seventies: The Great Shift in American Culture, Society, and Politics* (Free Press, 2004)

Taylor, Dallas, *Prisoner of Woodstock* (Thunder's Mouth, 1995)

Weller, Sheila, *Girls Like Us* (Atria, 2008)

Wenner, Jann, *Lennon Remembers* (Popular Library, 1971)

Weyler, Rex, *Greenpeace: How a Group of Ecologists, Journalists, and Visionaries Changed the World* (Rodale, 2004)

White, Timothy, *Long Ago and Far Away: James Taylor, the Life and Music* (Omnibus, 2001)

Zimmer, Dave, *Crosby, Stills & Nash: The Biography* (Da Capo, third edition, 2008)

Zimmer, Dave (ed.), *4 Way Street: The Crosby, Stills, Nash and Young Reader* (Da Capo, 2004)

Zollo, Paul, *Songwriters on Songwriting* (Da Capo, 2003)

SELECTED ARTICLES

Alterman, Laraine, "Paul Simon," *Rolling Stone*, May 28, 1970

Aronowitz, Alfred G., "In Paul's Own Write," *New York Post*, April 20, 1970

Aronowitz, Alfred G., "Phil Spector Finds a Group," *New York Post*, February 3, 1970

Bailey, Andrew, "George Does a Turn for Ravi," *Rolling Stone*, October 29, 1970

"Beatle Asked to Testify at Tate Trial," *Washington Post*, October 29, 1970

Bernstein, Carl, "Gentle James," *Washington Post*, July 29, 1970

Braudy, Susan, "James Taylor, a New Troubadour," *The New York Times Magazine*, February 21, 1971

Browne, David, "James Taylor: The Greats," *Entertainment Weekly*, December 7, 2001

Caldwell, Earl, "Tate Jury Denied Death-Site Visit," *New York Times*, January 19, 1971

Connolly, Ray, "The Party's Over, but None of us Wants to Admit It," *London Evening Standard*, April 21, 1970

Darnton, John, "20,000 Youths Attended Rock 'Festival for Peace' Here," *New York Times*, August 7, 1970

"Fatal U. of W. Blast Laid to Bomb in Truck," *Chicago Tribune*, August 25, 1970

Fong-Torres, Ben, "Art Garfunkel: The *Rolling Stone* Interview," *Rolling Stone*, October 11, 1973

Fong-Torres, Ben, "Hello Darkness, My Old Friend," *Rolling Stone*, January 12, 1971

"Frantic Filming of a Crazy Classic, The," *Life*, June 12, 1970

Fremer, Michael, "Veteran Recording Engineer Roy Halee on Recording Simon and Garfunkel and Others," Musicangle.com, July 1, 2005

Gould, Jack, "Ed Sullivan Devotes Show to Music by Beatles," *New York Times*, March 2, 1970

Harris, Lew, "Like Old Times Again," *Chicago Tribune*, July 6, 1970

Heckman, Don, "View from Simon's Bridge," *New York Times*, February 27, 1972

Kneeland, Douglas E., "Campuses Quiet but Not Content," *New York Times*, December 20, 1970

Landau, Jon, "Paul Simon: The *Rolling Stone* Interview," *Rolling Stone*, July 20, 1972

Large, Arlen J., "Gore, Brock and 'Southern Strategy,'" *Wall Street Journal*, October 20, 1970

Lee, Victoria, "Teen Songwriters Hit," *New York World-Telegram*, December 27, 1957

Montgomery, Paul L., "Slain Youths Lacked Time for 'Politics,'" *New York Times*, May 16, 1970

"New Rock: Bittersweet and Low, The," *Time*, March 1, 1971

"Nixon Requests Broadcasters to Screen Lyrics," *Billboard*, October 24, 1970

North, Patrick, "Ringo & Friends in Country Country," *Rolling Stone*, August 16, 1970

Pagliasotti, Jim, "Concert Proves Again CSN&Y Without Peers in Rock Music," *Denver Post*, May 13, 1970

Palmer, Tony, "Super-group Mythology," *London Observer*, January 11, 1970

Robinson, Douglas, "Manson Called a Megalomaniac by Prosecutor as Trial Begins," *New York Times*, July 25, 1970

Schultz, Terri, "Old Beatles Never Die; They Just —," *Chicago Tribune*, March 12, 1970

Siegel, Jules, "Midnight in Babylon," *Rolling Stone*, February 18, 1971

Taylor, Derek, "The Beatles Split: Report from a Front Row Seat," *Chicago Tribune*, July 26, 1970

Volsky, George, "Illicit Traffic in Cocaine 'Growing by Leaps and Bounds' in Miami," *New York Times*, February 1, 1970

Watts, Michael, "Stephen Stills," *Circus*, July 1972

Weiler, A. H., "Son of 'Help!'," *New York Times*, February 15, 1970

Wierzynski, Gregory H., "New Campus Mood: From Rage to Reform," *Time*, November 30, 1970

Wright, Robert A., "Youths Battle Police on Coast," *New York Times*, February 27, 1970

Yorke, Ritchie, "A Visit to Steve Stills' House," *Los Angeles Times*, June 14, 1970

Yorke, Ritchie, "John, Yoko, Kyoko Get Trimmed," *Rolling Stone*, February 21, 1970

ADDITIONAL DOCUMENTATION

Archives of New York University, Elmer Holmes Bobst Library, New York

Assorted documents and "President Richard Nixon's Daily Diary," Nixon Presidential Library and Museum

Catch-22, DVD commentary (Paramount, 2001)

"James Paul McCartney *vs.* John Ono Lennon, George Harrison, Richard Starkey, and Apple Corps Ltd.," court documentation and affidavits, National Archives, London

"James Taylor," Warner Brothers press bio, 1970

Two-Lane Blacktop, DVD commentary (Criterion Collection, 2007)

U.S. Department of Commerce, Bureau of the Census, "Current Population Reports," March 5, 1971

INDEX

Gundelfinger, Tom, 89–91, 101

Hair (musical), 19
Halee, Roy, 27–31, 39–40, 47, 299
Halverson, Bill, 98, 100, 106–107, 185, 287
Fillmore East and, 235–236
"Happiness Is a Warm Gun" (song), 218
A Hard Day's Night (film), 10, 74, 104–105
Harper, Peggy, 30, 156–158, 163–164, 295
Harrison, George
Abbey Road and, 70
All Things Must Pass and, 255–258, 262–264
Beatles breakup and, 142–143
Blue Jay Way and, 28
"Carolina in My Mind" and, 58
closeness to Starr, Ringo, and Lennon, John, of, 262–263
Crosby, Stills & Nash and, 89, 96
death of, 327, 330
Delaney and Bonnie and, 208–209
delay of *McCartney* and, 137–139
dissolution of Apple Corps and, 322–323
Dylan and, 150–151
Friar Park, 84–85
Hollies, The, and, 89–90
"I Me Mine" and, 8–9
Indian music and, 255
Kunkel and, 150–151
Langham and, 6–7
McCartney, Paul, and, 256
O'Dell and, 84
royalties and, 265
Starr, Ringo, and, 87
Stills and, 104–105
Vollmer and, 79
Wonderwall Music and, 81, 208
Hart, Mickey, 275–276, 318

Harvard Crimson, 323–324
Harvest (album), 318
Hashish, 242
Haskell, Jimmie, 29–30
Havens, Richie, 199
Winter Concert for Peace and, 19
Hawk, David, 17–21, 121, 200–201, 202, 323
Hayden, Tom, 108
Hazel, Jimi, 199
"Heart of Gold" (song), 328
Heider, Wally, 95, 98, 275
Heller, Joseph, 38, 191–192
Hellman, Monte, 127–129, 243–248, 303
Hell's Angels, 18
Help! (film), 74
"Helpless" (song), 98, 110–111, 175, 223
"Helplessly Hoping" (song), 95, 226
"Helter Skelter" (song), 129, 218–219
Hendrix, Jimi, 195, 224
death of, 274
drugs and, 106–107
Monterey Pop Festival and, 203
New York Pop concerts and, 199
"Old Times Good Times" and, 286
Stills and, 106–107
Winter Concert for Peace and, 20–21
Henry, Buck, 191, 293–294
"Here Comes the Sun" (song), 327–328, 334
Heroin, 85–87
Lennon, John, and, 146
Taylor, James, and, 55–56, 59, 250
"Hey, Schoolgirl" (song), 31–33, 190
"Hey Doll Baby" (song), 31
Hey Jude (album), 132
"Hey Jude" (song), 57, 257
"Hey Mister, That's Me Up on the